ALSO BY AMY GOODMAN AND DAVID GOODMAN

Standing Up to the Madness:
Ordinary Heroes in Extraordinary Times

The Exception to the Rulers:
Exposing Oily Politicians, War Profiteers, and the Media That Love Them

Static:
Government Liars, Media Cheerleaders, and the People Who Fight Back

ALSO BY AMY GOODMAN AND DENIS MOYNIHAN

Breaking the Sound Barrier

The Silenced Majority:
Stories of Uprisings, Occupations, Resistance, and Hope

DEMOCRACY NOW!

TWENTY YEARS COVERING THE MOVEMENTS
CHANGING AMERICA

AMY GOODMAN

with DAVID GOODMAN and DENIS MOYNIHAN

SIMON & SCHUSTER

NEW YORK   LONDON   TORONTO   SYDNEY   NEW DELHI

 Simon & Schuster
1230 Avenue of the Americas
New York, NY 10020

First Simon & Schuster hardcover edition April 2016

SIMON & SCHUSTER and colophon are registered trademarks
of Simon & Schuster, Inc.

For information about special discounts for bulk purchases,
please contact Simon & Schuster Special Sales at 1-866-506-1949
or business@simonandschuster.com.

The Simon & Schuster Speakers Bureau can bring authors to
your live event. For more information or to book an event, contact
the Simon & Schuster Speakers Bureau at 1-866-248-3049
or visit our website at www.simonspeakers.com.

Interior design by Ruth Lee-Mui

Manufactured in the United States of America

10 9 8 7 6 5 4 3 2 1

Library of Congress Cataloging-in-Publication Data has been applied for.

ISBN 978-1-5011-2358-0
ISBN 978-1-5011-2360-3 (ebook)

CONTENTS

DEMOCRACY NOW!

INTRODUCTION: GOING TO WHERE THE SILENCE IS

It was December 1995. I was at an underground safe house in Haiti during the presidential election there, interviewing members of a political party who feared for their lives. I got a phone call from a colleague at the Pacifica Radio network, asking if I would be interested in hosting a new daily news hour that we had been developing, covering the 1996 presidential election . . . in the United States. The importance of covering elections weighed heavily on me, especially from Haiti, a country where people took incredible risks simply to vote.

The political violence that had consumed Haiti since the US-backed coup in 1991, which ousted democratically elected President Jean-Bertrand Aristide, had left thousands of Haitians dead. Thousands more fled the Caribbean island nation, making the dangerous trip, often in unsafe boats, to land on the shores of

Florida. President Bill Clinton feared that this influx of refugees from Haiti would lose him the crucial swing state of Florida. He knew the only way to end the refugee crisis was to restore Aristide to his presidency. So Clinton reversed his support of the Haitian coup, and returned Aristide to power for the fifteen months that remained in his term. In return, he forced Aristide to give up his demand that he serve his full five years, since the coup had robbed him of three of them. As the 1995 Haitian elections approached, many Haitians were terrified, but went to the polls nevertheless. Yet in the United States, where that kind of violence at the polls is nearly unheard of, less than half of those eligible bother to vote in presidential elections, and even fewer turn out for midterms.

Many have attributed low participation in US elections to voter apathy. I have never believed this. The low turnout is directly related to the many obstacles put in place that deter people from voting (for example, holding elections on just one day when most people are working, limiting hours that polling places are open, or requiring photo identification that disproportionately disenfranchises poor people and people of color). And then there are those who feel that there isn't a significant difference between the candidates, or that money distorts the process so much that their vote doesn't really count. Yet people are engaged in their communities all over the country. If they aren't voting, what are they doing? These were the questions we would ask while covering each state primary—not to focus on polls but to focus on people at the grassroots and what they cared about.

On February 19, 1996, I began hosting *Democracy Now!*, the only daily election news hour in public broadcasting. This was the election in which President Bill Clinton ran against Republican Senator Bob Dole of Kansas and Reform Party candidate Ross Perot.

Our hope was that the issues in the presidential race were important enough and listeners cared enough that they would tune in to daily coverage that brought them voices and ideas not normally heard in the corporate media.

That's how we started: giving a voice to the grassroots. When the 1996 election wrapped up, with President Clinton easily re-elected, we thought that *Democracy Now!* would wrap up as well. But there was more demand for the show after the elections than before. Why? There is a hunger for authentic voices—not the same handful of pundits on the network shows who know so little about so much, explaining the world to us and getting it so wrong.

Twenty years later, after airing on nine community radio stations in 1996, *Democracy Now!* is broadcast on over 1,400 public television and radio stations around the world and on the internet. The show, which I have cohosted since the beginning with the remarkable journalist Juan González, is the largest public media collaboration in the United States. *Democracy Now!* is broadcast on Pacifica, community and college radio and television stations, as well as on many NPR radio stations, and can be seen on public access TV, PBS TV stations, and via satellite television on Free Speech TV and Link TV. Millions access the program at democracynow.org and by video and audio podcasts that are among the most popular on the internet.

Early on, we learned that giving voice to those who are outside the mainstream comes with risk. In 1997, just a year after *Democracy Now!* started, we dared to broadcast the commentary of prisoner Mumia Abu-Jamal, who had been on Pennsylvania's death row for fifteen years. As journalists, we didn't think this was that daring. It's our job to go to where the silence is.

Abu-Jamal did not talk about his case. He talked about his experience behind bars. Actually, bars behind bars, because he was on death row. How rare to have a voice from one of the most controversial spaces in the world.

A former journalist and Black Panther in Philadelphia, Abu-Jamal was sentenced to death after having been convicted of the 1981 murder of a police officer. Abu-Jamal maintains he is innocent of the charges, and an international solidarity movement has grown around his case. Among those who have called for a new trial have been the European Parliament and the late South African President Nelson Mandela. Amnesty International and many other human rights groups say Abu-Jamal never received a fair trial. After almost thirty years on death row, in 2011 the US Court of Appeals for the Third Circuit vacated Abu-Jamal's death sentence on the grounds that it was unconstitutional; he is now serving a sentence of life without parole.

Mumia Abu-Jamal has been an outspoken advocate for the thousands of people on death rows around this country. He has written articles for the *Yale Law Review*, among other publications. In 2014 he delivered a commencement address from prison to his alma mater, Goddard College in Vermont. His popular book *Live from Death Row*, published in 1995, is a collection of his commentaries.

Working with Prison Radio's Noelle Hanrahan, we taped thirteen commentaries with Abu-Jamal in October 1996, and *Democracy Now!* began airing the pieces in early February 1997. But minutes before the first broadcast, the twelve stations in Pennsylvania that are owned by Temple University and that aired *Democracy Now!* pulled our show entirely and ended their contract with the Pacifica Network. They said it was "inappropriate" to air the commentaries of Mumia Abu-Jamal; his voice should not be heard on the public airwaves. Temple is a quasi-public university, so for us it was not only an issue of freedom of the press but also an issue of academic freedom.

When Temple University took us off the air, the reason it gave was that listeners demanded more jazz. Being a jazz lover, this was doubly insulting.

A tremendous outcry followed. The president of Temple received more than a thousand calls, emails, letters, and faxes from academic groups and activists all over the country. The *Washington Post* and the *New York Times* both framed it as a free speech issue.

The day that *Democracy Now!* aired the first commentary, we interviewed two representatives of the Society of Professional Journalists (SPJ). (We'd also invited the Fraternal Order of Police to come on, but the organization declined.) The SPJ said that the commentaries were extremely important, and they were shocked at what happened.

"I am outraged that administrators at Temple University decided to silence an alternative voice," Steve Geimann, SPJ president, said to the *Washington Post*. "SPJ, like Pacifica Radio, isn't taking a stand on Abu-Jamal's guilt or innocence. This issue today is all about allowing him—and other prisoners—the right to be heard."

The problem for Jazz FM, the Temple station, was that it had already sent out its program guide stating that *Democracy Now!* was its most successful show and that it was using us as a model for its other programs.

That's some model: air alternative voices and get kicked off the air.

Temple University law school held a forum; it was packed. Students protested. Nevertheless, Temple stuck by its decision. So did we. *Democracy Now!* grew by leaps and bounds as station after station began broadcasting the show.

One of the reasons that Abu-Jamal's commentaries broke new ground is that you rarely heard voices from prison, because journalists were increasingly being blocked from going there. At the time, Pennsylvania, along with Virginia, California, Indiana, and Illinois, were among the states where journalists' access to jails was heavily restricted.

Abu-Jamal has faced multiple obstacles as he has tried to have his voice heard. On August 12, 1999, Abu-Jamal called in to *Democracy Now!* to comment on the release of sixteen Puerto Rican political prisoners. As he began to speak, a prison guard yanked the phone out of the wall. Abu-Jamal called back a month later and recounted that "another guard appeared at the cell door hollering at the top of his lungs, 'This call is terminated!' I immediately called to the sergeant standing by and looking on and said, 'Sergeant, where did this order come from?' He shrugged his shoulders and answered, 'I don't know. We just got a phone call to cut you off.' "

Abu-Jamal actually first recorded his commentaries for National Public Radio. Ellen Weiss, then the executive producer for the news program *All Things Considered*, said, "He is a good writer and brings a unique perspective to the air." She added that the commentaries were a way for public radio to broaden its coverage of crime and punishment.

But then the Fraternal Order of Police put enormous pressure on National Public Radio. NPR decided to kill the series of commentaries, though it had publicized them heavily.

We felt it was critical to air Abu-Jamal's commentaries on *Democracy Now!* The commentaries touched on a broad range of issues. He spoke of capital punishment being punishment for those without capital. And he talked about "father hunger": the idea that so many young black men in prisons don't know their fathers. Abu-Jamal mused on the irony of being a father figure to those prisoners, despite the fact that he couldn't be a father to his own children or grandchildren. He wrote:

"Here, in this restrictive place of fathers without their children and men who were fatherless, one senses and sees the social costs of that loss. Those unloved find it virtually impossible to love, and those who were fatherless find themselves alienated and at war with their own communities and families."

There's a reason why our profession is the only one explicitly protected by the US Constitution: journalists are supposed to be the check and balance on power, not win popularity contests. The United States has 5 percent of the world's population but 25 percent of the prisoners. It's the job of journalists to put our microphones between the bars and broadcast the voices of those inside.

ROOTS

I come originally from Pacifica Radio, which was founded in 1949 by a man named Lew Hill. He was a war resister who came out of the compulsory work camps for conscientious objectors in World War II. Hill said we need a media outlet that's not run by corporations that profit from war, but run by journalists and artists.

As George Gerbner, the late dean of the Annenberg School for Communication at the University of Pennsylvania and the founder of the Cultural Environment Movement, which advocates greater diversity in the media, would say, we need a media "not run by corporations that have nothing to tell and everything to sell that are raising our children today."

The first Pacifica station was KPFA, launched in Berkeley,

California, in 1949. In 1959 KPFK went on the air in Los Angeles, and in 1960 WBAI started broadcasting in New York. In 1970 KPFT went on the air in Houston, and WPFW came to the airwaves in Washington, DC, in 1977.

What happened to KPFT says a lot about how independent media threatens the status quo. It was the only radio station in the country whose transmitter was blown up. In May 1970, just two months after KPFT began broadcasting, the Ku Klux Klan dynamited the station's transmitter, knocking it off the air for several weeks. The explosion came in the middle of Arlo Guthrie's antiwar song, "Alice's Restaurant," just as he was singing, "Kill, kill, kill," as he spoofed the draft. Not long after the transmitter tower was rebuilt and the station returned to the air, the Klan blew it up again with fifteen times the dynamite used the first time, knocking the station off the air for more than three months. Jimmy Dale Hutto, the Grand Dragon of the local Ku Klux Klan, who was convicted of the bombing, said blowing up KPFT was his proudest act.

When KPFT finally went back on the air for the third time in January 1971, it was a national event. PBS broadcast its rebirth on television. Arlo Guthrie came back to Houston to pick up where he was so rudely interrupted: he finished singing "Alice's Restaurant" live on the air.

The Klan leader understood how dangerous independent media is. Because when you hear someone speaking for themselves—whether it's a Palestinian child or an Israeli grandmother, or an uncle in Afghanistan or an aunt in Iraq—it challenges the stereotypes that fuel the hate groups. It's not that you have to agree with what you hear. How often do we agree even with our family members? But you begin to understand where they're coming from. That understanding is the beginning of peace.

I believe the media can be the greatest force for peace on Earth. Instead, all too often, it is wielded as a weapon of war. That has to be challenged.

I come from the radio network where Chris Koch worked. Koch was sent by WBAI as the first American journalist to cover the war from North Vietnam. What he saw there changed him. The American people were being led to believe that the United States would prevail against the Vietcong. Koch saw something very different, and he dared to talk about it in his reports for Pacifica.

"When Koch returned home to the United States from that first trip in 1965, he became one of the first US journalists to conclude America should withdraw from Vietnam, and his own countrymen were not nearly as easy to get along with as those he met in North Vietnam," reported a Vietnamese news agency in 2012.

Koch recalled, "When I lectured at a university in Plattsburgh, New York, they had to lead me out the back door because people were getting very angry, beginning to shout at me. In Denver, Colorado, they really got angry. They began coming on the stage. I had to climb out a window in the back of the room and get in my car. Americans were not ready to listen to what I had to say."

When he returned from North Vietnam, Koch was interviewed by ABC, CBS, and NBC. None of the national networks ran the interviews. Koch didn't have official permission to go where he went and say what he saw. He was too controversial. That's why we need a media that is independent.

The first book I wrote was with my brother, journalist David Goodman, called *The Exception to the Rulers*. That's what the media should be: the exception to the rulers.

Our next book was called *Static*. Even in this high-tech digital age with high-definition television and digital radio, still all we get is static: that veil of distortion, lies, misrepresentations, and half-truths that obscure reality.

We need the media to give us the dictionary definition of *static*: Criticism. Opposition. Unwanted interference.

We need a media that covers power, not covers for power.

We need a media that is the fourth estate, not for the state.

And we need a media that covers the movements that create static and make history. That is the power of independent media. That is a media that will save us.

BREAKING GROUND AND BREAKING NEWS

In 1999 we headed to Seattle to cover one of the first meetings of the World Trade Organization (WTO). The corporate media had barely mentioned the WTO, a powerful, secretive body established in Geneva, Switzerland, in 1995 with the strong support of President Bill Clinton. It can overturn local laws in the name of "free trade"—or, more accurately, corporate-managed trade. As with the Trans-Pacific Partnership today, a trade agreement among twelve Pacific Rim countries and the United States, WTO trade bureaucrats from nearly 150 countries, as well as from many corporations, were saying, in effect, you can pass your laws in your democratically elected legislatures to protect workers or the environment, but supranational bodies such as the WTO can throw out those local laws on the grounds that they are barriers to trade and thus "WTO-illegal." This means that everything from Thailand putting a warning on cigarettes, to the requirement that genetically modified food be labeled, could be overturned.

Tens of thousands of people from around the world descended on Seattle to show this shadow corporate government how people feel when their democracy—and their jobs, environment, and right to participate—is stolen out from under them. They were religious people, trade unionists, doctors and nurses, students, environmentalists, and steelworkers in a global uprising against corporate power.

As all this was about to unfold, activists confronted a dilemma: What media would cover their actions? Protesters knew that the corporate media would belittle or misrepresent them—or ignore them completely.

Democracy Now! cohost Juan González also works at the New York *Daily News* as a news columnist. When he asked his editors to send him to Seattle to cover the WTO, they responded, "The what?"

The *Daily News* is one of the largest city newspapers in the country. But in the end, it wasn't the media behemoth, the *Daily News*, that sent him, but his other *DN*—the nonprofit *Democracy Now!* As this major global protest erupted, the *Daily News* called Juan repeatedly for reports from the front lines. His editors were proud that their reporter was on the scene, scooping the other New York papers. Privately, they kept asking him, "How did you know this was going to happen?"

A new kind of media was rising up. People came together with pens and pencils, tape recorders and video cameras, and established an Independent Media Center (IMC).

Tens of thousands of marchers were tear-gassed and shot with rubber bullets and pepper spray. The mayor of Seattle declared martial law for the first time since World War II. The city established "no-protest zones."

As the corporate media networks scrambled to buy plane tickets and book hotel rooms from which to cover the protest, this new independent media movement had already swung into action. When CNN, citing police sources, denied that protesters were being shot with rubber bullets, the IMC's new website at www.indymedia.org was showing photographs of people picking up rubber bullets by the handful. As one person carrying a video camera would get tear-gassed and arrested, he or she would hand that camera to someone else. The *Democracy Now!* team spent many long hours in the streets with journalists from the IMC, being gassed and harassed by police dressed in futuristic black body armor as we documented the explosion of anticorporate globalization activism onto the world stage.

People are hungry for unfiltered, real-time coverage from real people's perspectives. So hungry for the truth that during the "Battle of Seattle," there were more hits on indymedia.org than on CNN's website.

The Battle of Seattle resulted in over six hundred arrests and the eventual failure of the WTO talks in America's largest export city, then home to Boeing, Microsoft, Amazon, and Starbucks. Seattle police chief Norm Stamper resigned within days. Ten years later, Stamper admitted on *Democracy Now!* that he'd made some of the worst decisions of his career that week, among them "not vetoing a decision to use chemical agents, also known as tear gas, against hundreds of nonviolent demonstrators."

He now sounds more like the WTO protesters whom his forces tear-gassed: "We're now reaping what we have sown in the form of unbridled globalization and unfettered free trade . . . It's time for all of us in this country, as we attempt to pull ourselves out of this global economic meltdown, to really take a look at what issues of social and economic justice mean within the context of globalization."

AN INDEPENDENT REPORTER'S RAP SHEET

As reporters, we shouldn't have to get a record for putting things on the record. But here's my rap sheet for covering the news during the last twenty years:

1998: Detained with *Democracy Now!* producer Jeremy Scahill at Andrews Air Force Base in Maryland while covering nuns and priests from the pacifist Plowshares movement who threw blood on a B-1 bomber used to bomb Iraq in 1996. Several hundred thousand people had come to the base for an air show. We were released many hours later after being investigated by the judge advocate general (JAG) and the Federal Bureau of Investigation (FBI), among other levels of law enforcement. Our tape was confiscated but returned months later following legal action.

1999: Detained and deported by Indonesia twice while trying to reach Indonesian-occupied East Timor to cover a UN independence referendum.

2003: Arrested in front of the White House on International Women's Day with writers Maxine Hong Kingston, Alice Walker, Terry Tempest Williams, Honor Moore, and others while covering their protest against the impending Iraq War.

2008: Arrested at the Republican National Convention in Saint Paul, Minnesota, when demanding that police release

> *Democracy Now!* producers from custody. They had been
> filming antiwar protests.

2009: Detained by Canadian border guards while driving into
     Canada to speak about press freedom at the Vancouver
     Public Library and the University of Victoria.

Government crackdowns on journalists are a threat to democracy.

A disturbing example of this is what happened at the 2008 Republican National Convention, where police were systematically targeting journalists. In Saint Paul, the press was free to report on the official proceedings of the Republican National Convention but it was much more difficult to report on the police violence and mass arrests directed at those who had come to petition their government: to protest.

The Republican National Convention began on Labor Day. The Democrats had held their convention the week before, in Denver. Protests against war took place all week there, as Barack Obama prepared to accept his party's nomination. On the first day of the Republican National Convention, an even larger antiwar march took place. Ten thousand people joined in the march in Saint Paul, including local families, students, veterans, and concerned citizens from around the country. The protesters greatly outnumbered the Republican delegates.

There was a festive feeling as people gathered under a blue sky. Later in the day, after the march, as the crowd dispersed, the police—clad in full body armor, with helmets, face shields, batons, and canisters of pepper spray—charged. They forced marchers, onlookers, and working journalists into a nearby parking lot, and then surrounded the people and began handcuffing them.

Democracy Now! producer Nicole Salazar was videotaping.

Her tape of her own violent arrest is chilling. Police in riot gear charge her, yelling, "Get down on your face!" You hear her voice, clearly and repeatedly announcing "Press! Press! Where are we supposed to go?" She was trapped between parked cars. Suddenly she was hit from the front and behind. The camera dropped to the pavement amid Nicole's shouts of pain and shock. Her face was smashed into the pavement, and she was bleeding from her nose as an officer rammed a boot or knee into her back. Another officer was pulling on her leg. The police threw *Democracy Now!* senior producer Sharif Abdel Kouddous up against the wall and kicked him in the chest, and he was bleeding from his arm.

I was at the convention, interviewing delegates on the floor of the Xcel Energy Center when senior producer Mike Burke called my cell phone. He said that police had beaten and arrested Sharif and Nicole. Filmmaker Richard Rowley of Big Noise Films and I raced on foot to the scene. Out of breath, we arrived at the parking lot. I went up to the line of riot police and asked to speak to a commanding officer, saying that they had arrested accredited journalists.

Having just come from the convention floor, I had, in full view around my neck, my credentials that allow me to interview presidents, vice presidents, Congress members, and others. Within seconds, the riot police grabbed me, pulled me behind the police line, pushed me onto a car, forcibly twisted my arms behind my back, and handcuffed me, forcing me up against a wall and then onto the ground. The rigid plastic cuffs dug into my wrists. I saw Sharif across the parking lot. I demanded that the police take me to him. Standing next to each other in handcuffs, we kept repeating that we were journalists, whereupon a Secret Service agent came over and ripped our credentials from our necks. I was taken to the Saint Paul police garage, where cages were set up for protesters.

Nicole and Sharif were taken to jail, facing felony riot charges. I was charged with obstruction of a peace officer.

If only there was a peace officer in the vicinity.

There was an outcry as news spread of our arrest. Thousands of phone calls, emails, faxes, and tweets were directed at city officials, demanding our release. I was let go after a number of hours. Sharif's and Nicole's release took longer, but they did get out. I returned to the convention center, where I was ushered to the NBC skybox, to be interviewed about my arrest. Afterward, an NBC reporter came up to me and asked, "Why wasn't I arrested?"

I said, "Oh, were you out covering the protesters too?"

"No," he replied.

"I don't get arrested in the skyboxes either," I said.

Journalists have a special job. We have to cover the convention floor to question the delegates and politicians. We have to get into the corporate suites to see who is paying for the conventions. And we have to get out on the streets where the uninvited guests are—sometimes thousands of them. These protesters have something important to say as well. Democracy is a messy thing. And it's our job to capture it all. During the week of the 2008 Republican National Convention, more than forty journalists were arrested.

At these conventions, dissent is threatened by a massive array of paramilitarized police, operating under the US Secret Service, granted jurisdiction over the "National Special Security Events" that the conventions have been dubbed. Corporations pay millions to the host committees, earning exclusive access to lawmakers and candidates. The host committees in turn indemnify the city, which means that police can operate with impunity, all but guaranteeing injuries, unlawful arrests, and expensive civil litigation for years to come. More than just a campaign-finance loophole that must be closed, this is a national disgrace.

We brought a lawsuit against the Saint Paul and Minneapolis police departments and the Secret Service. The lawsuit took several years, but we ultimately won a $100,000 settlement, and an agreement that officers would receive training in First Amendment rights of the media and the public.

Throughout the convention week of 2008, one of the twenty-five original typeset copies of the Declaration of Independence was on display at Saint Paul City Hall—not far from where crowds were pepper-sprayed, clubbed, tear-gassed, and attacked by police with concussion grenades. As the clouds cleared, it is instructive to remember the words of one of the Declaration's signers, Benjamin Franklin:

"Those who would give up essential liberty to obtain a little temporary safety, deserve neither liberty nor safety."

9/11

By chance, *Democracy Now!* was slated to begin a daily television broadcast the week of September 11, 2001. It would air on the public access station Manhattan Neighborhood Network. We were operating from Downtown Community Television Center in a converted hundred-year-old firehouse, the closest national broadcast to what would become Ground Zero. Our small studio was in the garret. Yes, we did slide down the brass fire pole when in a hurry, but that is another story.

September 11, 2001, was mayoral primary day in New York. At that time, we broadcast live at 9:00 a.m. EST. (We now air at

8:00 a.m.) The first plane hit the World Trade Center at 8:47 a.m., the second at 9:03 a.m. We were preparing our show and didn't know what had happened.

We were doing a special segment that day on the connection between terror and September 11—that is, September 11, *1973*. In Chile, this was the day that democratically elected Chilean President Salvador Allende died in the palace as the forces of General Augusto Pinochet—sadly, the US-backed, ITT-backed Pinochet forces—seized power and ruled that country for seventeen years, killing thousands of Chileans and other Latin Americans.

No, this wasn't the first time that September 11 was connected to terror. Consider Guatemala, where anthropologist Myrna Mack, a vocal critic of the government, died at the hands of Guatemalan security forces on September 11, 1990—US-backed Guatemalan forces.

Then there was September 11, 1977. Steve Biko, founder of the Black Consciousness Movement in South Africa, was beaten severely in the back of a van by pro-apartheid forces—US-backed pro-apartheid forces. He died early the next morning.

And there's September 11, 1971, in Attica, New York. From September 9 to 13, prisoners rose up to protest conditions at the Attica State Correctional Facility. New York Governor Nelson Rockefeller called out a thousand state troopers and members of the National Guard on September 13. Under a cloud of tear gas, they stormed the prison and opened fire, killing forty-three men—prisoners and guards—and injuring hundreds more.

There's also September 11, 1988, in Haiti. On that date, at least thirteen people were murdered when the St. Jean Bosco church was attacked and burned by a group of former secret police while the charismatic priest named Jean-Bertrand Aristide was preaching. Aristide would soon be elected president. On the fifth anniversary of the massacre, September 11, 1993, in the midst of the US-backed coup that had ousted Aristide, Haitian businessman Antoine Izméry, an Aristide ally, led a memorial procession and was assassinated.

But September 11, 2001, is a date no one will ever forget. Almost three thousand people were incinerated in an instant. We'll never actually know how many people died that day, as those who go uncounted in life go uncounted in death: the homeless around the World Trade Center, and the undocumented workers who may have been there that day.

We stayed in the firehouse for four days. We were located inside the evacuation zone and feared that if we left, we would not be allowed back in. And we knew we needed to keep broadcasting. We saw people interviewed on other TV networks calling for revenge. But we saw very quickly that was not the general sentiment of people on the ground.

Photographs were pasted on every lamppost and every park bench with messages that read, "Have you seen my wife, last seen near Tower One?" "Have you seen my son, last seen in Tower Two?"

Those images connected us with people all over the world who suffer from terror—such as the mothers who walked the Plaza de Mayo in Buenos Aires, Argentina, bearing photos of their children who vanished during that country's US-backed "dirty war" in the 1970s and 1980s. "Mothers of the disappeared," they are called. The women's signs read, "Have you seen my son? Have you seen my granddaughter?"

September 11 united Americans with people around the world who have been victims of terror. Sadly, all too often, if those civilians were killed or bombed or tortured by a US ally, or by the US itself, the media coverage is often qualified. From Iraq, to Haiti, to Syria, to Yemen, to Afghanistan, if the media even reports on the atrocities, excuses are made: "It's more complicated than that . . ." "Collateral damage is part of war . . ." And so on.

But in the case of 9/11, there was a collective revulsion at the mass killing, as there should have been. The model of media coverage was to find the families who had lost loved ones, tell us their stories, give us their names. Those are the details that dignify a life; that's what makes us feel the loss. The portraits of grief, the profiles of children left without a parent, the deeds of unsung heroes—this kind of reporting should be the model for how all atrocities are covered. Whether it's a US bombing of a Doctors Without Borders hospital in Kunduz, Afghanistan, or the stories of millions of refugees fleeing their homes in Syria, Iraq, Afghanistan, or Libya, when people learn of others' pain, they are moved to act.

HOPE AND MOVEMENTS

What gives me hope? It's the movements.

Movements often start with a courageous act of resistance. These are not isolated acts. They are inspired by past movements. And they inspire future ones.

Take Jonathan Butler, an African American graduate student at the University of Missouri, also known as Mizzou. In the fall of 2015, African American students at the university staged weeks of demonstrations against what they called a lax response to racism. Then Butler decided to put his body, and perhaps his life, on the line: he launched a hunger strike that he said would end only with the resignation of University of Missouri President Tim Wolfe.

Butler laid out the grievances of African American students in a letter that he issued at the start of his hunger strike: "In the past 90 days alone we have seen the MSA (Missouri Students Association) President Payton Head being called the n-word on campus, graduate students being robbed of their health insurance, Planned Parenthood services being stripped from campus, #Concerned Student1950 peaceful demonstrators being threatened with pepper spray, and a matter of days ago a vile and disgusting act of hatred where a MU student drew a swastika in the Gateway residential hall with their own feces."

Butler was inspired and empowered by the Black Lives Matter movement and the protests in Ferguson, Missouri, in 2014, following the police killing of Michael Brown, an unarmed African American teenager. (See chapter 8, "When the Killer Wears a Badge.") Butler was among a group of Mizzou students who drove two hours back and forth to Ferguson to join the protests. He had never seen African Americans engage in mass protest in this way. "It was monumental in terms of how it influenced me," Butler said. The Mizzou protests, he explained, were part of "the post-Ferguson effect."

Mizzou students set up a campus encampment in support of Butler's action. They dubbed themselves Concerned Student 1950, a reference to the year that the school's first black student enrolled. The administration also faced opposition from graduate students who fought to win back their health coverage and activists who denounced a move to sever ties with Planned Parenthood under Republican pressure.

Then some powerful allies joined the fight. On November 7, 2015, a number of African American University of Missouri football players tweeted a photo of thirty African American team members linking arms alongside the statement "The athletes of color on the University of Missouri football team truly believe 'Injustice Anywhere is a threat to Justice Everywhere.' " They were quoting Dr. Martin Luther King Jr.

The Mizzou football players announced they would no longer take part in any football activities until President Wolfe resigned or was removed "due to his negligence toward marginalized students' experience." White players, the coach, and the athletic department quickly came out in support of the team.

The Mizzou football team is the center of power at the university. College football is a multimillion-dollar enterprise. Mizzou—which was cutting health care for graduate students as it invested $72 million in a new football stadium—stood to lose $1 million for every football game it forfeited, and the next game was days away. The football coach is paid $4 million per year—nearly nine times as much as the college president.

As sports commentator Dave Zirin observed on *Democracy Now!*, African American students comprise about 7 percent of the student body but almost 70 percent of the football team—these players, thus, "are at the fulcrum of the political, economic, social, and psychological life of campus, but none of those billion-dollar gears move at all if they choose not to play."

The pressure on President Wolfe snowballed. The following day, members of a "Concerned Faculty" group at the University of Missouri voted to stage a walkout, and the Missouri Students Association, representing twenty-seven thousand undergraduates, called on Wolfe to resign.

On November 9, 2015, the president announced that he was resigning, along with the chancellor of the campus in Columbia, Missouri, R. Bowen Loftin. Michael Middleton, an African American civil rights attorney and former vice chancellor of the university, was named interim president.

Concerned Student 1950 continued its activism, calling in a statement for "detailed plans to address issues such as minority student enrollment; faculty, staff and administration recruitment; and health resources for students."

Jonathan Butler ended his hunger strike when Wolfe resigned. He insisted that what brought about change "was not me alone. It was these people that I'm standing here on the stage with. It was the black community. It was the black faculty. It was the other faculty. It was the Forum on Graduate Rights. It was the people with Planned Parenthood. It was everybody who chose to stand up in this time who made this possible."

The uprising at the University of Missouri ignited Yale University, which held a march in solidarity with the Mizzou students. Yale students also raised questions about systemic racism on their own campus, which led Smith College to protest, then Columbia, Princeton, Stanford, and Ithaca College, among many others. #BlacksOnCampus was trending everywhere. In January 2016, the Ithaca College president, Tom Rochon, resigned as well.

"WE CANNOT REWRITE HISTORY, BUT WE CAN RIGHT HISTORY"

More than fifty years have passed since Bloody Sunday, that seminal event in US civil rights history when African Americans and their allies attempted to march from Selma to Montgomery, Alabama, demanding the right to vote. The date was March 7, 1965. As soon as they crossed the Edmund Pettus Bridge in Selma, they were violently attacked by the Alabama State Police, beaten with nightsticks and electric cattle prods, set upon by police dogs, and tear-gassed. They were chased off the bridge, all the way back to Selma's Brown Chapel AME Church, where the march began. News and images of the extreme and unprovoked police violence, in contrast to the conduct of the six hundred marchers, who practiced disciplined nonviolence, spread across the globe. Within months, President Lyndon Johnson would sign the 1965 Voting Rights Act, responding to the public outrage and the pressure applied by a skillfully organized mass movement.

In March 2015, the *Democracy Now!* team went to Selma to cover Bloody Sunday's fiftieth anniversary. Over a hundred thousand people came to Selma for the occasion. They came to march across the Edmund Pettus Bridge. Pettus was a US senator from Alabama. But he was also the Grand Dragon of the Ku Klux Klan, and a Confederate general who was captured three times and escaped.

On March 21, 1915, a motion picture was screened for the first time inside the White House. President Woodrow Wilson sat down to watch D. W. Griffith's *The Birth of a Nation*. The silent film, considered one of the most nakedly racist of all time, falsifies the history of post–Civil War Reconstruction, depicting African Americans freed from slavery as dominant, violent, and oppressive toward Southern whites.

President Wilson said of the film, "It's like writing history with lightning. My only regret is that it is all so terribly true." The film would serve as a powerful recruiting tool for the Ku Klux Klan.

One hundred years later, in January 2015, another film was screened at the White House, this time at the invitation of the first African American president. The film was *Selma*. Director Ava DuVernay watched it with the first couple. She told me, "It was beautiful to be in the White House in 2015 with a film like *Selma*, knowing that in 1915, the first film to ever unspool at the White House was *The Birth of a Nation*."

Selma highlights the story of Dr. Martin Luther King and a young John Lewis, then the twenty-five-year-old leader of the Student Nonviolent Coordinating Committee and one of the march organizers in 1965. Lewis would go on to be a longstanding member of Congress. On that Bloody Sunday in 1965, after Lewis told the Alabama troopers that the six hundred marchers were going to stop and pray, the state troopers didn't hesitate: they assaulted the protesters with full force. They fractured Lewis's skull.

DuVernay put the march into historical context. "*Selma* is a story of justice and dignity. It's about these everyday people. That's what I loved about it. It was about the power of the people," she told me. The story is also about Dr. King, who played a central role in organizing the marches after Bloody Sunday. He wasn't there in that initial march when Lewis was beaten down with so many others. But King led a second march two days later, and ultimately led the march that ended in a rally of 25,000 people on the steps of the State Capitol in Montgomery on March 25, 1965. It was there that King delivered his famous "How Long, Not Long" speech.

DuVernay told me, "There's been no major motion picture released by a studio—no independent motion picture in theaters with King at the center in the fifty years since these events happened—when we have biopics on all kinds of ridiculous people. Nothing on King? No cinematic representation that's meaningful and centered. It was just something I couldn't pass up."

Selma gained national attention. All over the country, students in middle schools and high schools could watch the movie for free. I think that inspired what happened on March 7, 2015, when so many people of all ages and races came out to reenact the crossing of the Edmund Pettus Bridge.

But when it came time for the Oscars in 2015, Ava DuVernay

was not nominated for best director, prompting a furor on social media under the Twitter hash tag #OscarsSoWhite. The following year, outrage mounted when the nominations were announced for the 2016 Academy Awards. Not one African American was nominated in any of the lead categories, which include best actors, best supporting actors, best picture, and best director. A 2012 survey conducted by the *Los Angeles Times* found that Oscar voters are 94 percent white and 76 percent male, with an average age of sixty-three. In response to the national outcry, Cheryl Boone Isaacs, the first African American president of the Academy of Motion Picture Arts and Sciences, announced that the Academy would double the number of women and members of color by 2020.

As for *Selma*, some critics called Ava DuVernay's portrayal of President Lyndon Johnson unfair—saying he'd led the voting rights movement, and yet she had shown him as a reluctant supporter of voting rights.

DuVernay responded, "I'm not here to rehabilitate anyone's image or be a custodian of anyone's legacy. We have to work without permission, especially as women in the industry. Who are we asking for permission to do what we want to do? That should be eradicated. You need to set a path and start walking."

Around the time that I interviewed Ava DuVernay at the annual Sundance Film Festival in Utah, another real-life modern drama was unfolding in South Carolina. It concerned a group of civil rights activists called the Friendship Nine. In 1961 these young African American men sat at a whites-only lunch counter in Rock Hill, South Carolina. They were arrested and sentenced to thirty days hard labor in a county prison camp.

In January 2015, the chief administrative judge for South

Carolina's Sixteenth Judicial Circuit, John C. Hayes III, over-turned their convictions. The judge addressed the activists, now elderly men, saying, "We cannot rewrite history, but we can right history."

Judge Hayes closed a circle: he is the nephew of the judge who'd sentenced the men fifty-four years earlier.

A few weeks after the Friendship Nine were convicted in 1961, South Carolina hoisted a Confederate battle flag over its statehouse. The flag would fly over the capitol or on its grounds for fifty-four years. It would take another nine people, known as the Beautiful Nine, victims of a horrific crime, to force the flag down forever. These were the eight African American parishio-ners and their pastor, Reverend Clementa Pinckney, who were murdered by a white supremacist in the historic Mother Emanuel AME Church in Charleston. (See chapter 9, "'This Flag Comes Down Today.'")

I went back and looked at the front page of the *New York Times* on March 8, 1965, the day after Bloody Sunday. Next to the top headline, "Alabama Police Use Gas and Clubs to Rout Ne-groes" and a photo of John Lewis and others being beaten by state troopers, captioned "Crushing Voter Demonstration," was another headline about the first US Marines sent to Vietnam.

John Lewis eloquently linked racism at home and militarism abroad when he declared, "President Johnson sent soldiers to Viet-nam, but he can't send federal troops to protect us in his own country, in Selma."

From the civil rights movement of half a century ago, to com-munities confronting police brutality today under the banner of Black Lives Matter, from the antiwar movement of the Vietnam War years to the peace movement today, broad movements are making valuable linkages across issues, demanding change. This is ultimately the hope.

How to capture the remarkable journey of the first two decades of *Democracy Now!*?

That was the challenge in writing this book. I found the answer by going back to our original mission: go to where the silence is and give voice to the movements that are shaping our world.

That mission was eloquently captured by my colleague Juan González when he was inducted into the New York Journalism Hall of Fame in November 2015, the first Latino journalist to receive the honor. Juan said of his quarter-century as a columnist:

> I figured my modest contribution would be . . . not writing *about* outcast neighborhoods, but *from* them. Not simply to entertain but to change. Not after the fact, but before it, when coverage could still make a difference.
>
> . . . I have tried to use as many of my columns as possible to probe the injustices visited upon the powerless. Yes, the rich and famous are also victims on occasion. But they have so many politicians, lobbyists, lawyers, gossip columnists and even editorial writers ready to jump to their defense that they'll always do fine without my help.
>
> I prefer the desperate unknown reader who comes to me because he or she has gone everywhere else and no one will listen. More often than not I come across unexpected gems, human beings whose tragedies illuminate the landscape and whose courage hopefully inspires the reader to believe that there is indeed some greater good served by a free press than just chronicling or influencing the ouster of one group of politicians by another.

This book celebrates some of the people and movements who have been making history during our first twenty years. This is not an exhaustive history, nor is it intended as a "greatest hits" of *Democracy Now!* This book is just our way of giving back by celebrating some of the ordinary heroes who have done extraordinary things to make the world a better place.

CHAPTER 1

THE WAR AND PEACE REPORT

As I have walked among the desperate, rejected, and angry young men, I have told them that Molotov cocktails and rifles would not solve their problems. I have tried to offer them my deepest compassion while maintaining my conviction that social change comes most meaningfully through nonviolent action. But they ask—and rightly so—what about Vietnam? They ask if our own nation wasn't using massive doses of violence to solve its problems, to bring about the changes it wanted. Their questions hit home, and I knew that I could never again raise my voice against the violence of the oppressed in the ghettos without having first spoken clearly to the greatest purveyor of violence in the world today: my own government.

—From "Beyond Vietnam: A Time to Break Silence"
speech by Dr. Martin Luther King Jr., April 4, 1967

The United States is engaged in what can only be called endless war. The war in Afghanistan is the longest in US history. The invasion and occupation of Iraq, launched in 2003 based on lies that are far too often described politely as "faulty intelligence," killed hundreds of thousands of people, if not over a million, and displaced many millions more. Despite the US troop withdrawal in 2011, Iraq is still consumed by violence, which has spilled over to further inflame the massively destructive Syrian civil war. Elsewhere, US special forces wage clandestine operations in the dark of night, killing and kidnapping. Guantánamo Bay's notorious prison complex exists outside the reach of courts, the press, or any sense of due process, as men arbitrarily swept off the dusty roads of distant countries and held without charge continue to engage in hunger strikes to protest their imprisonment.

The coverage of war is critical to our mission at *Democracy Now!* Our first broadcast was on Monday, February 19, 1996. It was the day before the New Hampshire primary. When we looked into that primary, into that state, we found a striking intersection of issues that would come to be central to our journalism at *Democracy Now!*: war, race, and the power of the media.

So much of US presidential electoral politics is shaped by two of the whitest states in the nation: Iowa, with its caucus vote taking place first in the nation every four years, followed by the New Hampshire primary. Presidential campaigns have now become, essentially, permanent, with presidential hopefuls visiting Iowa and New Hampshire years in advance, "testing the waters." As the primary elections near, the campaigns and their Super PAC supporters pour millions of dollars into organizing and advertising in these two states, setting the tone for the entire national election.

By 1996, New Hampshire was the last holdout against designating an official holiday in honor of Martin Luther King Jr., ten years after it first went into effect in the majority of states. It also had just one statewide newspaper, the *Manchester Union-Leader* (now called the *New Hampshire Union Leader*). It was considered one of the most conservative papers in the country, thanks to the vicious editorials penned by its owner and publisher, William Loeb III. Loeb had long railed against the civil rights movement, and against King in particular. King's assassination on April 4, 1968, prompted a flurry of invective from Loeb, splashed across his signed editorials on the paper's front page. "Dr. King was a brave man, a determined man, but also—in our carefully considered opinion—a clever demagogue," Loeb declared just two weeks after King's death, adding that he was "sick and tired of sentimental slop" about King. Loeb was the racist before whom every Republican presidential hopeful would prostrate himself in pursuit of his coveted endorsement.

Loeb died in 1981, as the fight for a day honoring King was beginning in New Hampshire. His widow, Nackey Scripps Loeb, continued his policy at the paper, inveighing against adoption of the holiday. The *Manchester Union-Leader* offered this odd rationale: King shouldn't be honored, its reasoning went, because he was opposed to the war in Vietnam, and thus unpatriotic. This rhetorical contortion failed to mask the publisher's racism, which was only amplified when, on Monday, January 15, 1996 (that year's federally recognized Martin Luther King Jr. Day), a racist group from Mississippi rallied at the New Hampshire state capitol, thanking the state for its stalwart stand against MLK Day.

The *Manchester Union-Leader* endorsed Republican candidate Patrick Buchanan that year, helping to propel him to victory in the critical New Hampshire primary. Buchanan had never held elective office, but he'd worked as an advisor in both the Nixon and Reagan administrations, and was an outspoken pundit on the far right of American politics, with regular appearances on PBS, CNN, and his own syndicated radio show. He was a principal architect of the "southern strategy," which he'd laid out in a 1971 memo to President Nixon, whereby the Republican Party captured white Democratic voters in the South by appealing to their racism. In a 1993 column, Buchanan wrote, "How long is this endless groveling before every cry of 'racism' going to continue before the whole country collectively throws up?"[1]

Buchanan's inflammatory rhetoric served him well when campaigning in New Hampshire. He pledged, "I promise you that I will tear out this whole diversity program root and branch: Affirmative Action, discrimination, and all racial set asides, they will all be gone."[2]

Among our guests on that first episode of *Democracy Now!* was Reverend Bertha Perkins, pastor at the New Fellowship Baptist Church and a board member of Southern New Hampshire Outreach for Black Unity, who explained, "When you talk about racism in New Hampshire, they have a very unique way of doing it. And they do it by—basically, just excluding us, a denial that we exist."

The state's position on the Martin Luther King Jr. holiday, and the *Manchester Union-Leader*'s disingenuous opposition to it, though, affords an opportunity to revisit that remarkable antiwar speech that King gave on April 4, 1967, one year to the day before he was assassinated. That landmark speech clearly marks the moment that King publicly embraced the antiwar movement, and eloquently expresses the importance of coalition building, of organizing across issues, of uniting disparate sectors. This type of organizing has become standard in recent years. Back then it was groundbreaking.

The "Beyond Vietnam" speech clearly struck a chord with William Loeb. Shortly after King's death, Loeb denigrated his memory: "King charged in a vicious address, sponsored by the Clergy and Laymen Concerned About Vietnam, that American GIs were killing innocent civilians," Loeb wrote, referencing the speech directly. In "Beyond Vietnam," King detailed the history of how the US role escalated in Vietnam. Then he linked the expense of the war to poverty at home, saying, "A few years ago, there was a shining moment in that struggle. It seemed as if there was a real promise of hope for the poor—both black and white—through the poverty program. There were experiments, hopes, new beginnings. Then came the buildup in Vietnam, and I watched this program broken and eviscerated, as if it were some idle political plaything of a society gone mad on war, and I knew that America would never invest the necessary funds or energies in rehabilitation of its poor so long as adventures like Vietnam continued to draw men and skills and money like some demonic destructive suction tube. So, I was increasingly compelled to see the war as an enemy of the poor and to attack it as such."

Over three thousand people had gathered to hear King speak that day, in the sanctuary of the Riverside Church in New York City. In his speech, King called the United States "the greatest purveyor of violence in the world today," and committed to oppose "the giant triplets of racism, extreme materialism, and militarism." Borrowing a phrase from John F. Kennedy, he said, "Those who make peaceful revolution impossible will make violent revolution inevitable." King's speech advanced the antiwar movement to a new level. Almost a year later, feeling the pressure from that movement, President Lyndon Johnson would announce his decision not to seek a second term—four days before King's assassination.

The mainstream backlash against King's "Beyond Vietnam" speech was immediate. *Life* magazine, in an editorial in its April 21 issue, accused King of "betraying the cause for which he worked so long," adding that "much of his speech was a demagogic slander that sounded like a script for Radio Hanoi." The establishment editorial page of the *Washington Post* opined, "Dr. King has done a grave injury to those who are his natural allies . . . He has diminished his usefulness to his cause, his country, and his people." Even the National Association for the Advancement of Colored People (NAACP) weighed in. Its sixty-member board unanimously approved a statement that read in part, "to attempt to merge the civil rights movement with the peace movement . . . is, in our judgment, a serious tactical mistake."

OBAMA'S WARS

From King, who won the Nobel Peace Prize in 1964, jump ahead to the next African American leader to win it: Barack Obama. The first-term senator from Illinois ran for president as the antiwar candidate, first in the Democratic primaries against Senator Hillary Clinton of New York. She refused to admit that her 2002 vote authorizing the invasion of Iraq was a mistake, giving Obama a vital edge throughout the primaries. Then Obama, maintaining his antiwar position, ran in the general election against Senator John McCain, a Vietnam veteran and POW, and won. Nine months into his administration, Obama was named the winner of the 2009 Nobel Peace Prize. Reuters reported that the news "was greeted with gasps from the audience at the announcement ceremony in Oslo." Obama had no major foreign policy accomplishments at that time, and even he admitted, "I do not feel that I deserve to be in the company of so many of the transformative figures who have been honored by this prize." Many accepted that the award for Obama was simply the Nobel committee's tacit repudiation of President George W. Bush and his administration.

On December 10, 2009, Obama went to Oslo, Norway, to receive the Nobel Prize. This was just over a week after he announced a troop surge in Afghanistan. In his thirty-six-minute acceptance speech, he invoked Martin Luther King's name six times. "As someone who stands here as a direct consequence of Dr. King's life's work, I am living testimony to the moral force of nonviolence," Obama said. Unlike King, though, Obama then made the case for war: "I am the commander in chief of the military of a nation in the midst of two wars . . . the instruments of war do have a role to play in preserving the peace." Obama went on to defend militarism: "We will not eradicate violent conflict in our lifetimes. There will be times when nations—acting individually or in concert—will find the use of force not only necessary but morally justified." He added, "To say that force may sometimes be necessary is not a call to cynicism—it is a recognition of history; the imperfections of man and the limits of reason."

In an indirect reference to King, President Obama said, "Our actions matter, and can bend history in the direction of justice." He was paraphrasing King, who said in his last speech before the Southern Christian Leadership Conference, entitled "Where Do We Go From Here?," on August 16, 1967, "Let us realize the arc of the moral universe is long, but it bends toward justice."

A *Washington Post* headline in late 2015 read, "After Vowing to End Two Wars, Obama May Leave Three Behind," pointing to his about-face on sending ground troops into Syria to fight against the so-called Islamic State, along with the continuing wars in Iraq and Afghanistan. Add to these other conflicts where US forces play a role, often clandestinely, in Somalia, Yemen, Sudan, central

African nations such as the Democratic Republic of the Congo, and in Colombia.

DRONES, DEATH, AND DEMONSTRATIONS

The aspect of Obama's wars that perhaps most distinguishes him from his predecessors is his unprecedented reliance on drones. In a remarkable series of articles published by the Intercept, the online news organization founded by Jeremy Scahill, Laura Poitras, and Glenn Greenwald, Scahill wrote, "From his first days as commander in chief, the drone has been President Barack Obama's weapon of choice, used by the military and the CIA to hunt down and kill." Scahill and colleagues obtained a trove of leaked secret documents detailing the Obama administration's assassination and targeted killing program. Intercept journalist Ryan Devereaux reported on a US military campaign in Afghanistan's Hindu Kush mountain range, from 2011 to 2013, called Operation Haymaker. Devereaux wrote, "The documents show that during a five-month stretch of the campaign, nearly nine out of 10 people who died in airstrikes were not the Americans' direct targets." Another analyst he interviewed found that, despite government assurances that drone strikes afford precise targeting, they were "10 times more likely to kill civilians than conventional aircraft."

Years before cofounding the Intercept, Jeremy Scahill was a long-time producer and correspondent for *Democracy Now!* and Ryan Deveraux was a *Democracy Now!* fellow. The Intercept's groundbreaking reporting adds to the work of others, like the London-based Bureau of Investigative Journalism. BIJ carefully amasses data on drone strikes in Pakistan, Yemen, and Somalia, and recently began gathering data in Afghanistan. Drawing from information "reported by US administration and intelligence officials, credible media, academics, and other sources," BIJ has documented more than seven hundred strikes in these regions, starting from 2002 in Yemen, 2004 in Pakistan, 2007 in Somalia, and 2015 in Afghanistan. Between 3,600 and 5,800 people have been killed, most, according to BIJ, only "suspected" militants. At least 532 were civilians, including children, although the upper range of their estimate is likely closer to the truth, with 1,174 civilians killed.

Juxtapose these casualty figures with Obama's stated policy on drones, which he delivered in a speech at the National Defense University on May 23, 2013, as Operation Haymaker was being waged: "Before any strike is taken, there must be near-certainty that no civilians will be killed or injured—the highest standard we can set."

Behind the statistics are real people: children, families, thousands of them. On October 24, 2012, for example, the CIA launched a drone strike in North Waziristan, Pakistan. One person was confirmed killed. Between six and nine were injured. Killed: Mamana Bibi, a sixty-seven-year-old grandmother who was picking okra. Among the wounded: Bibi's grandson, twelve-year-old Zubair Rehman, and his eight-year-old sister, Nabila. After multiple surgeries, Zubair and Nabila would come to the United States a year later, with their father, Rafiq, a schoolteacher, to testify before Congress. Their lawyer, Shahzad Akbar, was denied a visa to enter the United States. Akbar represents many drone strike victims in lawsuits against the United States and speaks fluent English. He would have helped this family navigate their way into the heart of the very nation that bombed them. No doubt, it was thought that denying Akbar a visa would discourage the family from coming as well. But they would not be deterred. They testified before Congress and then came to our studios in New York.

Rafiq Rehman told us, through an interpreter, "I had gone to Miranshah to buy some things from the bazaar. And so, then, when I returned, I noticed that in the graveyard on the outskirts of our village, they were preparing for a burial. I asked some little children who they were preparing the burial for. And they said, 'Latif Rehman's mother.' And that's my older brother. So I knew at that point that my mother had been killed by an American drone."

Nabila recalled that the attack came just before Eid, the Muslim holiday that marks the end of Ramadan, the holy month of fasting. "I was outside with my grandmother, and she was teaching me how to tell the difference between okra that was ripe and not ripe. We were going to prepare it for our Eid dinner the next day. And then I had heard a *dum-dum* noise. Everything became dark. And I had seen two fireballs come down from the sky." Zubair added, "I had seen a drone, and two missiles hit down where my grandmother was standing in front of me. And she was blown into pieces, and I was injured in my left leg." He went on, "My grandmother, there was no one else like her. She was full of love. And when she passed away, all my friends told me that 'You weren't the only one who lost a grandmother; we all lost a grandmother,' because everyone knew her in the village."

The BIJ provided a detailed summary of the strike, backed up with documentation and firsthand accounts. Mamana Bibi, the grandmother, was a midwife. At least five of her grandchildren were injured. There were no "militants" in the area.

"What I'd like to say to the American people is: Please tell your government to end these drones," Zubair told us. In his testimony before Congress, Zubair said, "I no longer love blue skies. In fact,

I now prefer gray skies. The drones do not fly when the skies are gray. And for a short period of time, the mental tension and fear eases. When the skies brighten, though, the drones return, and so, too, does the fear."

Months before the Rehman family spoke before Congress, another young man testified about trying to survive at the target end of US foreign policy. Farea al-Muslimi is a writer and activist from Yemen, currently working at the Carnegie Endowment for International Peace. He appeared before the US Senate on April 23, 2013, just six days after his home village was struck by a drone. His testimony was unforgettable:

> I am from Wessab, a remote mountain village in Yemen. Just six days ago, my village was struck by an American drone in an attack that terrified the region's poor farmers. Wessab is my village, but America has helped me grow up and become what I am today. I come from a family that lives off the fruit, vegetables and livestock we raise in our farms. My father's income rarely exceeded two hundred dollars. He learned to read late in his life, and my mother never did.
>
> My life, however, has been different. I am who I am today because the US State Department supported my education. I spent a year living with an American family and attending an American high school. That was one of the best years of my life. I learned about American culture, managed the school basketball team and participated in trick-or-treat on Halloween. But the most exceptional experience was coming to know someone who ended up being like a father to me. He was a member of the US Air Force. Most of my year was spent with him and his family. He came to the mosque with me, and I went to church with him. And he became my best friend in America. I went to the US as an

ambassador for Yemen, and I came back to Yemen as an ambassador of the US.

I could never have imagined that the same hand that changed my life and took it from miserable to promising would also drone my village. My understanding is that a man named Hamid al-Radmi was the target of a drone strike. Many people in Wessab know al-Radmi, and the Yemeni government could easily have found and arrested him. Al-Radmi was well known to government officials, and even local government could have captured him if the US had told them to do so.

At best, what Wessab's villagers knew of the US was based on my stories about my wonderful experiences here. The friendships and values I experienced and described to the villagers helped them understand the America that I know and that I love. Now, however, when they think of America, they think of the terror they feel from the drones that hover over their heads, ready to fire missiles at any time. What the violent militants had previously failed to achieve, one drone strike accomplished in an instant. There is now an intense anger against America in Wessab.

This is not an isolated incident. The drone strikes are the face of America to many Yemenis.

Farea al-Muslimi himself had a direct encounter with drones. He was visiting a Yemeni village when he heard a loud buzz overhead. Residents told him it was a drone. He recounted, "I felt helpless. It was the first time that I had truly feared for my life or for an American friend's life in Yemen. I couldn't help but think that the drone operator just might be my American friend with whom I had the warmest and deepest relationship. I was torn between this great country that I love and the drone above my head that could not differentiate between me and some AQAP [Al Qaeda on the Arabian Peninsula] militants."

Sadly, most US senators on the committee didn't even bother to show up for Farea al-Muslimi's testimony. As they shape US foreign policy, it would be instructive for them to hear just ten seconds of what this young man had to say: "What the violent militants had previously failed to achieve, one drone strike accomplished in an instant." On *Democracy Now!*, we broadcast Farea al-Muslimi's testimony in its entirety.

Antiwar activists have been organizing to stop this new form of remote-controlled killing. One of the most prominent groups challenging Obama's drone program is Codepink. Founded in 2002, Codepink was satirically named after the Bush administration's color-coded "terror alert" rating, which left New York City and other high-profile locations under a perpetual "Code Orange" level of enhanced security. The government has since dropped the color scheme, but Codepink persists. The group describes itself as "a women-led grassroots organization working to end US wars and militarism, support peace and human rights initiatives, and redirect tax dollars into health care, education, green jobs, and other life-affirming programs." It was cofounded by Medea Benjamin, activist and author of *Drone Warfare: Killing by Remote Control*. Dressed in pink, she and her sister activists are regular fixtures at congressional hearings, directly challenging those in power by interrupting them from the audience. These actions are often captured on C-Span, the cable television channel that televises Congress.

On the last weekend in April 2012, Benjamin and Codepink hosted the International Drone Summit in Washington, DC, to organize effective opposition to drone warfare. The next day, Monday, April 30, John Brennan, a top national security advisor to

President Obama—who would later become the director of the Central Intelligence Agency—spoke at the Woodrow Wilson International Center for Scholars. He made the first official public admission about the targeted killing program: "[T]he United States government conducts targeted strikes against specific Al Qaeda terrorists, sometimes using remotely piloted aircraft, often referred to publicly as drones. And I'm here today because President Obama has instructed us to be more open with the American people about these efforts."

As usual, Benjamin was there. She spoke out, declaring, "How many people are you willing to sacrifice? Why are you lying to the American people and not saying how many innocents have been killed? I speak out on behalf of Tariq Aziz, a sixteen-year-old in Pakistan, who was killed because he wanted to document the drone strikes. I speak out on behalf of Abdulrahman al-Awlaki, a sixteen-year-old born in Denver, killed in Yemen, just because his father was someone we don't like. I speak out on behalf of the Constitution, on behalf of the rule of law. I love the rule of law. I love my country. You are making us less safe by killing so many innocent people."

The two victims she mentioned were both sixteen-year-old boys. Tariq Aziz, from Pakistan, had volunteered to learn photography to begin documenting drone strikes near his home. He attended an antidrone conference in Islamabad, and participated in a news conference where he and others decried the practice of drone strikes. On October 31, 2012, just seventy-two hours after returning home to his rural community to begin the work of documenting the attacks, Aziz himself was killed in a US drone strike, along with his twelve-year-old cousin.

Abdulrahman al-Awlaki was a US citizen who was living with his grandfather in Sana'a, Yemen's largest city. His father, Anwar al-Awlaki, had been a respected Muslim scholar and cleric in the United States, with dual Yemeni-American citizenship. In the wake of 9/11, Anwar al-Awlaki frequently appeared in the media, as he eloquently explained Islam while also extolling American freedoms. He even lectured at the Pentagon. But he became radicalized, in part due to increasing FBI and police harassment of the Muslim community in the United States, and the killing of Muslims in Afghanistan and later in Iraq. He returned to Yemen, bringing his family to join him. From Yemen, Anwar al-Awlaki preached jihad against America and became a key target of the US government. He fled the city to avoid capture. In 2011 his son Abdulrahman decided to go out on his own to find his father. While he searched, his father was killed in a drone strike. Unaware of his father's death, he continued searching. Two weeks later he too was killed in a drone strike, along with his cousin and at least five other civilians, while sitting at an outdoor café. The US government would never admit publicly that it killed the young US citizen in a drone strike, let alone why.

In June 2013, I had a chance to interview Abdulrahman's grandfather, Nasser al-Awlaki, from Yemen. The former Fulbright scholar and Yemeni government official had desperately sued to block the targeted killing of his son Anwar al-Awlaki before the Obama administration succeeded in assassinating him, but the US courts offered no protection. As for his grandson, he told me, "Abdulrahman did nothing against the United States. He's only sixteen years old, and he is an American citizen. He was born in America. And he was killed by his own government. . . . What we are asking for is just that we know exactly why Abdulrahman was killed."

In May 2013, President Obama delivered a speech at the National Defense University that was billed as an announcement of a major shift in drone policy. Medea Benjamin was again there. As

Obama spoke, Benjamin's voice could be heard from the audience. After engaging the president on why he hadn't closed the Guantánamo Bay prison, she shouted:

MEDEA BENJAMIN: How about Abdulrahman al-Awlaki, sixteen-year-old American citizen—

PRESIDENT BARACK OBAMA: When we—

MEDEA BENJAMIN:—killed [*inaudible*]

PRESIDENT BARACK OBAMA: We went—

MEDEA BENJAMIN: Is that the way we treat a sixteen-year-old American?

PRESIDENT BARACK OBAMA: He went on to—

MEDEA BENJAMIN: Why was he killed?

PRESIDENT BARACK OBAMA: We went on—

MEDEA BENJAMIN: Can you tell us why Abdulrahman al-Awlaki was killed? Can you tell the Muslim people their lives are as precious as our lives? Can you take the drones out of the hands of the CIA? Can you stop the signature strikes that are killing people on the basis of suspicious activities?

PRESIDENT BARACK OBAMA: We're addressing that, ma'am.

MEDEA BENJAMIN: Will you apologize to the thousands of Muslims that you have killed? Will you compensate the innocent family victims? That will make us safer here at home. I love my country. I love the rule of law. Drones are making us less safe. And keeping people in indefinite detention in Guantánamo is making us less safe. Abide by the rule of law. You're a constitutional lawyer.

PRESIDENT BARACK OBAMA: You know, I think that the—and I'm going off script, as you might expect, here. The voice of that woman is worth paying attention to. Obviously I do not agree with much of what she said. And obviously she wasn't listening to me in much of what I said. But these are tough issues, and the suggestion that we can gloss over them is wrong.

The next day, Medea Benjamin was our guest on *Democracy Now!* to talk about why she repeatedly interrupted Obama's address. "I was very disappointed. He said that his policy is to capture, not kill. That's just not true. I know personally of many incidents where it would have been very easy to capture people, like the sixteen-year-old Tariq Aziz in Pakistan, who was in Islamabad at a well-known hotel, but instead was killed by a drone strike two days later," Benjamin said. "I think the president is really justifying the use of drones, which will continue to happen under his administration and be passed on to the next."

Benjamin told me that President Obama "said that I wasn't listening to him. I was hanging on every single word. I really expected to hear some major policy changes, and I didn't know whether I was going to speak up or not. If he had said something like, 'To show my commitment to Guantánamo, next week we will start releasing those prisoners who have been cleared,' or if he had said, 'We're taking drones out of the hands of the CIA immediately,' or, 'We're going to immediately say that signature strikes, where people are killed on the basis of suspicious behavior, will no longer be allowed'—if he had said anything like that, I wouldn't have spoken up."

I then asked her why she objected to the *New York Times* describing her as a "heckler." "I think a heckler is a very negative term, and I think it's a positive thing when people find the courage to speak up to leaders who are not leading. And I didn't do what I did to embarrass the president. I did it because I feel that he needs to be pushed more, that it has been over four years now of policies that have been killing innocent people with drones. It has been now over eleven years that innocent people are still being held in Guantánamo and now being force-fed. These are crisis situations, and it requires more from us as citizens."

BODY OF WAR

On May 1, 2003, President Bush delivered his "Mission Accomplished" speech aboard the aircraft carrier USS *Abraham Lincoln*, dressed in a military flight suit that was cinched tightly around his crotch. The war was over, he boasted.

Only, it wasn't. Eleven months later, on April 4, 2004, Tomas Young was just five days into his first deployment to Iraq when he was struck by a sniper's bullet in Baghdad's Sadr City. The single shot paralyzed him from the chest down.

Tomas Young's remarkable story was told poignantly in a feature-length documentary, *Body of War*, directed by legendary TV talk-show host Phil Donahue and filmmaker Ellen Spiro. In the film, Tomas talks about the day he was injured:

"I only managed to spend maybe five days in Iraq until I got picked to go on my first mission. There were twenty-five of us crammed into the back of a two-and-a-half-ton truck with no covering on top or armor on the sides. For the Iraqis on the top of the roof, it just looked like, you know, ducks in a barrel. They didn't even have to aim."

This was just eleven days after President Bush had been yukking it up before hundreds of journalists and members of the Beltway elite at the annual Radio and Television Correspondents Dinner in Washington, DC. He showed photos of himself in the Oval Office, down on all fours, looking for WMDs behind curtains and under his desk. "Those weapons of mass destruction have got to be somewhere," Bush joked. It was incomprehensible that the pretext used to send thousands of young men and women to their deaths, for a war that cost, by some estimates, upwards of a million people their lives, had become a punch line.

"Nope, no weapons over there . . . maybe under here," he said. Many in the press corps guffawed.

The film *Body of War* documents Tomas Young's struggle, coping with paralysis and life in a wheelchair, its impact on his psyche, his wrecked marriage, his family, and his political development from military enlistee into a member of Iraq Veterans Against the War. IVAW held its inaugural press conference at the Boston Public Library in the summer of 2004, during the annual convention of another, older antiwar veterans group, Veterans for Peace (VFP). IVAW formed to give voice and structure to the widespread opposition to the Iraq invasion and occupation that existed within the ranks of the US military and its new, growing population of young veterans. *Democracy Now!* was at that first press conference and has followed IVAW's work ever since.

Soldiers, sailors, marines, Coast Guard, the National Guard: we have covered the torrent of GI resistance that was sweeping all the US services, yet went almost entirely unreported. Soldiers were refusing to deploy or to redeploy, were filing applications for conscientious objector status (which were all too often rejected), active duty service members were fleeing to Canada, and many soldiers were going AWOL, desperate to avoid the carnage and inhumanity of the wars in Iraq and Afghanistan. From these many, IVAW formed.

It was appropriate that the group publicly launched at the Veterans for Peace convention. That group's members today are predominantly veterans of the Vietnam War. They welcomed their new brothers and sisters. VFP was formed in the 1980s and has included veterans of all the US wars and conflicts from before World War II on. Among its members have been veterans of the Abraham Lincoln Brigade, Americans who went to Spain to defend the democratically elected government against the forces of the fascist general Franco, during the Spanish Civil War of 1936–39. The VFP chapter in Madison, Wisconsin, is named after one of those Lincoln "Brigadistas," Clarence Kailin, who organized for social justice from his twenties, when he went to fight in Spain, until he died at age ninety-five in 2009. The Madison VFP chapter states on its website, "It is our fervent wish that we have no more wars from which we add to our membership."

Phil Donahue was no stranger to covering antiwar views. He had been producing and hosting a daily, prime-time news program on MSNBC. In early 2003, Donahue's program was MSNBC's top-rated show. Then, just weeks before the March 19, 2003, invasion of Iraq, his show was abruptly canceled. Shortly afterward, a leaked internal memo from NBC said Donahue presented a "difficult public face for NBC in a time of war. He seems to delight in presenting guests who are antiwar, anti-Bush, and skeptical of the administration's motives . . . at the same time that our competitors are waving the flag at every opportunity."

I was invited to appear on MSNBC for the cable channel's tenth anniversary. It was the last day of July 2006, and MSNBC host Chris Matthews was broadcasting outside 30 Rockefeller Plaza in New York City. As we came back from a commercial break, Matthews pointed up to the top of NBC's headquarters, called the Top of the Rock, and said he would be joining the network executives there shortly to celebrate. I responded, "I want to congratulate you, Chris, on ten years of MSNBC. But I wish standing with you was Phil Donahue. He shouldn't have been fired for expressing an antiwar point of view on the eve of the invasion."

Matthews replied, "I don't know what the reasons were, but I doubt it was that."

But the leaked NBC memo was clear: Donahue was fired because he brought antiwar voices to prime-time TV. At the time of his program's cancellation, back in 2003, a majority of Americans supported both more time for weapons inspections in Iraq and more time for diplomacy to solve the crisis.

So Phil Donahue turned his media talents to telling the story of a remarkable patriot, Tomas Young.

I first met Tomas Young in the summer of 2005. He was with the grieving mother-turned-peace-activist Cindy Sheehan at Camp Casey, the protest encampment in Crawford, Texas, not far from the ranch of President George W. Bush. Sheehan named the encampment after her dead son, Casey, who was killed on April 4, 2004, the same day that Tomas was shot, both in Sadr City.

Bush took extended vacations at his "ranch," and a servile press corps followed dutifully, broadcasting images of him cutting brush and chopping wood. At the start of his 2005 vacation, Bush delivered a speech to the annual convention of the American Legislative Exchange Council (ALEC). The nonprofit Center for Media and Democracy writes that at these ALEC meetings, "corporate lobbyists and state legislators vote as equals on 'model bills' to change our rights that often benefit the corporations' bottom line at public expense. . . . Participating legislators, overwhelmingly conservative Republicans, then bring those proposals home and introduce them in statehouses—without disclosing that corporations crafted and voted on the bills." ALEC is the source of many state laws that restrict gun control, limit a woman's right to choose whether or not to have an abortion, and roll back environmental, workplace safety, and any number of other sensible regulations.

In his speech at the ALEC meeting, Bush declared, "Our men and women who have lost their lives in Iraq and Afghanistan and in this war on terror have died in a noble cause, in a selfless cause."

Cindy Sheehan was outraged. She was slated to give the keynote address several days later at a different conference in Dallas: the 2005 annual convention of Veterans for Peace. After the convention ended, she drove to Crawford to ask President Bush directly: "For what noble cause did my son die?" A dozen or so Veterans for Peace accompanied her, setting up "Camp Casey" outside the entrance to the Bush ranch.

The protests grew, attracting international attention, as Bush's vacation continued. *Democracy Now!* broadcast live from the site, interviewing Sheehan and others who had lost loved ones in Iraq, as well as some who had loved ones still deployed there. We interviewed organizers, activists, elected representatives, members of the clergy, commissioned officers, a senior diplomat, an FBI whistleblower, and others. We also interviewed Tomas Young.

The film *Body of War* premiered in the spring of 2008. A grim milestone was marked at that time, as the number of US soldiers killed in Iraq had just surpassed four thousand. Typically unmentioned alongside the count of US war dead are the tens of thousands of wounded, to say nothing of the Iraqi dead. The Pentagon doesn't tout the number of Americans injured, but the Iraq Coalition Casualty Count project (www.icasualties.org) had reported 32,223 US service-members wounded between the March 2003 invasion and the troop pullout in November 2011.

In an interview on ABC News at the time, Vice President Dick Cheney was asked about the four thousand soldiers killed. "The president carries the biggest burden, obviously," he said. "He's the one who has to make the decision to commit young Americans, but we are fortunate to have a group of men and women, an all-volunteer force, who voluntarily put on the uniform and go in harm's way for the rest of us."

Just after the film premiered, I interviewed Tomas Young from his home in Kansas City, Missouri. I asked him what he thought about the vice president's comments. Tomas replied, "From one of those soldiers who volunteered to go to Afghanistan after September 11, which was where the evidence said we needed to go, to [Cheney], the master of the college deferment in Vietnam: many of us volunteered with patriotic feelings in our heart, only to see them subverted and bastardized by the administration and sent into the wrong country."

In one of the most moving scenes in the film, Young meets Democratic Senator Robert Byrd, the longest-serving senator with the most votes cast in Senate history (more than eighteen thousand). Byrd said his "no" vote on the Iraq War resolution was the most important of his life. Young helped him read the names of the twenty-three senators who voted against the resolution. Byrd, who died in 2010 at age ninety-two, still representing West Virginia, reflected: "The immortal twenty-three. Our founders would be so proud." Turning to Young, he said, "Thank you for your service. Man, you've made a great sacrifice. You served your country well."

Young replied, "As have you, sir."

At about the same time as the film's premiere, IVAW held a remarkable event just outside Washington, DC, called "Winter Soldier: Iraq and Afghanistan—Eyewitness Accounts of the Occupation." Military veterans from Iraq and Afghanistan who opposed the ongoing occupations spoke candidly about their experiences, describing in brutal detail the violence, potential war crimes, the post-traumatic stress disorder (PTSD), and the epidemic of suicide.

The weekend of testimonials was based on a similar event in 1971, the original Winter Soldier hearings, held by antiwar veterans of the Vietnam War. The name "Winter Soldier," coined by Vietnam Veterans Against the War (VVAW), was inspired by Thomas Paine's *The American Crisis*, a series of essays Paine wrote during the American Revolution. Paine opened the first in the series, "These are the times that try men's souls. The summer soldier and the sunshine patriot will, in this crisis, shrink from the service of their country; but he that stands by it now, deserves the love and thanks of man and woman." The phrase "Winter Soldier" was explained during testimony before the Senate Committee on Foreign Relations by a young US Navy lieutenant named John Kerry, who would later become a US senator from Massachusetts and then secretary of state. Kerry spoke about a report produced by VVAW that detailed alleged war crimes witnessed by, or in many cases perpetrated by, the soldiers themselves. He said, "We who have come here to Washington have come here because we feel we have to be winter soldiers now. We could come back to this country; we could be quiet; we could hold our silence; we could not tell what went on in Vietnam, but we feel because of what threatens this country, the fact that the crimes threaten it—not reds and not redcoats, but the crimes which we are committing that threaten it—that we have to speak out."

His testimony would be best remembered for two questions he posed before the Senate committee: "[H]ow do you ask a man to be the last man to die in Vietnam? How do you ask a man to be the last man to die for a mistake?"

Several months after the release of *Body of War*, a blood clot lodged in Tomas's arm, causing severe complications. He lost most of the use of his arms, and suffered diminished ability to speak. He never lost his deep commitment to peace or his hope that those responsible for the war would be held accountable.

In February 2013, appearing via video stream before an audience of *Body of War* in Litchfield, Connecticut, he shocked the crowd by telling them that he intended to end his own life. The thirty-three-year-old veteran said he would simply stop eating.

At the screening, Tomas was asked how he wanted to be remembered. He replied, "That I fought as hard as I could to keep young men and women away from military service. I fought as hard as I could to keep another me from coming back from Iraq. That is what I want to be remembered for."

Soon after announcing his intent to commit suicide, Tomas Young released "The Last Letter: A Message to George W. Bush and Dick Cheney from a Dying Veteran." We sent a TV satellite truck to his house in Kansas City. Tomas struggled to sit upright, to face the camera for our broadcast, then he read his letter aloud: "You may evade justice, but in our eyes you are each guilty of egregious war crimes, of plunder and, finally, of murder, including the murder of thousands of young Americans—my fellow veterans— whose future you stole."

I asked Young if anything would change his mind about his decision to end his life. "No," he said, adding that if he were not in such intense, constant pain, he would not be taking this course. "We wouldn't be having this conversation," he told me.

Phil Donahue stayed in touch with Young after making *Body of War*. Donahue told me that making the film was a "spiritual experience . . . a chapter of our lives." He said he understood Young's decision: "[H]e struggles now to speak, although you can understand him. He has difficulty grasping silverware, his opposable thumbs are at a serious deficit . . . so he has to be fed. When he and his [second] wife, Claudia, have gone out to dinner, she would look for a corner of the restaurant, so when she fed him, they wouldn't be stared at. He now has pressure sores, with exposed bone. He recently had a colostomy, so he has a bag on the side of his body. He is fed through a tube, and every other commercial he sees on television is about food. It is beyond awful what Tomas has sustained. He now lies immobile, in a dark bedroom in Kansas City, dutifully cared for by his wife, Claudia, who has been with him for five years.

"Throughout this whole ordeal, I have been with him often enough to know, he wanted to live," said Donahue. "That is what makes it extra sad. He wanted to live. He has fought back against every setback, from the inadequate treatment at the Veterans Administration, to his own PTSD. Now the situation is so dire that no one who is close to him can claim to not understand: He has given up.

"When I look down on this young man," Donahue reflected, "all I can think of is President Bush saying, 'Bring 'em on.' There is almost no remorse."

Claudia told us that Tomas found some relief from marijuana, which is illegal in Kansas and Missouri. So they moved to Oregon, where medical marijuana is legal. Unfortunately, Claudia felt the Veterans Affairs (VA) hospital in Portland did not support his use of marijuana, and punitively reduced his prescription pain medications in response. Seeking a safe, compassionate place, they moved to Seattle, another place with legal medical (and now, recreational) marijuana. Tomas and Claudia felt the VA dragged its heels, leaving them to ration his pain pills.

In his open letter to George W. Bush and Dick Cheney, Tomas concluded "My day of reckoning is upon me. Yours will come.

I hope you will be put on trial. But mostly I hope, for your sakes, that you find the moral courage to face what you have done to me and to many, many others who deserved to live. I hope that before your time on Earth ends, as mine is now ending, you will find the strength of character to stand before the American public and the world, and in particular the Iraqi people, and beg for forgiveness."

Just before Veterans Day 2014, Young died at home in Seattle, with his wife by his side. He was just one soldier, one veteran, out of the more than 2.3 million deployed to the wars in Afghanistan and Iraq since 2001. The Iraq Coalition Casualty Count project maintains a detailed online database of troop fatalities for both the Iraq and Afghan wars. As of January 2016, there had been 6,873 US soldiers killed. This doesn't count several thousand more from the coalition partner nations, and hundreds more private military contractors. Based on the Pentagon's own numbers, from 2001 through June 2015, there were over 320,000 traumatic brain injuries in the military. Actual rates could be twice as high as that. The occurrence of PTSD is epidemic among veterans, both those from the Vietnam era and from the recent wars.

HONOR THE DEAD, HEAL THE WOUNDED, STOP THE WARS

IVAW organized a march in Chicago on May 20, 2012, to confront a summit of the North Atlantic Treaty Organization, or NATO, where close to thirty heads of state were meeting. Hundreds of veterans in camouflage uniforms marched through the streets, to the high fences that had been erected to protect the

NATO leaders. One by one, fifty of these antiwar veterans ascended a simple stage, declared their opposition to the wars, and hurled their combat medals over the fence. Like Winter Soldier, this protest was also inspired by an earlier protest. Vietnam veterans, including John Kerry, stood in front of the Nixon White House in 1971 and threw their medals over the fence as a statement against war.

In the midst of the NATO protests in Chicago, two filmmakers, Haskell Wexler and James Foley, had a chance encounter. Wexler was there documenting the protests, at the age of ninety. He made scores of films, won an Emmy and two Oscars. His most iconic film was *Medium Cool,* released in 1969, which included footage from the protests at the 1968 Democratic National Convention in Chicago.

Foley volunteered to help Wexler document the protests for the film that Wexler later released, *Four Days in Chicago.* The Chicago protest was in late May 2012. Foley had just returned from war reporting in Syria.

By August, James Foley was back in Syria reporting on the civil war for GlobalPost. He went missing on November 22 and was held captive by ISIS for two years. Sometime in mid-August 2014, ISIS beheaded him, then released a gruesome video of the execution.

Wexler's exchange with Foley was captured on camera:

HASKELL WEXLER: What countries recently have you been filming, taping?
JAMES FOLEY: Libya, Syria. I was in Afghanistan with US troops in 2010. And I'm really interested in the young guys, the ones that are just coming back from Iraq and Afghanistan, those

guys' perspectives, you know, because that has a huge impact, you know. And if they're giving their medals back, that harkens back to the Winter Soldiers, essentially in Vietnam and Kerry and what those guys did, right? So, I'm really interested in that young mentality. I've seen young vets that are in Occupy in DC and New York, and kind of gravitated toward them a little bit, because . . . they have the most authentic voice to criticize NATO right now. They were inside the beast.

In 2016, I interviewed James Foley's parents and several of his colleagues, shortly after the premiere of a documentary about his life, *Jim: The James Foley Story*. I asked his mother, Diane Foley, if it was fair to say that Jim covered war to end war.

"I think that's very true," she said. "He wanted to understand the issues, and certainly particularly the issues of the civilians and the children. And he really felt our world, the Western world, really needed to know those stories."

The corporate media rarely told that side of the James Foley story. The documentary, filmed by James Foley's childhood friend Brian Oakes, captured his dedication and commitment to peace.

Freelance journalist Clare Gillis, who worked with Foley in Syria and in Libya before that, told me about a 2014 *Wall Street Journal*/NBC poll that showed that 94 percent of Americans knew about the beheadings of American journalists by ISIS—higher than any other news event the poll has measured in the past five years. "It would have been very disturbing to him . . . he never wanted his face to be anywhere near what he went there for. He went there to show the suffering of the Syrian people. He devoted, quite literally, his life to doing that."

FIGHTING FOR PEACE IN THE MIDST OF WAR

There is nothing more dangerous than to enter a war zone, unarmed, to advocate for peace. Sami Rasouli did just that. He grew up in An Najaf, Iraq, considered one of Shia Islam's holiest cities. After finishing his degree in the 1970s, he taught math in the United Arab Emirates and then moved to Germany, where he met his Palestinian wife. In 1985 they traveled to the United States, seeking a cure for their eldest child's deafness. The treatment failed, but Rasouli and his family decided to settle in Minneapolis. By 1990, he had opened a restaurant, Sinbad's, which became one of the most popular spots in town. He was featured on the cover of *Minneapolis* magazine. Then, in November 2003 he made the journey to his home city, his first time back in twenty-seven years. There he witnessed firsthand the catastrophe of the US invasion and occupation of Iraq.

"I was really destroyed by seeing the amount of the destruction and devastated country after the war and also the effects of the sanctions the last twelve years," he told me after returning from his trip. He recounted the killings, the kidnappings.

The next year he made the difficult decision to sell his restaurant, leave his community in Minneapolis, pack up, and head home to Iraq for good. Rasouli founded Muslim Peacemaker Teams (MPT), an organization whose mission, he said, is to "bring Iraqis together in peace to work for the good of the country, and encourage Iraqi people to be self-sufficient in the face of the violence across the country."

I asked him how he could move into a war zone, and what he would actually do in Iraq. He replied humbly, "I would do anything, anything. Probably I will start cleaning the streets where my sister lives." He did that, and then joined with allied Christian Peacemaker Teams to clean up Fallujah. The city had been devastated twice by the US military in 2004: the United States not only bombed and occupied, but dropped the napalm-like chemical weapon white phosphorous. "We went knocking [on] the doors of the residents to [take] away refuse and waste," he said. "And the people there were touched. They actually haven't seen any garbage collectors for the previous two years, since the war started. So they invited us to pray with them . . . We prayed in the Al Furqan Mosque in the area of Saba Nissan. There were close to two thousand worshippers, where the sheikh changed his sermon to [one of] unity. People learned about us, that we were among them, Sunni and Shiites worshipping together, same God, having the same holy book, the Quran."

Soon the Minneapolis City Council voted unanimously to make Rasouli's home city, Najaf, a sister city, and a Minnesota partner organization formed to foster person-to-person contact between the two distant cities that were united by one courageous activist. He consulted on the creation of the new Iraqi constitution and then worked to overcome an outbreak of cholera.

Over the years, in our interviews with him, Rasouli has called consistently for the United States to leave Iraq, from 2007, in response to the so-called surge and its oft-touted success, all the way up to 2014, as ISIS made rapid strikes against the Iraqi national army and scored victory after victory. Rasouli told me, "I think the US should get out of the area. But what's going on is controlled by the huge embassy in Baghdad, run by at least five thousand employees. They have nothing to do except monitor Iraq, advising the Iraqi government what to do, and also monitoring the area surrounded by Iraq. The five thousand, this is [in addition to] the estimated ten thousand military forces who are stationed there to protect the interest of the embassy and the US. So, I think they should leave the area, not to intervene, end the war in Afghanistan, and pull out their forces, and let the Arabs and the countries of the area solve their problem. But it's not going to be easy. It's going to take some time, but eventually they will figure out a way.

"My home is Mother Earth," Rasouli told me. "Peace should prevail, wherever there is violence—not only in Iraq, Afghanistan, but beyond that, and we keep continuing our efforts."

A FORCE MORE POWERFUL THAN WAR

What if war were not an option? What if people had to resolve conflicts nonviolently?

This is a central question that we pursue in our news reporting on *Democracy Now!* From individuals taking principled action, to efforts of small community groups that meet in churches, mosques, union halls, and campuses, to national coalitions, the peace movement is a broad mosaic. The mainstream, corporate media typically ignores it. Despite this, the daily work of building organizations, researching issues, and discussing and debating them to determine positions and strategies, writing to elected officials, maintaining vigils and organizing marches—all the hard work of building grassroots power—happens every day in this country. Unfortunately, many in the media don't consider this collective effort to be very newsworthy.

But if you consider the key movements on which US history has hinged, they have always required mass mobilization; people coming together to demand change. The effort to stop the invasion of Iraq was one such movement.

Democracy Now! and a number of other independent media

outlets covered the succession of lies that came out of the Bush-Cheney administration, interviewing dissenters and critics; people who challenged the dominant narrative that Iraqi dictator Saddam Hussein was developing weapons of mass destruction. President George W. Bush said in a speech in Cincinnati on October 7, 2002, "Facing clear evidence of peril, we cannot wait for the final proof—the smoking gun—that could come in the form of a mushroom cloud." The day after that major prowar address, we invited several guests on *Democracy Now!*: Cleveland's Democratic Congressman Dennis Kucinich, who was leading the effort in the House to block the war; Jay Bookman, deputy editorial page editor of the *Atlanta Journal-Constitution*; and Sister Alice Gerdeman of the Intercommunity Justice and Peace Center, which organized protests outside the Cincinnati Museum Center where Bush spoke.

In his speech, the president read a laundry list of threats he claimed were posed by Saddam Hussein, saying that "the Iraqi dictator must not be permitted to threaten America and the world with horrible poisons and diseases and gases and atomic weapons." Hundreds gathered outside. Sister Alice told me, "The crowd outside had one message that I think we held in unison: no war." Yet their presence never made it to the evening news.

Dennis Kucinich's experience in his own congressional offices confirmed the results of research we conducted at *Democracy Now!*: namely, that the telephone calls flooding Congress against a military invasion of Iraq outpaced calls in support many times over. Polling the offices of fifty senators, we found that antiwar calls were coming in at a rate of a hundred to a thousand times those of prowar callers. Jay Bookman, one of the few editorialists from a major newspaper to critically question the drumbeat for war, told me, "There is clear evidence that this war was contemplated long before 9/11 . . . September 11 has become the excuse, the motivation. The administration, instead of trying to reassure America, is trying to scare the hell out of America."

We went on to broadcast voices from a rally in New York's Central Park that occurred on the same day Bush spoke in Cincinnati. Over twenty thousand people attended the rally, yet it didn't register on the national news. There were strong antiwar currents in the country and around the world, for any news organization that was willing to look for them.

A couple of weeks later, on Saturday, October 26, 2002, *Democracy Now!* reported from a major antiwar protest in Washington, DC. The police told us that between 150,000 and 200,000 people attended. The next day, the *New York Times* reported that "fewer people had attended than organizers had hoped for . . . even though the sun came out." NPR reported "fewer than 10,000" showed up.

We had to ask: Were the reporters even there?

It was clear to all of us who were actually *there* that the size of the crowd was significant. In addition to our broadcast, C-SPAN was carrying the protest live. Anyone watching from home could clearly see the masses of people. The *Washington Post* headline read, "Antiwar Protest Largest Since '60s; Organizers Say 100,000 Turned Out."

Democracy Now! producer Mike Burke noticed that the people quoted in the *Times* article had spoken at a press conference a few days earlier. So he tracked down each person quoted in the story. There was an MIT professor, a student from the University of North Carolina (UNC), and Eli Pariser with MoveOn.org.

Pariser confirmed that the *Times* reporter had interviewed him a few days earlier. The MIT professor said the same thing. The UNC student said, "She did interview me at the rally—on my cell phone. I asked her why she wasn't here. She said she was working on another story."

Three days later, the *New York Times* ran another story on the same protest. "The turnout startled even organizers, who had taken out permits for 20,000 marchers," it read. "They expected 30 buses, and were surprised by about 650, coming from as far as Nebraska and Florida." The article continued, "The demonstration on Saturday in Washington drew 100,000 by police estimates and 200,000 by organizers'." An accompanying photo caption noted that the rally was "the biggest antiwar protest since the Vietnam War era."

Who do you believe: the *New York Times* . . . or the *New York Times*?

Democracy Now! attempted to question the reporter and her editors at the *Times* about their coverage, but the *Times* declined to comment. Finally, after we reported on their misreporting, the reporter called us and confirmed that she had left the protest before it had even started. She had seen only the early crowds trickling in, not the actual demonstration. When she realized that the rally was much bigger, she called in a correction to her editors, but they didn't change the numbers.

On October 30, NPR aired a correction: "We erroneously reported on *All Things Considered* that the size of the crowd was fewer than 10,000. While Park Service employees gave no official estimate, it is clear that the crowd was substantially larger than that. . . . We apologize for the error."

Democracy Now! called the *New York Times* and asked why the newspaper of record hadn't issued a correction. An editor told us that the paper hadn't made a mistake. The difference, he said, was only a matter of emphasis.

WAR & PEACE PLANNING

As the war planning and the propaganda from the Bush White House accelerated, so too did the planning to stop it. Press accounts, when they did report on antiwar efforts, often compared them to similar events during the Vietnam War. But those accounts missed a very important point: the antiwar organizing in 2002 was happening *before* the invasion of Iraq had even started. This is one of the most significant achievements of the modern peace movement.

During the Vietnam era, there were some prescient activists who saw the buildup in Vietnam early, such as the twelve college students in New York City who burned their draft cards on May 12, 1964. The first teach-in against the war was held on March 25, 1965, at the University of Michigan, Ann Arbor. Faculty organizers there developed the "teach-in" tactic from their experiences with the sit-ins used in the civil rights movement. But the mass marches and organizing against the Vietnam War took years to build, intensifying only as the number of US casualties increased, and as the images of the war dead, on both sides, became daily fare in the newspapers and on evening news programs in the United States.

In 2002, the organizing began almost immediately after Bush and British prime minister Tony Blair held a press conference on September 7, clearly indicating they would try to overthrow Saddam Hussein. Coalitions formed quickly, harnessing the power of the internet and calling for a global day of protest on February 15, 2003. In the United States, United for Peace and Justice had formed to ensure that the first anniversary of 9/11 would not be exploited for nationalistic or war-making causes but rather commemorated "in the hopes of transforming that day into an occasion that promotes a more just and peaceful world." The group became an organizing hub for the February mass mobilization. In the United Kingdom, the Stop the War Coalition formed just after 9/11, explicitly to challenge the so-called War on Terror. When it became clear that Prime Minister Tony Blair stood shoulder to shoulder with George Bush in planning for an invasion of Iraq, the coalition began working immediately in opposition. Stop the War's work included, it wrote, "thousands of public meetings across the country, direct action in the run-up to UK wars—including walk-outs from schools, colleges, and workplaces—two People's Assemblies, international peace conferences, vigils, lobbies of Parliament, and antiwar cultural events."

Among the members of Stop the War's steering committee in 2003 was Jeremy Corbyn, a member of the British parliament. In 2015, twelve years after the invasion of Iraq, Corbyn would shock the British establishment with his election as leader of the Labour Party, making him the principal opposition leader to the conservative government and thus one of the most powerful figures in the UK. Also in 2015, Tony Blair, who was, at the time of the invasion in 2003, the UK Prime Minister and leader of the Labour Party, would make a critical admission in an interview with CNN's Fareed Zakaria:

> **FAREED ZAKARIA:** When people look at the rise of ISIS, many people point to the invasion of Iraq as the principal cause. What do you say to that?
> **TONY BLAIR:** I think there are elements of truth in that. . . . Of course, you can't say that those of us who removed Saddam in 2003 bear no responsibility for the situation in 2015.

On Saturday, February 15, 2003, the global day of action began, first as dawn broke over the international date line in the Pacific.

In Sydney, Australia, over six hundred thousand marched, with smaller protests around the country. There were marches in Auckland, New Zealand, and in Fiji, Japan, and Korea. In Malaysia, three thousand people violated an official ban and protested. Also violating a ban on protests were scientists and staffers at the United States' McMurdo Station in Antarctica, which at the time was run by the defense contractor Raytheon Company. They had posted three separate group photos in the lead-up to the war, with people forming a peace sign. In one, after being prohibited from including any station buildings, vehicles, uniforms, or insignia in their photo, ten people disrobed and sent a nude protest photo, joining other nude actions around the globe under the heading "Baring Witness." Computer technician Robbie Liben and other protest organizers were eventually fired for their actions.

The global day of action continued, with protests across India, Pakistan, and in Moscow. Thousands marched in Beirut, Lebanon; Amman, Jordan; Damascus, Syria; and Baghdad itself, the target of the intended "Shock and Awe" assault. Tens of thousands marched in South Africa, with separate events in Johannesburg, Cape Town, and Durban, among others. In Europe, the numbers swelled, with thousands in the Czech capital of Prague, as well as in Hungary, Poland, and Ukraine. Muslims and Christians joined together in protest in the Bosnia and Herzegovina city of Mostar, which was itself besieged by war just a decade earlier.

In Rome, three million people marched against war, setting a world record. Huge numbers continued to turn out across Western Europe. In Madrid, where conservative prime minister José María Aznar supported the war, an estimated two million people marched. Over one million people marched in London, breaking that city's record for the largest march in its history.

In New York City, a federal judge had banned the planned

march. Peace demonstrators sought to gather at the United Nations Plaza and then march to Central Park for a rally. US District Court Judge Barbara Jones apparently took the word of the New York City assistant police chief, who said he feared that the police department couldn't provide sufficient security for a moving crowd of up to a hundred thousand people. Judge Jones ruled that the First Amendment guarantees the right to protest but does not ensure the right to march. She said the peace activists could accept the city's counteroffer of a rally at the UN Plaza.

February 15, 2003, was a brutally cold morning in New York. The NYPD, Judge Jones, and the Republican billionaire Mayor Michael Bloomberg had done all they could to minimize the size and impact of the rally. Now the winter weather was doing its part. Yet, despite all the obstacles thrown in front of the organizers, hundreds of thousands of people turned out. Among them was antiapartheid activist and Nobel Peace Prize laureate Archbishop Desmond Tutu from South Africa, legendary performer and civil rights activist Harry Belafonte, anti-prison activist and former Black Panther Angela Davis, and actors Susan Sarandon and Danny Glover, all of whom spoke from the stage.

Not satisfied with barring a march, the NYPD, out in full force in riot gear and supported by intimidating horse-mounted officers, erected barricades across the side streets needed to access First Avenue, Second Avenue, and Third Avenue, thus denying entry to the "stationary rally" to hundreds of thousands of people. We had a live TV broadcast position set up outdoors, behind the stage, with a satellite uplink truck beaming our coverage to the world. Pacifica Radio had ordered a special high-quality phone line from the phone company and had it installed on-site in order to provide live, broadcast-quality radio coverage of the rally. Before the first speaker began, two surly NYPD officers found the phone line, which Verizon had run from a nearby phone booth, and ripped it out of the ground. This was New York's finest, in the media capital of the world, doing everything they could to ensure that voices for peace, against war, were silenced. Pacifica's engineer managed to repair the line, and the rally went out globally over radio, TV, and the internet. Despite the official harassment, organizers estimate that between a half million and a million people turned out that cold winter's day.

People rallied in cities across the United States, Canada, Mexico, and across Latin America. A French academic studied the turnout and estimated that between thirty million to thirty-six million people around the world rose up to oppose war, making it the largest organized mass event in human history.

HUMAN FALLOUT

Endless wars have now spawned the largest migration of human beings since World War II. Europe has been the first stop for this wave of humanity.

In December 2015, my *Democracy Now!* colleagues and I visited a massive, makeshift refugee camp called "The Jungle" on the outskirts of the northern French town of Calais. The camp grows daily, swelling with asylum-seekers fleeing war in Afghanistan, Syria, Iraq, Sudan, and beyond. Their countries of origin are a map of the targets of US bombing campaigns. More than six thousand people in this, France's largest refugee camp, hope for a chance to make the last, dangerous leg of their journey through the nearby Channel Tunnel to England. Wind whips off the North Sea, blasting the shelters made of tarps, tents, plastic sheeting, and scrap lumber in this sprawling, ramshackle end of the line. The roads in the camp are muddy; the portable toilets are filthy. The charity health clinic had been closed since mid-November. The main entrance to the camp is below a freeway, with several police vans parked with lights flashing and armed officers stationed above.

Most who arrive here have endured arduous journeys of thousands of miles, hoping to cross to the United Kingdom. The Channel Tunnel offers asylum-seekers a way to make it to the UK without risking a dangerous crossing of the English Channel, by stowing away on either a high-speed passenger train or a freight train. Accessing either type of train involves significant risk, and accidental deaths occur almost weekly when people leap onto moving trains or stumble under truck tires.

A few days before *Democracy Now!* visited the camp, a Sudanese man named Joseph was killed when he was run over by a car on the highway. Camp residents were protesting that the police had not stopped the driver, holding signs reading "We are Humans, Not Dogs" and "Do survivors of war not have the right to live in peace?" We asked a young man named Majd from Damascus, Syria, why he fled his country: "I escaped from the war. I don't want to die. This war is not my war." We asked him who was attacking his country. He said: "Who? Everyone. Russia and America and Iran—everyone."

Days before we met Majd, the British Parliament voted to attack Syria and began bombing immediately. In the few months prior, the British government built multiple layers of high, razor-wire-topped fences in Calais, sealing off the tunnel entrance and the rail line for miles before the tunnel, as well as the staging area where freight trucks line up to drive onto the rail cars that will carry them through the tunnel. Each truck is also subjected to an infrared scan to look for stowaways. Before the enhanced security, scores of asylum-seekers might get through the tunnel nightly.

Now, it is almost impossible. The more the West bombs their countries, the more it shuts out those who flee its wars.

In the Afghan section of the refugee camp, Sidiq Husain Khil was eager to speak about the fourteen-year-old US war in Afghanistan—the longest war in US history. Like many, he did not want his face to be filmed. We asked him about the effects of US bombing and drone strikes on Afghanistan. He replied: "If they are killing one person or ten persons, one hundred of them are joining the group of Taliban. . . . The war is not the solution for finishing terrorism. They have to talk face-to-face."

As we roamed the camp, pulling our coats tightly around us in the cold, we looked for a woman who would be willing to speak. We met Dur, an Afghan professor of English, who also did not want her face shown. She traveled more than three thousand miles with her four children, by car, bus, horse, foot, and boat. In almost perfect English, her twelve-year-old daughter described their unimaginable route: "First we go to Nimruz province of Afghanistan. Then we went to Pakistan. Then we walked to Saravan, Balochistan. Then Iranshahr, Kerman, Shiraz, Tehran, Kurdistan, and Turkey. Then we start walking in mountains. Then we went to Istanbul, Izmir. Then we arrived to the sea." Dur hired a smuggler to take them in a leaky boat from Turkey to Greece. She told me, "When I saw that boat . . . I called all my children and I start to cry . . . I spent all my money to buy them death." Miraculously, they survived. Whether they make it to their destination, Britain, is another question.

As we left the camp, a man named Najibullah raced up to us. An Afghan who worked with the US Marines as a translator, he applied for a special visa for Afghans who put themselves at risk by working for the United States. He said he was turned down because he hadn't worked for the marines for a full year. "Working with the US government . . . just one day or a year . . . it doesn't matter to the Taliban," he told me. "As long as you work with them just one hour, you're condemned to death."

"Today, Joseph. Tomorrow, who?" read one of the many signs at the protest earlier that day. These refugees are the roadkill of war.

A few days after we left the camp, a painting appeared on the concrete wall of the underpass, where the protest had occurred. It was painted by the globally renowned street artist Banksy, whose identity has never been revealed. Banksy painted a life-size depiction of Steve Jobs, the visionary founder of Apple, with a bag slung over his shoulders. Banksy released a statement to accompany the painting of Jobs:

"We're often led to believe migration is a drain on the country's resources but Steve Jobs was the son of a Syrian migrant. Apple is the world's most profitable company, it pays over $7 billion a year in taxes—and it only exists because they allowed in a young man from Homs."

A NOBLE ENDEAVOR

Working for peace is among the most important and noble of human endeavors. Individuals might feel powerless when confronted with a nation intent on going to war, but history shows that movements matter; that small acts of defiance and dissent can ripple out and create change. Noam Chomsky is a Massachusetts Institute of Technology professor emeritus of linguistics, a field of science that he revolutionized. He is perhaps best known, though, as one of the world's most prolific analysts of US foreign policy. He has authored over a hundred books and still, in his late eighties, is a tireless writer and speaker on issues of war and peace. In the early 1990s, Chomsky wrote an essay called "What You Can Do," which reads in part,

> One of the things [people in power] want is a passive, quiescent population. So one of the things that you can do to make life uncomfortable for them is not be passive and quiescent. There are lots of ways of doing that. Even just asking questions can have an important effect. Demonstrations, writing letters and voting can all be meaningful—it depends on the situation. But the main point is—it's got to be sustained and organized. If you go to one demonstration and then go home, that's something, but the people in power can live with that. What they can't live with is sustained pressure that keeps building, organizations that keep doing things, people who keep learning lessons from the last time and doing it better the next time.

Covering social movements like those Chomsky was writing about, reporting on efforts to effect lasting change—the movements that make history—that is our daily labor at *Democracy Now!* The global protest on February 15, 2003, didn't stop the invasion of Iraq. We can't know for sure what impact it had, or continues to have, as the demands of those thirty million marchers continue to reverberate. Thousands of individuals and groups around the world continue to work for peace, each contributing a small share to what Martin Luther King Jr. called, in his "Beyond Vietnam" speech, "the long and bitter, but beautiful, struggle for a new world."

CHAPTER 2

THE WHISTLEBLOWERS

In the aftermath of the 9/11 attacks, the US government embarked on war abroad and mass surveillance at home. In this national security state, torture, spying, and the killing of innocent civilians became normalized. These abuses would have continued unknown and unchecked were it not for the courageous whistleblowers who unmasked what was taking place in America's name. This is the story of the modern-day patriots who are defending democracy, at great personal cost.

Tucked away on a side street in one of London's toniest neighborhoods, just across the street from the sprawling department store Harrods, sits a Victorian-style brick apartment building. A white oval plaque indicates that the building is home to the Embassy of Ecuador. As my *Democracy Now!* colleagues and I approach the building, we see the ever-present police outside. Soon after walking into the embassy, British police officers in the foyer speak to embassy security, saying they want to see our identification. Under the Vienna Convention, authorities of the host nation may not enter a foreign embassy or question its staff, who enjoy diplomatic immunity.

We choose to ignore the request.

The police want to know who has come to speak with one of the world's most famous whistleblowers, Julian Assange. The Australian internet activist founded WikiLeaks in 2007 and remains its editor. WikiLeaks is an independent nonprofit media organization that publishes leaked information—often secret, and often from government sources. The group says its goal "is to bring important news and information to the public . . . One of our most important activities is to publish original source material alongside our news stories so readers and historians alike can see evidence of the truth."

To the US government, though, revealing information without permission can be tantamount to terrorism.

In April 2010 WikiLeaks released a US military video that it named *Collateral Murder*. The video, taken from an American helicopter gunship flying over Baghdad, captures graphically the killing of at least a dozen Iraqi civilians. Then, in July, WikiLeaks released the Afghan War Logs: more than ninety thousand secret US military communications that laid out the official record of the violent invasion and occupation of Afghanistan, the scale of civilian deaths, and likely war crimes. In October the site released more than 390,000 similar military records from the Iraq War.

The magnitude and pace of the leaks brought unprecedented global attention to WikiLeaks. As its public face, Julian Assange became, almost overnight, a primary target of the Obama administration and a number of other governments around the world, and the subject of the wrath of a broad swath of the US establishment.

In the midst of this, in mid-August 2010, Assange was invited to Sweden to give several talks about WikiLeaks. There, he admits, he had sex with two women on separate occasions. Based on analysis of police reports that followed, which are redacted, at least one of the two women later tried to contact Assange, wanting him to get tested, for assurance that he did not give her a sexually transmitted disease. Unable to reach Assange, they both went to the police for help. Duty Prosecutor Maria Häljebo Kjellstrand received the report and issued an arrest warrant for Assange, for questioning involving suspicion of rape, unlawful coercion, and sexual molestation.

The circumstances of the case are clouded in controversy. Assange's lawyers were subsequently allowed to see, but not make copies of, text messages that one of the women sent from the police station. One message, as written down by the lawyers after being shown it, read "[I] did not want to put any charges on JA but . . . the police were keen on getting a grip on him." Another message, sent hours later after charges had initially been filed, read (as related by the lawyers), "chocked [sic] when they arrested JA because [I] only wanted him to take a test." Assange's lawyers have attempted to obtain the entire text message archive taken by the police, but have been denied by the Swedish authorities for years.

The next day, Chief Public Prosecutor Eva Finné reviewed the cases and decided quickly to cancel the arrest order, saying in a press release, "I consider that there is no reason to suspect that he has committed rape." On suspicion of sexual molestation and coercion, however, the investigation continued, and Assange was questioned by police on August 30.

Two days later, on September 1, another prosecutor, Marianne Ny, got involved and resurrected the case. Through his lawyer, Assange made himself available for questioning for four weeks, to no avail. He then asked for and was granted permission to leave Sweden in order to give a talk in Berlin. The day he left, Prosecutor Ny issued an arrest warrant for him. Assange returned to London, which prompted Ny to issue a European Arrest Warrant, or EAW. According to journalist John Pilger, EAWs are "a draconian product of the 'war on terror' supposedly designed to catch terrorists and organized criminals. The EAW had abolished the obligation on a petitioning state to provide any evidence of a crime. More than a thousand EAWs are issued each month; only a few have anything to do with potential 'terror' charges . . . Many of those extradited face months in prison without charge. There have been a number of shocking miscarriages of justice, of which British judges have been highly critical." [1]

Ny sought Assange's extradition to Sweden for questioning, even though there were never any formal charges made against him. Assange offered to meet the Swedish authorities in their embassy in London, or in Scotland Yard, but was refused. Even though he had not been charged with any crime, he was placed under house arrest in England from 2010 to 2012 as he contested the warrant. He had to wear an electronic ankle shackle so that his whereabouts could be monitored constantly, and he was under a nightly curfew.

It was in the middle of this period, on the weekend of July 4, 2011, that I flew to London to interview Assange at a public event hosted by the Frontline Club, a war correspondents' organization there. Two venues had agreed previously to host the event, only to cancel abruptly. Exceeding all expectations, and after days of rain, more than two thousand people streamed into East London's historic Roxy Theatre on a sunny Saturday afternoon to hear Assange speak. The event had a firm end time, though, as he had to race to catch the last train in order to report to the police and return to the home of the Frontline Club's founder, Vaughan Smith, where he was confined for curfew each night.

On May 30, 2012, the UK Supreme Court ruled against Assange's attempt to have the EAW invalidated and upheld his extradition to Sweden.[2] Despite the fact that he had one further ground for appeal, the wheels were in motion to extradite him. The terms of the EAW treaty required that he be extradited within ten days. Then, four days later, in a highly unusual move, US Secretary of State Hillary Clinton visited Sweden to meet with the foreign minister and minister of defense. It was the first visit to Sweden by a US secretary of state in thirty-six years.[3] The publicly stated reason for her visit, ironically, was to discuss "internet freedom," but the timing, so close to Assange's potential return there as a prisoner, was suspicious.

In early 2012 WikiLeaks began posting documents from another massive leak. These were emails from a private intelligence firm called Stratfor. Someone had leaked more than five million Stratfor emails to WikiLeaks. One of them contained the first proof that the United States was developing a case against Assange. The firm's vice president for intelligence, Fred Burton, wrote in a January 26, 2011, email: "Not for Pub—We have a sealed indictment on Assange. Pls protect." If an indictment had been issued in secret, then Assange could have found himself in US custody shortly after landing in Sweden. He feared he would be charged with espionage, especially since the Obama administration had already invoked the espionage law against whistleblowers more times than all previous US administrations combined.

On June 19, 2012, two weeks after Clinton's visit to Sweden, Assange, believing that the United States was intent on putting him behind bars, fled to the Ecuadorian Embassy in London. He appealed to that country's government for political asylum, which it granted. He has been there ever since, a prisoner inside the embassy, denied even the hour of time outside that most prisoners are guaranteed. If he so much as steps outside the embassy's front door, he will be arrested.

"Julian would have gone to Sweden a long time ago had he gotten a guarantee from Sweden that they will not forward him to the United States for standing trial on the espionage charges," said Assange's attorney, Michael Ratner, president emeritus of the Center for Constitutional Rights. Ratner explained: "Sweden has never been willing to give that guarantee. And Sweden has a very bad reputation of complying with US demands, whether it was sending some people from Sweden to Egypt for torture or whether it's guaranteeing people who are asylees in Sweden that they won't be deported."

Assange has other reasons to fear for his safety if he is sent to the United States. So many public figures have called for Assange's assassination that a website was created to catalog the threats. Former Arkansas governor, perennial presidential candidate, and former Fox News commentator Mike Huckabee said, "Anything less than execution is too kind a penalty."

Prominent conservative political commentator Bill Kristol said, "Why can't we use our various assets to harass, snatch, or neutralize Julian Assange and his collaborators, wherever they are?"

Assange told me, "The US case against WikiLeaks is widely believed to be the largest-ever investigation into a publisher. It is extraterritorial. It's setting new precedents about the ability of the US government to reach out to any media publisher in Europe or the rest of the world, and try and achieve a prosecution. They say the offenses are conspiracy, conspiracy to commit espionage,

Computer Fraud and Abuse Act, computer hacking, conversion, stealing government documents." The espionage charges, if they materialize, could carry the death penalty.

In May 2015 the Swedish Supreme Court, in a 4-to-1 vote, declined to quash the arrest warrant lodged against him in late 2010. Justice Svante Johansson, dissenting, wrote that Assange's de facto detention, with both house arrest and his asylum in the embassy, was "in violation of the principle of proportionality."

There is no technical or legal reason why prosecutors cannot question Assange while he is in the Ecuadorian Embassy, either in person or via video. Yet Marianne Ny has proven intransigent—to the point that the statute of limitations for the coercion and molestation accusations expired in August 2015. The rape accusation still stands, though, and won't expire until 2020.

"WE HAVE NO RIGHTS"

Sitting across from me in the conference room of the small embassy that has served as his home, refuge, and jail for over three years, Assange described the Kafkaesque netherworld he inhabits: "We have no rights as a defendant because the formal trial hasn't started yet. No charges, no trial, no ability to defend yourself . . . [You] don't even have the right to documents, because you're not even a defendant."

Despite Assange's failure to have his Swedish arrest warrants quashed, the Svea Court of Appeals, one of Sweden's highest courts, admonished Marianne Ny for declining to question Assange in the Ecuadorian Embassy. The court noted that "the investigation into the suspected crimes has come to a halt and considers that the failure of the prosecutors to examine alternative avenues is not in line with their obligation—in the interests of everyone concerned—to move the preliminary investigation forward."

Western governments have failed so far to prosecute Julian Assange in court, but they continue to persecute him. In October 2015 the British government refused Ecuador's request to grant him "safe passage" out of the Ecuadorian Embassy so that he could go to a hospital for an MRI. Assange's doctor said that he has constant, severe shoulder pain that requires a Magnetic Resonance Imaging scan to diagnose. Assange's lawyer Carey Shenkman said, "By claiming that Mr. Assange must give up his asylum in order to receive medical treatment, the UK government is forcing him to choose between the human right to asylum and the human right to medical treatment. No one should ever have to face that choice."

This is not the first time that Assange was denied medical care as a result of being trapped in the embassy. The Italian magazine *L'Espresso* obtained a tranche of emails from the Swedish government as a result of a Freedom of Information Act (FOIA) request. In one exchange, Paul Close, an attorney with the UK's Crown Prosecution Service, wrote to Marianne Ny, "By chance I heard the BBC World Service radio report earlier this morning about his health . . . There is no question of him being allowed out of the Ecuadorian Embassy, treated and then allowed to go back. He would be arrested as soon as was appropriate."

When I interviewed Julian Assange in May 2015, I was shocked by how his condition had deteriorated in the year since I had seen him last. His skin was pale from years without sunlight, matching his prematurely white hair, which was long and tied back. But Assange's resolve remains unbroken, and the leaks he originally sought to publish when he founded WikiLeaks in 2007 are still reaching the light of day.

COLLATERAL MURDER

The *Collateral Murder* video—the first of the prominent US military leaks that WikiLeaks released in 2010—was part of a massive transfer of classified information allegedly provided by an American soldier serving in Iraq. That soldier was known at the time as Bradley Manning. Private Manning was ultimately arrested and tried in a court martial proceeding and was convicted. Immediately after the verdict was announced, Manning stated publicly that she had begun a transgender transition, and changed her name to Chelsea Manning.

I say that the information was "allegedly provided" because after being arrested, Manning was held in harsh solitary confinement at the Quantico Marine Corps Base in Virginia for close to a year. Thus, any confession that Manning might have given while at the marines base was made under what amounts to torture and should be viewed as coerced. Manning's confinement that prompted an investigation by Juan Mendez, the UN Special Rapporteur on Torture. Mendez concluded, "I believe Bradley Manning was subjected to cruel, inhuman, and degrading treatment in the excessive and prolonged isolation he was put in during the eight months he was in Quantico."

The original video was recorded on July 12, 2007, by a US Apache helicopter gunship flying over New Baghdad, an area of Baghdad, and includes audio of the helicopter's radio transmissions. The stark, grainy black-and-white video shows a group of men in an open square in Baghdad leading two Reuters employees, to show them an area that had been recently bombed. The Reuters staffers, photographer Namir Noor-Eldeen and his driver, Saeed Chmagh, are shown, each carrying a camera with a telephoto lens. A US soldier in the helicopter says: "Okay, we got a target fifteen coming at you. It's a guy with a weapon." There is much back-and-forth between two helicopters and ground troops in armored vehicles nearby:

"HAVE FIVE TO SIX INDIVIDUALS WITH AK-47S. REQUEST PERMISSION TO ENGAGE."

"ROGER THAT. UH, WE HAVE NO PERSONNEL EAST OF OUR POSITION. SO, UH, YOU ARE FREE TO ENGAGE. OVER."

The helicopter circles around, with the crosshairs squarely in the center of the group of about eight men. WikiLeaks and its partner for this story, the Icelandic National Broadcasting Service, added subtitles to the video, as well as arrows indicating the Reuters employees.

The helicopter opens fire with machine guns, killing most of the men instantly. Noor-Eldeen runs away, and the crosshairs follow him, shooting nonstop until he falls, dead.

The radio transmission continues: "All right, hahaha, I hit 'em . . ." And then: "Yeah, we got one guy crawling around down there."

Chmagh, seriously wounded, can be seen dragging himself away from the other bodies. A voice in the helicopter, seeking a rationale to shoot, says: "Come on, buddy. All you gotta do is pick up a weapon . . . If we see a weapon, we're gonna engage."

A van pulls up, and several men, clearly unarmed, come out and lift Chmagh to carry him to medical care. The soldiers on the Apache seek and receive permission to "engage" the van and opened fire, tearing apart the front of the vehicle and killing the men. The weapon used is a 30-millimeter machine gun, which can pierce armor.

With everyone in sight apparently dead, US armored vehicles move in. When a vehicle drives over Noor-Eldeen's corpse, an observer in the helicopter says, laughing, "I think they just drove over a body."

The troops discover two children in the van, who, miraculously, have survived. One voice on the military radio requests permission to evacuate them to a US military hospital. Another voice commands them to hand over the wounded children to Iraqi police for delivery to a local clinic, ensuring delayed and less-adequate treatment.

One of the soldiers on the ground was Ethan McCord, who rushed to the scene of the slaughter and helped save the two children injured in the attack. He ran cradling a boy's bloody body in an effort to get him to a hospital.

Today McCord suffers from PTSD; he has also attempted suicide.

McCord told *Democracy Now!* that he sought mental health counseling after rescuing the wounded children. "I went to my staff sergeant and asked to see mental health, so that I can talk about my feelings. They told me I needed to suck it up and that there would be repercussions if I was to go see mental health, and I would be charged with malingering. And I was rather shocked that just by me needing to speak to somebody about what was going on and what I was feeling could constitute a crime in the army." McCord is the subject of an Oscar-nominated documentary about this attack, *Incident in New Baghdad*. He received death threats for speaking out against the Iraq War and he now champions soldiers suffering from PTSD.

The radio transmissions show not only the utter callousness of the soldiers, laughing and swearing as they kill, but also the strict procedure they follow, ensuring that all of their attacks are clearly authorized by their chain of command. The leaked video is a grim depiction of how routine the killing of civilians has become and is a stark reminder of how necessary journalism is—and how dangerous it is in practice.

After its two employees were killed, Reuters demanded a full investigation. Noor-Eldeen, despite his youth at the age of twenty-two, had been described by colleagues as one of the preeminent war photographers in Iraq. Chmagh, forty, was a father of four.

The US military inquiry into the attack that killed these twelve civilians cleared the soldiers of any wrongdoing. Reuters's requests for the video under the Freedom of Information Act were repeatedly denied for years. Despite the Pentagon's whitewash, the attack was brutal and might have involved a war crime, since the people attempting to rescue Chmagh were protected under the Geneva Conventions. WikiLeaks says it obtained the video "from a number of military whistleblowers."

Pentagon Papers whistleblower Daniel Ellsberg, a marine veteran who trained soldiers on the laws of war, told me: "Helicopter gunners hunting down and shooting an unarmed man in civilian clothes, clearly wounded . . . that shooting was murder. It was a war crime. Not all killing in war is murder, but a lot of it is. And this was."

When WikiLeaks published the Iraq War Logs in October 2010, we learned of another attack by the same Apache helicopter unit in February 2007, five months before the *Collateral Murder* attack. There is no video of this earlier event, but evidence exists in the form of a single report, one of close to a half million records leaked from both the Afghanistan and Iraq wars, dating between 2004 and 2010.

Here is an excerpt, which details the final moments of two lives, as they flee a vehicle, attempt to surrender then run to a building, and are blown to pieces by the helicopter called Crazy-horse 18. The acronym AIF is military jargon meaning "Anti-Iraq Forces":

221233FEB07: CRAZYHORSE 18 REPORTS AIF GOT INTO A DUMP TRUCK HEADED NORTH, ENGAGED AND THEN THEY CAME OUT WANTING TO SURRENDER.

221239FEB07: CRAZYHORSE 18 CLEARED TO ENGAGE DUMP TRUCK. 1/227 LAWYER STATES THEY CAN NOT SURRENDER TO AIRCRAFT AND ARE STILL VALID TARGETS.

221250FEB07: CRAZYHORSE 18 REPORTS THEY MISSED WITH HELLFIRE AND INDIVIDUALS HAVE RAN INTO ANOTHER SHACK.

221303FEB07: IH6 APPROVES CRAZYHORSE 18 TO ENGAGE SHACK.

221303FEB07: CRAZYHORSE 18 REPORTS ENGAGED AND DESTROYED SHACK WITH 2X AIF. BDA IS SHACK / DUMP TRUCK DESTROYED.

Perhaps if the public had been able to read these logs earlier, then maybe the killing would not be allowed to continue with impunity. If that war crime—the killing of people with their hands in the air, trying to surrender—had gotten the exposure immediately after it happened, then perhaps the perpetrators would have been brought up on charges, or at least investigated. With that increased scrutiny, what happened five months later in New Baghdad might never have happened, and Saeed Chmagh, Namir Noor-Eldeen, and the ten other people with them might be alive today.

WikiLeaks released the War Logs along with three mainstream media partners: the *New York Times*, the *Guardian* of Britain, and the German news magazine *Der Spiegel*. The reports were written by soldiers on the ground immediately after military actions and represent a true diary of the Afghan and Iraq wars from that five-year period, detailing everything from the killing of civilians, including children, to the growing strength of the insurgencies in each country, to Pakistan's support of the Taliban.

After these documents were released, Assange told me, "Most civilian casualties occur in instances where one, two, ten, or twenty people are killed—they really numerically dominate the list of events . . . The way to really understand this war is by seeing that there is one killed after another, every day, going on and on."

Assange described a massacre in an Afghan village, what he called a "Polish My Lai," a reference to My Lai, a notorious 1968 massacre by US troops during the Vietnam War that was exposed by journalist Seymour Hersh. On August 16, 2007, Polish troops returned to an Afghan village where they had suffered an improvised explosive device (IED) roadside bomb that morning. The Poles launched mortars into the village, striking a house where a wedding party was under way. Assange suspects that the Poles, retaliating for the IED, committed a war crime, concealed in the dry bureaucratic language in the report:

"Current Casualty list: 6x KIA (1x male, 4 female, one baby) 3x WIA (all female, one of which was 9 months pregnant)."

The tens of thousands of classified reports are dense with KIAs (killed in action) and WIAs (wounded in action). The reports document over sixty-six thousand civilian deaths in Iraq and thousands more in Afghanistan. Prisoner abuse—including bruising, burns, and frequently death—is often attributed to either Iraqi or Afghan army units, but with no proof that the overseeing US authorities took any real action. Other entries describe Task Force 373, a US

Army assassination unit that allegedly captured or killed people believed to be members of the Taliban or Al Qaeda.

Following the WikiLeaks revelations, the Obama administration ran for cover. National Security Advisor General James Jones condemned the disclosure of classified information, saying it "could put the lives of Americans and our partners at risk, and threaten our national security." White House press secretary Robert Gibbs said, "There's no broad new revelations in this."

The disclosures in this historic leak were not a threat to the lives of American soldiers, but to a policy that puts those lives at risk. With public support waning, this massive leak of documents strengthened the call for an end to the wars in Iraq and Afghanistan.

Assange told me, "We are transparency activists who understand that transparent government tends to produce just government. That is our modus operandi behind our whole organization: to get out suppressed information into the public where the press and the public and our nation's politics can work on it to produce better outcomes."

A GLOBAL "APOLOGY TOUR"

In November 2010 WikiLeaks began a rolling release of more than a quarter-million classified US State Department diplomatic cables, dating from as far back as 1966 up to early 2010. This became known as Cablegate. The contents of these cables, which included details of how the United States was making deals with dictators, proved highly embarrassing to the US government and sent shock waves around the world.

One cable revealed how the United States had made a deal with President Ali Abdullah Saleh of Yemen to cover up the use of US warplane and cruise missile attacks inside Yemen against alleged terrorist targets. "We'll continue saying the bombs are ours, not yours," President Saleh told General David Petraeus in 2010.[4] Yemen's deputy prime minister, Rashad al-Alimi, joked at the meeting that he had just "lied" by telling parliament that bombs on supposed Al Qaeda targets in Arhab, Abyan, and Shebwa were American made but deployed by Yemen.

The United States had good reason to want to cover up its attacks in Yemen: they were killing innocent people. On December 17, 2009, the Joint Special Operations Command (JSOC) launched a cruise missile attack on the Yemeni village of al-Majalah. The Yemeni government initially took credit for the strike, saying that it had targeted an Al Qaeda training camp. But it was later revealed through WikiLeaks cables that it was in fact a US attack. Investigative journalist and *Democracy Now!* correspondent Jeremy Scahill reported extensively on this attack in his book and Oscar-nominated film *Dirty Wars: The World Is a Battlefield*.

Among the first to arrive at the scene of the bombing was Yemeni tribal leader Sheikh Saleh bin Fareed, at the time a member of the Yemeni parliament. He went there to investigate who was behind the bombing. He says the victims were Bedouin villagers, not Al Qaeda members. Sheikh Fareed told *Democracy Now!*:

It was unbelievable . . . They told us that they were training fields, there were huge storage, stores for the ammunition and arms. When we reached there, we found nobody at all except those poor Bedouin people who live just across the road from the main road. And, of course, we have to collect all the bodies and bury them in the village after that. And I challenge anybody in the United States of America, especially the American government, to prove that there was anybody from Al Qaeda at that site at all, when they bombed it with about seven huge rockets from the navy in the sea.

Sheikh Fareed said that this and other missile attacks in Yemen "turned the people to be completely against the American government. And they should really think twice about it, and they should stop it."

In January 2011 Secretary of State Hillary Clinton embarked on what she called an "apology tour" to Middle East leaders. Her tour included a visit to Yemeni President Saleh, who would be toppled the following year in the wave of prodemocracy protests known as the Arab Spring.

Clinton told reporters, "I think I will be answering concerns about WikiLeaks for the rest of my life, not just the rest of my tenure as Secretary of State." [5]

She joked, "I've told my team that I want to get one of those really sharp-looking jackets that rock 'n' roll groups have on tours. And I could have a big picture of the world, and it could say 'The Apology Tour.' "

Clinton's apologies did not stop the flow of WikiLeaks exposés. In 2011 a Cablegate release exposed details of an alleged 2006 massacre by US troops in the Iraqi town of Ishaqi, north of Baghdad. Eleven people were killed, including a woman in her seventies and a five-month-old infant. In the initial investigation, US military spokesmen insisted that a member of Al Qaeda in Iraq "had been seized from a first-floor room after a fierce fight that had left the house he was hiding in a pile of rubble." [6]

But the confidential State Department cable released by WikiLeaks told a different story: "Neighbors said the US troops had approached the house at 2:30 a.m. and a firefight ensued. In addition to exchanging gunfire with someone in the house, the American troops were supported by helicopter gunships, which fired on the house . . . US forces entered the house while it was still standing . . . The American forces gathered the family members in one room and executed 11 persons, including five children, four women, and two men. Then they bombed the house, burned three vehicles, and killed their animals."[7] Iraqi TV aired grisly footage of the aftermath.

Citing attacks like these, the Iraqi government said it would no longer grant immunity to US soldiers there. The Obama administration promptly ended negotiations with the Iraqi government about keeping US troops in Iraq past a 2011 deadline.

The impact of the WikiLeaks disclosures has been far reaching. Among the diplomatic cables released were those detailing US support for the corrupt Tunisian regime. The revelations helped fuel the uprising there and sparked the Arab Spring.

Noting that *Time* magazine named "The Protester" as its 2011 Person of the Year, Daniel Ellsberg said that Chelsea Manning should be the face of that protester, since the leaks for which she was accused "sparked the uprising in Egypt . . . which stimulated Occupy Wall Street and the other occupations in the Middle East and elsewhere. So, one of those 'persons of the year' is now sitting in [jail]."

Manning is now serving thirty-five years in prison for her disclosures. Later, in an opinion piece in the *New York Times*, she wrote, "I believe that the current limits on press freedom and excessive government secrecy make it impossible for Americans to grasp fully what is happening in the wars we finance."

TRAITOR OR PATRIOT?

In January 2013 journalist and filmmaker Laura Poitras received an email that turned into a five-month exchange with a whistle-blower. One of the emails read in part,

> Laura,
>
> At this stage I can offer nothing more than my word. I am a senior government employee in the intelligence community. I hope you understand that contacting you is extremely high risk . . . This will not be a waste of your time.

The writer went on to explain technical procedures to encrypt electronic communications, and continued:

> In the end, if you publish the source material, I will likely be immediately implicated. This must not deter you from releasing the information I will provide.
>
> Thank you, and be careful.
> Citizen Four

Citizen Four was the code name that the whistleblower chose. Earlier, this person tried to communicate with journalist Glenn Greenwald, who was then reporting for the *Guardian*. Green-wald didn't respond, in part because he didn't know how to use the encryption standards demanded by the whistleblower. Poi-tras did, and later recruited Greenwald and Barton Gellman of the *Washington Post* to help, given the great volume of material the source promised. The *Guardian* assigned Ewen MacAskill to help as well.

Poitras and Greenwald followed the source's instructions and traveled to Hong Kong, where a face-to-face meeting was to take place. The *Washington Post* considered the venture too risky and refused to send Gellman. The duo met with their source for the first time on June 3, 2013. The meeting, in a hotel, had all the elements of a cloak-and-dagger story. They were to look for a man holding a Rubik's Cube. They were instructed to ask him when the restaurant would open. He would tell them, but advise them that the food was bad. After making contact, they went to his hotel room. On camera, he identified himself: Edward Snowden.

Snowden was a twenty-nine-year-old former CIA staffer and analyst for the private consulting firm Booz Allen Hamilton, which does extensive defense and intelligence work. He proceeded to provide the journalists with one of the most, if not *the* most, significant leaks in US history, providing documentary evidence that the US government, primarily the National Security Agency (NSA), was conducting massive, unconstitutional, global surveillance. Perhaps most controversially, the NSA was spying on all, or almost all, US citizens. Snowden had collected the trove of files over time, it appears, even applying for and obtaining specific jobs and assignments that he knew would grant him access to more key documents.

Snowden's historic leak revealed what he calls an "architecture of oppression": a series of top-secret surveillance programs that went far beyond what had been publicly known. The first was an order from the US Foreign Intelligence Surveillance Court requesting that a division of the phone company Verizon hand over "all call detail records" for calls to or from the United States and locations abroad, or all calls within the United States, including local calls. Another document was a slide presentation revealing a program dubbed Prism, which allegedly empowers NSA snoops access to all the private data stored by internet giants such as Microsoft, AOL, Skype, Google, Apple, and Facebook, including email, video chats, photos, files transfers, and more.

Snowden also released Presidential Policy Directive 20—a top-secret memo from President Barack Obama directing US intelligence agencies to draw up a list of targets for American cyber attacks. Then came proof of the existence of a program called Boundless Informant, which creates a global "heat map" detailing the source countries of the 97 billion intercepted electronic records collected by the NSA in the month of March 2013. Among the top targets were Iran, Pakistan, Egypt, and Jordan. The leaked map color codes countries: red for "hot," and then yellow and green. That month, the United States was yellow, providing the NSA with close to 2.9 billion intercepts. A program called XKeyscore, according to Snowden, allows the NSA and its partners around the world, like the British spy agency Government Communications Headquarters, or GCHQ, to conduct global searches of any individual's internet activity. Glenn Greenwald and colleagues at the news organization he helped found in 2013, the Intercept, wrote in July 2015 that XKeyscore "sweeps up countless people's internet searches, emails, documents, usernames and passwords, and other private communications . . . NSA documents indicate that tens of billions of records are stored in its database." These records are available for searching by countless NSA and allied technicians, they write, with "no built-in technology to prevent abuse." [8]

The American Civil Liberties Union (ACLU) filed a lawsuit immediately after the programs were revealed in 2013, arguing that the "practice is akin to snatching every American's address book—with annotations detailing whom we spoke to, when we talked, for how long, and from where. It gives the government a comprehensive record of our associations and public movements, revealing a wealth of detail about our familial, political, professional, religious, and intimate associations." Parallel lawsuits were filed by the Electronic Frontier Foundation, the New York Civil Liberties Union, and the Center for Constitutional Rights. In May 2015 a federal appeals court ruled that the NSA bulk phone data collection program was indeed illegal, calling it "unwarranted and unprecedented." [9]

Snowden's revelations have had far-reaching implications, exploding the debate on warrantless wiretapping and mass surveillance, and alerting not only American citizens but also people around the world that the US government is aggressively spying on whomever it wants, wherever it wants.

Snowden knew he might go to jail, but that was not his biggest fear. "The greatest fear that I have regarding the outcome for America of these disclosures," he said, "is that nothing will change. People will see in the media all of these disclosures. They'll know the length that the government is going to grant themselves powers, unilaterally, to create greater control over American society and global society. But they won't be willing to take the risks necessary to stand up and fight to change things, to force their representatives to actually take a stand in their interests."

After meeting with Poitras, Greenwald, and MacAskill in Hong Kong and revealing his identity to the world, Snowden needed to find a safe place. He was granted political asylum in Bolivia, Nicaragua, and Venezuela. Ecuador was considering it. With help from Julian Assange in the Ecuadorian Embassy in London and other members of the WikiLeaks organization, Snowden managed to board a plane headed for one of the Latin American safe havens, with a flight connection in Moscow. While he was en route to Moscow, however, the US government revoked Snowden's passport. He became stranded in the airport's transit zone, where he stayed for thirty-nine days, along with WikiLeaks staff editor Sarah Harrison. Russia granted him temporary political asylum, so rather than proceeding to his intended destination, Snowden has been living in Russia ever since.

The scale of his disclosures, the impact he had, and his ability to avoid arrest provoked a chorus of establishment condemnation. Jeffrey Toobin, a legal analyst for CNN and the *New Yorker*, blogged quickly that Snowden is "a grandiose narcissist who deserves to be in prison."

New York Times columnists chimed in, with Thomas Friedman writing, "I don't believe that Edward Snowden, the leaker of all this secret material, is some heroic whistleblower."

Fellow *Times* columnist David Brooks engaged in speculative psychoanalysis of Snowden, opining, "[t]hough obviously terrifically bright, he could not successfully work his way through the institution of high school. Then he failed to navigate his way through community college." Others critiqued Snowden's military service. In 2004 he enlisted in the army in a special program that fast-tracks applicants to the Special Forces. He broke both of his legs while at Fort Benning, Georgia, and left the army after five months.

Secretary of State John Kerry declared in 2014, "There are many a patriot—you can go back to the Pentagon Papers with Dan Ellsberg and others who stood and went to the court system of America and made their case. Edward Snowden is a coward, he is a traitor, and he has betrayed his country." [10]

Daniel Ellsberg is perhaps the most famous whistleblower

in US history. In 1971 he released the Pentagon Papers, a seven-thousand-page top-secret history of US involvement in Vietnam. Ellsberg scoffs at the distinction between today's whistleblowers and himself. He told *Democracy Now!*, "If I released the Pentagon Papers today, the same rhetoric and the same calls would be made about me. I would be called not only a traitor—which I was then, which was false and slanderous—but I would be called a terrorist . . . Assange and Bradley Manning are no more terrorists than I am." Ellsberg has called Snowden "a hero." [11]

Daniel Ellsberg was an advisor to President Richard Nixon and Secretary of State Henry Kissinger. In the 1960s, while Ellsberg worked as a military analyst for the RAND Corporation, he was asked to join an internal Pentagon group tasked with creating a comprehensive, secret history of US involvement in Vietnam. Ellsberg, who was working at a RAND office in Santa Monica, California, at the time, removed sections of the massive report each day. He and a RAND colleague, Anthony Russo, began the painstaking work of photocopying page after page of the secret documents at night.

Ellsberg first offered the documents to key officials in Washington, such as Senators William Fulbright and George McGovern. The antiwar senators were interested and sympathetic, but they were not willing to disclose top-secret information. Finally, he leaked the Pentagon Papers to the *New York Times*, which began publishing extensive excerpts on June 13, 1971.

Nixon immediately got a restraining order, stopping the newspaper from printing more. It was the first time in US history that presses were stopped by federal court order. The *Times* fought the injunction and won in the Supreme Court case *New York Times Co. v. United States*. Following that decision, the *Washington Post* and other papers also began running excerpts.

Ellsberg wanted to be sure that all of the Pentagon Papers were in the public record, because he knew the newspapers would run only excerpts. So he gave the Pentagon Papers to the *Washington Post* on the condition that one of its editors, Ben Bagdikian, deliver a copy to Senator Mike Gravel of Alaska. Gravel could then read the papers into the public record on the Senate floor. What happened next was like something out of a John Grisham thriller.

Gravel recalled the exchange with Bagdikian, which he set up at midnight outside the storied Mayflower Hotel in Washington, DC: "I used to work in intelligence; I know how to do these things." Gravel pulled his car up to Bagdikian's, the two opened their trunks, and Gravel heaved the boxes personally, worried that only he could claim senatorial immunity should they get caught with the leaked documents. His staff aides were posted as lookouts around the block. Gravel first brought the documents home, then carrried them into his Senate office, where he had them guarded by members of Vietnam Veterans Against the War, who were in wheelchairs as a result of injuries sustained in combat.

Gravel attempted to read the Pentagon Papers into the public record. He went to the floor of the Senate to filibuster a bill he opposed that would extend the military draft, but a Senate quorum was not present, so that ploy failed. He then called a late-night meeting of the Subcommittee on Buildings and Grounds, which he chaired, and began reading the papers aloud there. He opened with a statement:

"Recently I gained possession of the Pentagon Papers. I do not have all of them, but I believe that I possess more than half the work. I did not seek these papers. When they were offered I accepted them . . . It is a remarkable work." He continued, "As I speak now, the war goes on. Immediate disclosure of these papers will change the policy that supports the war. If we act today, perhaps one life will be saved, one village not bombed."

Senator Gravel broke down crying while reading the details of Vietnamese civilian deaths, and could not go on. But because he had begun the reading, he was legally able to enter all of the pages of the top-secret Pentagon Papers that he had in his possession into the public record.

Though ridiculed by the press for his emotional display, Gravel was undaunted. He wanted the Pentagon Papers published as a book so that Americans could read what had been done in their name. Only Beacon Press, the publishing arm of the Unitarian Universalist Association, accepted the challenge.

Unitarian Universalist Association President Robert West approved the publication. With that decision, he said, "We started down a path that led through two and a half years of government intimidation, harassment, and threat of criminal punishment." As Beacon weathered subpoenas, FBI investigations of its bank accounts, and other chilling probes, Gravel attempted to extend his senatorial immunity to the publisher. The bid failed in the US Supreme Court (the first time that the US Senate appeared before the court), but not without a strongly worded dissent from Justice William O. Douglas: "In light of the command of the First Amendment, we have no choice but to rule that here government, not the press, is lawless."

Meanwhile, Ellsberg was charged under the Espionage Act of 1917 with theft and conspiracy, and faced up to 115 years in prison. It was one of the first times the act had been used against someone who was not actually spying for a foreign government. During Ellsberg's trial in 1973, it was revealed that President Nixon authorized a break-in at the office of Ellsberg's psychiatrist in an attempt to smear him. Other revelations followed, including one that the FBI was wiretapping phone calls between Ellsberg and National Security Council aide Morton Halperin without a court order; the government later claimed the records of the wiretap were lost. Under questioning by Ellsberg's attorneys, Judge William Matthew Byrne revealed that he had met twice during the trial with Nixon aide John Ehrlichman, who offered Byrne the directorship of the FBI, which he declined.

The illegal government actions finally brought down the case. Judge Byrne dismissed all charges against Ellsberg and Russo, ruling, "The totality of the circumstances of this case which I have only briefly sketched offend a sense of justice. The bizarre events have incurably infected the prosecution of this case."

Henry Kissinger, Nixon's national security advisor and secretary of state, who was an architect of the Vietnam War, called Ellsberg "the most dangerous man in America," which later became the title of an Oscar-nominated documentary film about him.

THE HIGH PRICE OF WHISTLEBLOWING

The Obama administration has charged more whistleblowers under the Espionage Act than all previous presidential administrations combined. Pulitzer Prize–winning investigative reporter James Risen of the *New York Times* has called Obama "the greatest enemy to press freedom in a generation." [12]

In addition to Edward Snowden and Chelsea Manning, others have been charged under the Espionage Act:

THOMAS DRAKE, NSA. Revealed the existence of a widespread illegal program of domestic surveillance. His house was raided by the FBI in 2007, and he was charged in 2010 under the Espionage Act. In

2011 he pled guilty to a minor misdemeanor of unauthorized use of a government computer. He did not serve jail time.

JEFFREY STERLING, CIA. Sentenced to three and a half years in prison in 2015 for leaking information to journalist James Risen about a botched CIA operation to deliver faulty nuclear bomb blueprints to Iran. Risen vowed he would go to jail rather than divulge his confidential source, but the US Supreme Court denied his appeal. In January 2015 the Justice Department stated in court filings that Risen would not be called to testify at Sterling's trial.

STEPHEN KIM, STATE DEPARTMENT. Sentenced to thirteen months in prison in 2014 for leaking information about North Korea's plan to test a nuclear bomb in a conversation with Fox News reporter James Rosen.

JOHN KIRIAKOU, CIA. Sentenced to two and a half years in prison in 2013 for revealing to journalists the names of two colleagues who used harsh interrogation techniques on prisoners, including waterboarding. He is the only high-level official sent to prison over torture—not for engaging in it, but for exposing it.

The Espionage Act has been the weapon of choice against whistleblowers partly because of its unusual penalty: those charged with violating the Espionage Act are gagged. They cannot even tell a court why they took the actions they did.

"You can raise no defense," explains attorney Jesselyn Radack, director of national security and human rights at the Government Accountability Project (GAP), which represents whistleblowers. She is counsel for Snowden, Drake, Kiriakou, and other targets of Espionage Act investigations and prosecutions. "It does not matter whether you were leaking secrets to a foreign enemy for profit or whether you were giving information to journalists in the public interest to give back to the people who have a right to know what's been done in their name."

Edward Snowden is the most famous of her clients. Former secretary of state Hillary Clinton said that Snowden should return to the United States, where he could mount a vigorous legal and public defense. Secretary of State John Kerry said that Snowden "should man up and come back to the United States" to face charges.

The comments are absurd. As Daniel Ellsberg said, Snowden "would have no chance whatsoever to come home and make his case—in public or in court. Snowden would come back home to a jail cell—and not just an ordinary cell block but isolation in solitary confinement . . . probably [for] the rest of his life." By contrast, Ellsberg noted, "I was out on bond, speaking against the Vietnam War, the whole twenty-three months I was under indictment." [13]

Ellsberg concluded, "[N]othing excuses Kerry's slanderous and despicable characterizations of a young man who, in my opinion, has done more than anyone in or out of government in this century to demonstrate his patriotism, moral courage, and loyalty to the oath of office the three of us swore: to support and defend the Constitution of the United States."

Whistleblowers also challenge members of the corporate media, who often can't decide which side they are on: the ruling elite or those who reveal truths that threaten the elite. That's why when journalist Glenn Greenwald, who was reporting for the *Guardian*, published Edward Snowden's explosive revelations, he was confronted by David Gregory, then the host of NBC's agenda-setting Sunday talk show *Meet the Press*. Gregory demanded: "To the extent that you have aided and abetted Snowden, even in his current movements, why shouldn't you, Mr. Greenwald, be charged with a crime?"

It was a stunning accusation, laying bare the way that some elite journalists view their proper role as partners in power.

Greenwald shot back: "I think it's pretty extraordinary that anybody who would call themselves a journalist would publicly muse about whether or not other journalists should be charged with felonies . . . It means that every investigative journalist in the United States who works with their sources, who receives classified information, is a criminal."

Gregory responded, "Well, the question of who's a journalist may be up to debate with regards to what you're doing."

Others were not so confused about "who's a journalist." In April 2014 the Pulitzer Prize for Public Service was awarded to the *Guardian* for its reporting on NSA surveillance by Glenn Greenwald, filmmaker Laura Poitras, and Ewen MacAskill, and to the *Washington Post* for its reporting on this subject by Barton Gellman.

Gregory's plunging ratings might have improved had he challenged those in power instead of aiding and abetting them. In August 2014, NBC fired him.

A DOUBLE STANDARD ON LEAKS

Leaking information is punishable by jail or exile—unless you are a high-level government official, in which case you get a free pass to the White House.

David Petraeus, the retired four-star general and former head of the CIA, did not leak information to expose government wrongdoing. Instead, in 2012 Petraeus gave classified material to his mistress, Paula Broadwell, who was writing a fawning biography of him.

Petraeus let Broadwell access thousands of emails on his CIA email account and other sensitive material, including the names of covert operatives in Afghanistan, war strategies, and quotes from White House meetings. The FBI and federal prosecutors recommended felony charges and a possible prison sentence for the general.

But Petraeus was too big to jail.

In April 2015 General Petraeus reached a plea deal, admitting to one count of unauthorized removal and retention of classified information. Prosecutors did not seek prison time but instead requested two years probation and a $100,000 fine. Petraeus remains a trusted administration insider, advising the White House on the war against ISIS.

Attorney Abbe Lowell reacted to the sweetheart deal for Petraeus by demanding the immediate release of his client, imprisoned State Department whistleblower Stephen Kim. In 2010 Kim was charged under the Espionage Act for a conversation he had with Fox News reporter James Rosen, in which Kim allegedly disclosed that North Korea might test a nuclear bomb—information that was widely known. In 2014, after endless investigations and legal maneuvers, Kim pled guilty to a single felony count of disclosing classified information to an unauthorized person. He was sentenced to thirteen months in prison.

In a letter to the Justice Department, Lowell wrote, "The decision to permit General Petraeus to plead guilty to a misdemeanor demonstrates more clearly than ever the profound double standard that applies when prosecuting so-called 'leakers' and those accused of disclosing classified information for their own purposes."

Lowell said prosecutors dismissed his offer to have Kim plead guilty to the same misdemeanor that they ended up offering to Petraeus. He wrote, "You rejected that out of hand, saying that a large reason for your position was that Mr. Kim lied to FBI agents."

But Petraeus also lied to the FBI, telling agents falsely that he never provided classified information to Broadwell.

Lowell concluded, "Lower-level employees like Mr. Kim are prosecuted under the Espionage Act because they are easy targets and lack the resources and political connections to fight back. High level officials . . . leak classified information to forward their own agendas (or to impress their mistresses, in the case of Petraeus) with virtual impunity." [14]

The lenient treatment of Petraeus falls in line with similar responses to leaks from other administration insiders:

SECRETARY OF DEFENSE ASHTON CARTER used his personal email account to conduct some government business, in violation of Defense Department rules. When the *New York Times* reported this in December 2015, Carter acknowledged that he had made "a mistake." The Senate Armed Services Committee promised to review the matter. Joe Kasper, chief of staff for Rep. Duncan Hunter (R.-Calif.), a member of the House Armed Services Committee, said "Carter is the type of guy who can be taken at his word when he says it was a mistake, and no classified information passed through." [15]

SECRETARY OF STATE HILLARY CLINTON used her personal email account on a private server to conduct government business. Some emails included classified information. In October 2015, during an FBI investigation into Clinton's emails to determine whether she broke any laws, President Obama told *60 Minutes*, "I don't think it posed a national security problem." [16]

CIA DIRECTOR LEON PANETTA helped provide secret information to the filmmakers of *Zero Dark Thirty*, the blockbuster Hollywood film about the Navy SEAL raid that killed Osama bin Laden. Panetta never faced punishment.

JAMES "HOSS" CARTWRIGHT was a top-ranking Pentagon general and close advisor to President Obama who was investigated for allegedly leaking highly classified information to the *New York Times* about a US cyber warfare operation against Iran. According to the *Washington Post*, the probe of General Cartwright ended in 2015 because he had authorization to speak to reporters. The Obama administration was concerned that defense attorneys "might try to put the White House's . . . use of authorized leaks on display, creating a potentially embarrassing distraction for the administration." [17] Meanwhile, CIA analyst Jeffrey Sterling was treated far differently for allegedly revealing information to *Times* reporter James Risen about a failed CIA operation against Iran: he was sentenced to three and a half years in prison.

Even General Petraeus believes that leaking secret information is terrible—when others do it. In 2010 he said on *Meet the Press* about Chelsea Manning's revelations: "This is beyond unfortunate. I mean, this is a betrayal of trust . . . that is very reprehensible."

Attorney Jesselyn Radack responded on *Democracy Now!*, "The government has gone to great lengths in every single case of whistleblowing to claim that great harm occurred from the disclosures of Chelsea Manning . . . I went to the court-martial, and when it came time for the government to present a damage assessment, it in fact could not come up with one. So, although in all of these cases—Snowden; Tom Drake [who] was said . . . to have blood of soldiers on his hands; John Kiriakou was said to have caused untold damage now and into the future—the government waves its hands and screams and cries about damage, when none has occurred."

Leaks by high-level officials are not only overlooked, they require our sympathy. Senator Dianne Feinstein said about Petraeus, "This man has suffered enough . . . He, I think, is a very brilliant man. People aren't perfect. He made a mistake. He lost his job as CIA director because of it. I mean, how much do you want to punish somebody?"[18]

Radack, who has seen the lives of her whistleblowing clients unravel, responded, "I think they're right that people have suffered enough, and this is a life-crushing thing to be charged with espionage or to be under any kind of criminal cloud whatsoever. However, with a number of my clients, we approached Congress, who did nothing . . . There were no crocodile tears. There were no public statements.

"Tom Drake and John Kiriakou . . . lost their careers, their life savings, their pensions, their marriages and families—same with Stephen Kim. People have paid a huge price and suffered tremendously, far more than Petraeus, who . . . enjoys a lucrative speaking career, still has his security clearance, and is, in fact, advising the White House on ISIS. He has suffered no damage from this. Whereas John Kiriakou and Stephen Kim have both spoken about being suicidal over having the sword of Damocles over their head for so many years."

Edward Snowden saw what happened to the other whistleblowers at the NSA. He knew that raising concerns about illegal surveillance with his superiors at the NSA would likely bring charges against him, not against those breaking the law. So in 2013 he went directly to the press. Snowden pointedly declined to go to the *New York Times* with his revelations because of how the newspaper spiked an exposé about widespread NSA domestic wiretapping in October 2004. The story could have cost George W. Bush reelection that year, but the *Times* delayed the story at the request of the Bush administration. The *Times* did publish the story over a year later because its star reporter, James Risen, was about to release it in his own book. It would have been embarrassing for the *New York Times* to have a story as big as Risen's NSA exposé released somewhere other than in its pages.

"He had a gun to their head," *New York Times* reporter Eric Lichtblau, coauthor of the story with Risen, told PBS's *Frontline*. If the story came out in Risen's book before the *Times* published it, Lichtblau predicted "the paper is going to look pretty bad." [19]

Risen faced possible jail time as he refused to testify in the trial against Jeffrey Sterling. His bank, email, and phone records were monitored by the federal government. Despite this, he continued reporting while waging a seven-year legal battle to protect his sources. After furious protests by news organizations, the Obama administration finally announced in January 2015 that Risen would not be called to testify.

Current *New York Times* executive editor Dean Baquet conceded that Snowden's decision to avoid the *Times* "meant that somebody with a big story to tell didn't think we were the place to go, and that's painful. And then it also meant that we got beaten on what was arguably the biggest national security story in many, many years." [20]

Radack, one of Snowden's attorneys, has negotiated with the Obama administration regarding his possible return to the United States from Russia. She has been unable to extract many promises from the government, other than that he would not face the death penalty.

"They also promised he would not be tortured," she added. "I think that's setting a very low bar."

TRUTH TELLER IN THE PUZZLE PALACE [21]

Thomas Drake is in a hurry. He apologizes that he has to be at his job at the Apple Store in Bethesda, Maryland, by ten o'clock in the morning. He agrees to meet and talk in a hotel lobby in Washington, DC, at eight.

Drake is a decorated navy and air force veteran whose previous job was as a top official at the National Security Agency running secret electronic surveillance programs, supposedly against foreign enemies. When he discovered that the NSA was breaking the law and spying on Americans, he did what any law-abiding person should do: he said no. He notified his superiors. He trusted that America was a nation of laws. He figured that when he alerted senior officials that laws were being violated, he could bring a halt to the illegal activity.

Instead, the full weight of the law was turned against Drake. His career came to a screeching halt.

Thomas Drake is a tall, earnest man who carries himself with the posture and discipline from his years of military service. He is full of nervous energy, eager to talk, but hyperalert to the people coming and going in the room where we sit. A single question is all it takes for him to burst forth with his incredible story.

"My first day at the job after I started [at the NSA] at the end of August 2001, I had to take the oath again to support and defend the Constitution for the fourth time in my government career . . . The day I reported to my new duty station was the morning of 9/11 . . . Those weeks and months after 9/11 are the basis for what took place years later with me."

Drake was in a meeting in the legislative affairs office at the NSA when an executive assistant opened up a back door and said there had been a freak accident: an airplane had hit one of the World Trade Center towers. It was disturbing news, but the people in the meeting were not alarmed. The assistant returned a short time later with news that the second World Trade Center tower had been hit. Drake stood up and declared to all those assembled, "America is under attack."

"Those four months [after 9/11] and all the secret decisions that were made at the highest levels of the government that I knew were fraught with enormous strategic consequences would change history," Drake says. "9/11 had already changed history, but it was used as an excuse for the government to unchain itself from the Constitution in ways that I don't think are yet fully appreciated. We were basically put under emergency decree . . . Raw executive authority was invoked.

"What that meant in terms of the NSA is they were granted a special license. They were designated the executive agent for a mass domestic electronic surveillance program—basically turning the United States into the equivalent of a foreign nation for a data dragnet on a scale that still has not been fully revealed in spite of all the Snowden disclosures.

"The United States as a country became the petri dish for dragnet electronic surveillance. . . . It didn't matter that you're in total violation of the Fourth Amendment . . . It didn't matter that you were in violation of the Foreign Intelligence Surveillance Act. It didn't matter that the NSA had been caught in previous decades . . . The scale and scope that have occurred after 9/11 is far, far more pervasive."

I ask Drake when he first began to suspect something was wrong.

"Within days after 9/11—just days. This is the dirty knowledge that I'm burdened by.

"The moment in which I knew that I could not remain silent . . . was that first week in October when I confronted [NSA deputy general counsel] Vito Potenza . . . I still shiver and shudder when I think about his response. He says, 'You don't understand, Mr. Drake. The White House has approved the program . . . It's all legal.'

"And as soon as he said, 'It's all legal,' I'm thrown right back to when I was a very, very young teenager growing up in the 1970s. When the president said, 'If the president says it's okay, it's not illegal.' That was the Nixon era. This is now making that era look like pikers by comparison; this is now the government saying the Constitution is in the way; that the Constitution itself no longer applies."

Drake continues recounting his conversation with the NSA attorney. "I said, 'Wait a minute . . . If the law doesn't work, there's a constitutional means in our form of governance in which you change the law.' "

Drake says Potenza scoffed at the idea. He recounts Potenza saying, "If we go to Congress, you know what they'll do? They'll say 'No.' "

"Say 'No'?" Drake just shakes his head. "I shiver again when I think about that.

"I knew in that moment when I ended that conversation that I was now confronted by Pandora's box. I'm looking into the abyss that Frank Church warned the nation about in 1975." Senator Church headed the Church Committee, which investigated abuses by the CIA, FBI, NSA, and other national security agencies. Church said famously about the NSA: "I don't want to see this country ever go across the bridge . . . I know the capacity that is there to make tyranny total in America, and we must see to it that this agency and all agencies that possess this technology operate within the law and under proper supervision, so that we never cross over that abyss. That is the abyss from which there is no return." [22]

Drake reflects, "It was almost prophetic what Church said: that with advances in technology, could we reach a point where effectively we'd cross the Rubicon and could we ever come back across? I'm confronted by that moment.

"What do you do? I decided in that moment that my fidelity to the oath took primacy over everything else . . . National security has clearly become for elite power the deep state religion. You don't dare question it. 'If you question it, then we'll excommunicate you.' "

There were swift consequences for questioning. "I became identified early on as a dissident. And when you become a dissident within the system, they begin to do everything they can to isolate you."

Feeling that he was being targeted by the NSA, Drake took his concerns to investigators on the congressional intelligence committees. But strange things kept happening. "No one can find any of the evidence I provided them or any of the formal notes that were taken. In fact, as I found out later, they considered what I gave them so sensitive a state secret that it couldn't even be in the secret report. All have been suppressed and censored."

What Drake revealed was details about a program called Stellar Wind, a vast domestic surveillance program in which the emails, phone calls, and other communications of American citizens were being data mined and monitored without a court order. "That's the thing they really wanted to cover up," he says.

Drake also told investigators what the NSA knew prior to

the 9/11 attacks. "It's an absolute lie by the US government to continue to say that we didn't know about the two hijackers living in San Diego. The fact is, they knew. It was in the database, and then there was this critical report that the NSA had done. I remember I was given this report shortly after 9/11, and when I presented it to [the NSA's third-highest-ranking official] Maureen Baginski, it was just one of these moments where she got incredibly rigid."

"I wish you had never brought this to my attention," Drake recalls Baginski telling him.

"She wanted plausible deniability," he explains. "It was extremely damaging to the NSA that they had actually done this comprehensive report on Al Qaeda and associated movements, yet had refused to share it with the other critical intelligence community partners. We're talking months and months prior to 9/11."

Drake remained at the NSA for several years, pursuing his complaint about agency abuses with the Department of Defense inspector general and with his superiors. Then in December 2005 the *New York Times* published its explosive exposé by Eric Lichtblau and James Risen revealing the NSA's secret warrantless surveillance program—which, Drake says, "was just the tip of the iceberg." Following the public revelation of the surveillance program, the government stepped up its attack on Drake and other NSA whistleblowers.

On July 26, 2007—two days after US Attorney General Alberto Gonzales underwent a testy Senate Judiciary Committee hearing about warrantless wiretapping—FBI agents raided the homes of NSA whistleblowers Bill Binney and Kirk Wiebe, who also revealed details about illegal NSA surveillance, as well as former House Intelligence Committee staffer Diane Roark. In 2002 the three of them had filed a formal complaint with the Department of Defense inspector general about problems at the NSA.

Binney, a senior NSA official and forty-year veteran who was largely responsible for automating the agency's worldwide eavesdropping network, described the early-morning raid in an interview on *Democracy Now!*:

There were, like, twelve FBI agents with their guns drawn. My son opened the door . . . and they pushed him out of the way at gunpoint. And they came upstairs to where my wife was getting dressed, and I was in the shower, and they were pointing guns at her, and one of the agents came into the shower and pointed a gun directly at me, at my head, and of course pulled me out of the shower. So I had a towel, at least, to wrap around [me].

And then they took me out and interrogated me on the back porch . . . They said they wanted me to tell them something that would implicate someone in a crime . . . I said I didn't really know about anything. And they said they thought I was lying.

Well, at that point, I said, "Okay, I'll tell you about the crime I know about." And that was that [NSA director Michael] Hayden, [CIA director George] Tenet, [President] George Bush, [Vice President] Dick Cheney—they conspired to subvert the Constitution and the constitutional process of checks and balances, and here's how they did it.[23]

Afterward, Binney contacted Drake. He delivered a chilling warning: "Tom, you're next."

A KNOCK AT THE DOOR

Four months later, at seven o'clock on a cool morning in November 2007, Thomas Drake's twelve-year-old son was getting ready to go to middle school when there was a loud knock at the door. The boy opened the door and was greeted by heavily armed agents. He called to his father. "There's someone here to see you!"

"I knew who it was," recounts Drake. "My family didn't know. All the whistleblowing, they didn't know."

For nine hours, about a dozen agents were "just shredding the house . . . I'm being treated as a spy, so they were everywhere. They were down in the basement. They were looking for hidden compartments. They were looking for something like a Robert Hanssen"—an FBI agent who spied for the Soviet Union and later for Russia—"where he had a locked room, safes, all of that. They went through everything."

The raid on Drake and most of the other NSA whistleblowers occurred under President Bush. But it was the Obama administration that pursued the legal cases against them with a vengeance. In 2010 the government ultimately charged Drake under the Espionage Act—the first time in forty years, since Daniel Ellsberg, that the act had been used to go after a whistleblower.

Sometime later, Drake was brought to an FBI facility. "There's someone here to meet you," he was told. It was the chief prosecutor.

The two men looked across a table at each other. The prosecutor said, "How would you like to spend the rest of your life in prison, Mr. Drake, unless you cooperate with our investigation? We have more than enough information to put you away for a long, long time. You better start talking."

Drake returned the prosecutor's stare. "I'm not going to plea bargain with the truth."

Drake recounts, "I found myself defending the Constitution against my own government. So who's the threat now? The government is now a threat to the constitutional form of government."

Drake tells me, "I consider myself a human being who has inalienable rights, and as a citizen of the United States, I've taken an oath four times to support and defend the Constitution . . . I was not going to break the oath that I had taken to that Constitution. Because if we don't have the Constitution, then what are we?"

Drake refused to cooperate with the FBI. He was scheduled to go to trial on June 13, 2011. The date was significant: it was the fortieth anniversary of the publication of the Pentagon Papers, and also the very day that the US National Archives and Records Administration was declassifying and releasing the full forty-seven volumes of the Pentagon Papers.

On May 22, 2011, Drake told his gripping story on CBS's *60 Minutes*. The publicity might have saved him: in early June the government dropped all of the serious charges against Drake and did not seek any jail time. A case that began with a dramatic charge of espionage ended with Drake agreeing to plead guilty to a misdemeanor of misusing the NSA's computer system. He was sentenced to one year of probation and community service.

"It was an extraordinary victory against the government," he says proudly.

But whistleblowing has taken a staggering toll on Drake. He spent nearly $1 million to defend himself, draining his retirement funds and all his assets. He says that he is "essentially broke—I'm in severe debt." And then there are "the personal costs with family and colleagues and friends. You're being cut off. All your social networks that you previously had are essentially gone. They're just destroyed."

He recalls one moment that softened some of the pain of his ordeal. It was when his son told him, "Thanks for standing up for our rights. They do matter."

Drake has been unable to find a job beyond being an hourly employee at a neighborhood Apple Store. "One of the prices you pay as a whistleblower is that you become radioactive," he says. But people come to the store and occasionally acknowledge him quietly. "They'll thank me for my service; thank me for standing up. They're extraordinarily grateful that I didn't end up in prison. I realize increasingly that I'm an example that you can in fact stand up to power and survive, even at extraordinary cost. You can keep your freedom."

He reflects, "The media, in the end, became my saving grace. The judge was not immune to what was happening in the press." The media shined "enough light to say what was [true]."

In 2011 Thomas Drake was awarded the Ridenhour Truth-Telling Prize, named for Ron Ridenhour, the Vietnam veteran who wrote to Congress in 1969 to expose the My Lai massacre that happened the year before. Drake also received the Sam Adams Award, a prize for intelligence professionals who have taken ethical stands. In 2013 he traveled to Moscow with fellow government whistleblowers Jesselyn Radack (Justice Department), Coleen Rowley (FBI), and Ray McGovern (CIA) to present the Sam Adams Award to Edward Snowden.

Drake continues to speak around the world in support of transparency, whistleblowers, and government accountability.

"This is a fundamental break of the social governance compact with the people," he says. "It is in the end about We the People— and We the People is what's been absolutely defiled by government.

This is the pathology of power. You just can't have this kind of power essentially saying, 'No, we know what's best. This is for your own good, but don't question and don't ask us to account for ourselves.' . . . This is a clear, compelling danger to democracy.

"You can't have a national security state—sort of this dual state, this secret dark state. It can't coexist with a democracy in the special form that we have called the 'constitutional republic.' . . . I really fear for the republic. I really fear that what we're seeing is you have an extraordinary, almost a blanket immunity that's granted the secret and elite powers, and anybody who dares come forth, particularly in a post-9/11 context, is considered criminal."

Hunted, persecuted, and nearly destroyed, Thomas Drake nevertheless considers himself lucky. "I'm extremely fortunate that I'm sitting across from you as a free human being . . . I wake up every morning, and I pinch myself . . . because what does it mean to be free? It means more to me now. It's more precious now than ever."

Drake concludes our conversation with an urgent plea for open government, free media, and an end to secrecy: "Democracy dies behind closed doors."

CHAPTER 3

UNDOCUMENTED AND UNAFRAID

Give me your tired, your poor,
Your huddled masses yearning to breathe free,
The wretched refuse of your teeming shore.

These are the most famous lines from the sonnet "The New Colossus," written by Emma Lazarus in 1883 as a tribute to the new Statue of Liberty. John F. Kennedy, while still a senator in 1958, wrote in his short volume *A Nation of Immigrants*, "Under present law it is suggested that there should be added: 'As long as they come from Northern Europe, are not too tired or too poor or slightly ill, never stole a loaf of bread, never joined any questionable organization, and can document their activities for the past two years.' " He was pointing out basic flaws in US immigration policy that he saw almost sixty years ago. Today immigration policy is a political quagmire that inflames passions and incites racism and xenophobia. The condition of immigrants in the United States, especially of the more than eleven million people who live and work here without legal status or documentation, has sparked a massive movement demanding change.

On March 10, 2006, over a hundred thousand people took to the streets of Chicago to protest a bill before Congress. The bill, HR 4437, also called the Sensenbrenner Bill after the Wisconsin Republican congressman who sponsored it, would have criminalized undocumented immigrants while accelerating the militarization of the US-Mexico border. It even made it a felony to provide aid to an undocumented immigrant targeted for deportation. Abel Nuñez of Chicago's Centro Romero, an organization that serves the refugee immigration population, told me on *Democracy Now!*:

"A lot of people that are undocumented feel fear about coming out, and in the past that's why they haven't really demonstrated. But now they feel like they have nothing to lose; that for the first time this country is telling them, 'You are not wanted.' It's not about just not being able to adjust your status. It's now about, 'We want you out.' "

The Chicago march was soon followed by many more. On March 25, 2006, an estimated five hundred thousand people marched in Los Angeles. By May 1, May Day, a national day of action had been organized, with hundreds of separate events across the country. Over one million people turned out in Los Angeles, and hundreds of thousands in other major cities. These were peaceful gatherings, with entire families marching together.

The mass mobilizations had an impact. The Senate version of the bill passed, but only with a provision that would have offered a path to legal status for up to seven million undocumented immigrants in the United States. The House and the Senate could not resolve the differences between their separate versions, and the bill died.

This expression of political power in the streets paralleled a rise in the electoral power of traditionally marginalized communities. In 2008 a broad coalition succeeded in electing Barack Obama to be the first African American president of the United States. Women, Latinos, African Americans, Asian Americans, and the LGBT community all turned out in unprecedented numbers to achieve this historic victory. After eight years of the Bush-Cheney regime, the world heaved a sigh of relief with the election of Obama.

But for the undocumented among us, the promise of hope and change was short lived, as the Obama administration soon ramped up deportations to record levels.

Immigration is a central and enduring pillar of the United States. Without immigration, there is no United States. We all know the phrase "We are a nation of immigrants." Put aside for the moment that this trope ignores the indigenous people, who are neither immigrants nor are they descended from them. According to the US Census Bureau's 2014 statistics (and using that agency's nomenclature), American Indian, Native Alaskan, and Native Hawaiian and other Pacific Islanders number almost 8 million, out of a total population of 318 million. Nevertheless, most people here can trace their ancestry to one or more immigrants. Currently, a majority of those connections lead back to Europe, based in part on the preferences that Kennedy criticized, which were given to Northern Europeans.

Then there are those who are now too often referred to as "illegals": undocumented immigrants. The Pew Research Center estimates that as of 2014, there were 11.3 million undocumented people in the United States. That figure has roughly stabilized over the past five years, after climbing steadily for decades. According to Pew, there were 3.5 million undocumented immigrants in America in 1990, with the number reaching 12.2 million in 2007, the seventh year of the George W. Bush administration. There are various explanations for why the number plateaued since then, among them the global financial crisis of 2008 and the recession that followed. But a significant factor has been the massive number of deportations under President Obama. During each year of his first term, close to 400,000 people were deported, or an average of 1,100 people per day.

It was in the throes of this deportation crisis that a new generation of immigrant-rights activists rose to the fore. They call themselves Dreamers.

The 2012 Democratic National Convention was gaveled into session on Tuesday, September 4, in Charlotte, North Carolina. Charlotte is where some of the first lunch counter sit-ins against segregation occurred in the fifties and early sixties. Protest helped shape modern Charlotte. As routinely happens now at major political gatherings like the two main party conventions, the city center had been put under the control of the US Secret Service and heavily militarized.

A march set out for the convention center, led by Dreamers and their family members. One young woman, Kitzia Esteva, told *Democracy Now!*, "I'm undocumented and unafraid. We're risking arrest right now to tell President Obama that he needs to have a position on our side—on the side of immigrants—to stop deportations, to stop the collaboration between the police and ICE, and to recognize our civil rights and to defend them." ICE is the acronym for US Immigration and Customs Enforcement.

"We are here to ask President Obama what his legacy will be," Rosi Carrasco said as she climbed down from the "UndocuBus," an old school bus painted colorfully with butterflies, which the activists traveled in from Arizona. "What we want to say to President Obama is, on which side of history is he going to be? Is he going to be remembered as the president that has been deporting the most people in US history? Or is he going to be on the side of immigrants?" Rosi's husband, Martin Unzueta, said, "I am undocumented. I've been living here for eighteen years. I pay taxes, and I'm paying more taxes than Citibank."

Amid roadblocks and armed checkpoints, Rosi and nine other undocumented immigrants blocked an intersection, risking arrest and possible deportation.

The border state of Arizona has become ground zero in the national immigration crisis. In 2010 Governor Jan Brewer signed the notorious law known as SB 1070, which sought to criminalize people for simply being in the state without documentation. Immigration is governed by federal law, and violations are actually civil offenses, not criminal. With SB 1070, Arizona preempted federal immigration policy—at least until most of its provisions were struck down in federal court.

The Arizona law gained added notoriety thanks to long-running persecution of Latinos at the hands of Maricopa County Sheriff Joe Arpaio. The controversial Arpaio is known for the severe conditions he imposes on county jail prisoners. Many are forced to live in cramped canvas tents in the sweltering Phoenix heat. He puts them in vintage-style black-and-white-striped prison garb and subjects them to public humiliation on chain gang work details. He has forced male inmates to wear humiliating pink underwear, and has reportedly bragged about serving rotten food to the prisoners, including green bologna. Arpaio is an inveterate media hound, never far from a camera. Adoring media outlets have produced countless profiles, amplifying Arpaio's self-appointed title of "America's Toughest Sheriff." He became a darling of the Tea Party movement when he launched an investigation into whether President Obama's birth certificate was valid.

Arpaio's biggest claim to fame, though, has been his tireless persecution of the Latino population. In 2007 he managed to get a joint operating agreement with ICE to assist the federal government with immigration enforcement and detention under Homeland Security's 287(g) program. Stephen Lemons, who has reported on Arpaio for the *Phoenix New Times* for many years, told us, "Arpaio used that authority to begin sweeps of Latino communities and almost instantly turned his law enforcement agency into a mini version of ICE . . . terrorizing large segments of Maricopa County." A class action lawsuit filed by the ACLU and a federal lawsuit filed by the Justice Department found that the Maricopa County Sheriff's Office (MCSO) engaged in systemic racial profiling of Latinos and other people of color, especially in its frequent, harassing traffic stops that often led to the arrest and jailing of people with no probable cause, violating their constitutional protections against illegal search and seizure.

So controversial and patently unconstitutional was Arpaio's treatment of the Phoenix Latino population that the MCSO's 287(g) status was stripped. The court told Arpaio to stop the racial profiling and to get out of the immigration law enforcement business. He ignored the court order for eighteen months and was hauled before the federal judge again, this time for contempt of court.

Sheriff Joe was in trouble. Not only had he defied the federal court order but also he was alleged to have run a covert investigation into federal judge G. Murray Snow—and into the judge's wife as well. The details, if accurate, defy credulity. Arpaio is accused of dispatching at least three officials—two of his staff and a third who worked for one of his nonprofit "posses"—to Seattle to meet with a self-described hacker to obtain CIA and NSA data that would confirm an anti-Arpaio conspiracy among the judge, US Attorney

General Eric Holder, and a cast of others whom Sheriff Joe deemed to be his sworn enemies. The hacker is alleged to be a fraud who received at least $250,000 of public money that Arpaio controlled.

The Arizona law, SB 1070, prompted similar bills in Republican-controlled state legislatures across the country. When a draconian anti-immigrant bill was signed into law in Alabama, Latinos fled east to Georgia and Florida, while Alabama farmers, unable to find hired help willing to do the backbreaking, low-wage work typically reserved for migrants, saw their crops rot in the fields.

Across the United States, well-organized immigrant-rights activists, especially youth, increased their civil disobedience. It was the young people in North Carolina more than a half century ago who defied the advice of their elders to be more patient in the fight against segregation. Now youths were targeting key politicians with sit-down actions as one way to advance the struggle for immigrant rights. In 2010 a group in graduation caps and gowns engaged in a sit-in at Washington, DC's Hart Senate Office Building and were arrested. As Obama's 2012 reelection campaign progressed, scores of sit-down protests took place in his campaign offices around the country.

The DREAM Act was first introduced in the US Congress in 2001, and several times thereafter, but never passed. DREAM, an acronym for Development, Relief, and Education for Alien Minors, would establish a process for qualified people who entered the United States as children without documentation to pursue an education or military service, and to potentially obtain legal permanent residency and thereafter US citizenship. A version of the DREAM Act passed the House of Representatives in 2010, but in the Senate it obtained fifty-five votes—five short of the number needed to overcome a Republican filibuster. It failed to become law.

President Obama responded to the pressure exerted by the

young people known as Dreamers in June 2012, when he announced a decision within the Department of Homeland Security to free eight hundred thousand of them from the threat of potential deportation proceedings. Obama declared, "Imagine you've done everything right your entire life—studied hard, worked hard, maybe even graduated at the top of your class—only to suddenly face the threat of deportation to a country that you know nothing about, with a language that you may not even speak . . . It makes no sense to expel talented young people who, for all intents and purposes, are Americans—they've been raised as Americans, understand themselves to be part of this country."

This was the first of President Obama's controversial executive orders on immigration, called Deferred Action for Childhood Arrivals, or DACA. It is not a path to citizenship, nor is it amnesty. Rather, DACA formalizes a bureaucratic decision to make deportation of certain young people a nonpriority and uses administrative measures to offer work permits to qualified applicants. Thus, as the president said in his White House Rose Garden address on DACA, the government would be using "discretion about whom to prosecute, focusing on criminals who endanger our communities rather than students who are earning their education . . . Effective immediately, the Department of Homeland Security is taking steps to lift the shadow of deportation from these young people."

Many celebrated the announcement—and then challenged the president to act on his pledge. Several activists got themselves detained so they could enter the Broward Transitional Center, a predeportation jail in Florida, to interview detainees. They found dozens of people who were eligible for release under President Obama's policies but were languishing in the jail nevertheless.

Another problem with DACA was that, while it safeguarded a select population of young people from deportation, it offered no relief for parents, or grandparents, and thus could potentially cause families to be split up. It was theses concerns that brought these impacted families to Charlotte and the Democratic National Convention.

Just as the convention was being gaveled into session, ten of these brave souls—among them a young woman and her mother, and a couple and their daughter—sat down outside in the pouring rain on a large banner they placed in the middle of the intersection. The banner read, "No Papers, No Fear," along with the same in Spanish, "Sin Papeles, Sin Miedo," with a large butterfly painted in the center.

As the police surrounded them, I asked one of the young women about to be arrested, "Why a butterfly?" "Because butterflies have no borders," she told me. "Butterflies are free." With that, the police handcuffed her and dragged her into the patrol wagon.

After the 2012 presidential election, the balance of power in the federal government stayed basically the same: the House of Representatives remained solidly controlled by the Republicans, while the Democrats held on to the Senate, but with their agenda hamstrung by constant Republican filibusters. In other words, any significant policy objectives of the Obama administration were dead on arrival. In the meantime, a half million young people took advantage of DACA. But still the machinery of deportation continued to churn away.

Five months after the election, on April 10, 2013, a major grassroots rally took place in front of the Capitol Building in Washington, DC. Tens of thousands gathered to demand, yet again, comprehensive immigration reform and a pathway to citizenship for the nation's eleven million undocumented people. The speakers represented a true cross section of US society, including undocumented immigrants themselves, speaking in their own voices.

Leaders of groups such as the NAACP. Labor unions, ranging from the Service Employees International Union (SEIU), to the National Education Association (NEA). Environmental groups such as Greenpeace. National LGBT organizations. The atmosphere was festive, yet the demands were unwavering. Seventeen-year-old Katharine Tabares was among those who spoke:

> My mother and I migrated from Colombia almost three years ago . . . She works as a home health aide from Monday until Sunday. And every afternoon when I am at school dedicating my soul to education, she is at home getting ready to go to work to do an arduous job that is very hard to do.
>
> It is unacceptable that the system does not recognize my mother for who she is because we don't have a regular immigration status. I am tired, just as many of you are tired, of seeing our parents being oppressed and denied work opportunities, not because of their skills—because they are very talented—but because of a nine-digit [Social Security] number that supposedly defines a person in the United States, when it should not.
>
> That's why we are here today, to fight for our rights, to fight for a change in the current immigration policy. We're sending a message that the time to do right has come, to pass an immigration reform with a path to citizenship that will include every single member of our community and will not leave anybody behind. We're fighting for equality for all undocumented and documented immigrants, for families that are here today, for families that are back home, and for families that have been separated because of our immigration system right now.

Tabares called out, *"¿Qué es lo qué queremos?"* ("What do we want?")

The crowd responded loudly, *"¡Reforma migratoria!"* ("Immigration reform!")

Luis Gutiérrez also spoke. He is a native Chicagoan of Puerto Rican descent, and a Democrat who serves his Chicago district as a member of Congress. He is an activist, a firebrand, and is acknowledged as a leading expert on comprehensive immigration reform. Surrounded at the podium by many colleagues from the Congressional Hispanic Caucus, and a number of allied Congress members who support immigration reform, Gutiérrez addressed the crowd:

> Like many of you, if we are citizens, we voted in November, and we watched on election night as the votes came in. And I don't care if you are watching on English TV, or Spanish, or in some other language. You saw how the very educated TV experts, one after another, said it was Latinos and Asian and African immigrants, it was their children and their friends and their families committed to their communities that returned Barack Obama to the White House. We delivered the votes that delivered the states like Nevada and Colorado and Nuevo Mexico and Florida to the Democrats, and these votes came with a great deal of hope and trust. The people who returned President Obama to the White House put trust in him and in the Democratic Party to deliver on what was promised. And it was not simply that they rejected the other candidate's approach.
>
> Yes, they rejected the call that every state pass laws like SB 1070 that was passed in Arizona. They rejected the threatened veto of a DREAM Act. Yes, we are all aware that the other candidate and the other party had based their approach to immigration on driving eleven million undocumented immigrants out of the United States by forcing them to self-deport.
>
> Latinos, Asian, African immigrant citizens and their families

and allies voted in record numbers for President Obama despite the most tremendous increase in deportations of any president in history. Despite 1,400 deportations a day, and 1.6 million people forcibly removed from the United States. They knew that that was the road and that was the way to stop the deportations, and today we are here to say:

"*Que se pare las deportaciones! Permite la legalización!*"
"Stop the deportations! Permit legalization!"

And we are here to make a simple and clear demand: that the promises of immigration reform go beyond the Dreamers. Now we have five hundred thousand young men and women, undocumented youth, who are safe from deportation. And now we say, bring your moms and your dads out of the shadows too!

The crowd responded with a chant made famous by the United Farm Workers of America during protests led by Cesar Chavez beginning in the 1960s: *Si se puede! Si se puede!* (Yes we can!)

Representative Gutiérrez continued: "I will tell you what I have been telling people across the country: Work hard. Push us! Keep pushing us! And together we will deliver immigration reform this year! You need to guarantee that you will give me and my colleagues in the Congress of the United States no place to hide. There are no acceptable excuses for failing to pass immigration reform this year, and no excuses will be accepted!"

After his rousing address, which continued for some minutes in both English and Spanish, Luis Gutiérrez and his colleagues left together, returning to the Capitol Building behind them.

The point on which he ended was significant: "Push us! Keep pushing us!" This is the same imperative laid out by President Franklin Roosevelt to the legendary labor and civil rights organizer A. Philip Randolph. Eleanor Roosevelt brought Randolph to meet with her husband, FDR. Randolph was a major force behind the black train conductors' union, the Brotherhood of Sleeping Car Porters, from 1925 through the 1960s, and was a key organizer of the 1963 March on Washington, at which Martin Luther King delivered his historic "I Have a Dream" speech.

Randolph, a lifelong Socialist, described what needed to happen to improve the condition of black and working people in the country. Roosevelt said he did not disagree with anything Randolph said, but he said to Randolph, "Go out and make me do it."

A *Democracy Now!* viewer approached me in the summer of 2008, while Senator Barack Obama was campaigning against Senator John McCain for the presidency. The viewer told me that he had been at an Obama fund-raiser in a backyard in New Jersey, where the candidate was taking questions. Someone asked Obama what he would do to help solve the Israel/Palestine conflict. According to this eyewitness, Obama told the story of A. Philip Randolph's meeting with FDR, and ended with FDR's response: " 'Make me do it.' "

THE STRUGGLE CONTINUES

The immigration movement had an impact in key states in the 2012 presidential election. After President Obama soundly defeated GOP challenger Mitt Romney, the Republican National Committee commissioned an internal report, a postmortem on the election, to assess the damage and map a road forward. The report suggested that the Republican Party was "driving around in circles on an ideological cul-de-sac," and warned that it "must focus its efforts to earn new supporters and voters in the following demographic communities: Hispanic, Asian and Pacific Islanders,

African Americans, Indian Americans, Native Americans, women, and youth . . . Unless the RNC gets serious about tackling this problem, we will lose future elections."

Throughout 2013, activists worked, lobbied, protested, and engaged in a national effort to force the immigration issue. In October 2013 close to thirty Dreamers, along with three parents—all of them undocumented—left the relative safety of Laredo, Texas, for their native Mexico. Then they marched back in unison, crossing into the United States. The Dreamers wore caps and gowns and chanted, "Undocumented and unafraid!" They were protesting the failure to resolve their immigration status, as well as the burden it puts on families who are separated, when undocumented relatives in the United States are effectively trapped here, unable to cross back for family visits or emergencies.

The following month, another group launched a thirty-one-day fast on the National Mall. Invoking the memory of the great labor leader who organized farm workers, the protesters' statement read, "Where Cesar Chavez ended his 36-day fast for the rights of farm workers in 1988, we continue decades later to sacrifice our own comfort to underscore the moral crisis afflicting workers, children, mothers and fathers, living under an immigration system unwilling to recognize their existence and the legitimacy of their familial ties with integrity and empathy . . . Our voluntary sacrifice represents the urgency, the passion and commitment of a community of all religions, races, and political affiliations, to enact commonsense immigration reform this year."

Among those fasting was Eliseo Medina, who a month earlier had left a career in labor organizing, retiring from his job as international secretary-treasurer of the large and politically powerful union SEIU. He wanted to devote himself full-time to the pursuit of immigration reform. He began as a farm worker in California and, at the age of nineteen, started organizing fellow workers under the guidance of Cesar Chavez. His fast on the mall attracted so much attention that even President Obama and First Lady Michelle Obama visited him there.

Medina ended his fast just after the House of Representatives ended its session for the year on December 12, 2013. We spoke to him on *Democracy Now!* the next morning. I asked him what motivated him to engage in a month-long water-only fast. He replied:

> We were haunted by the fact that last year four hundred sixty-three people died in the desert trying to come to the United States in search of a better life. Over two million people have been deported from the United States. These are numbers, but beyond those numbers there's real people, real human beings, with families who love them and who they love. And they will never be back with their families because they died in the desert. Or children are left behind when their mom or dad are deported, and they cry themselves to sleep wondering when they will see their parents again. And we just couldn't stand to continue to see this human suffering that's going on in our community. So we decided that we would go on a fast to dramatize—to put a human face on—this moral crisis facing our country. I feel very fortunate that we touched the heart of America.

But Medina failed to touch the heart of the US House of Representatives. John Boehner, the Speaker of the House, refused to address immigration reform in 2013.

The Fast for Families, as it was called, continued into 2014, traveling coast to coast, visiting communities, and appealing to members of Congress in their district home offices. When attempting to visit Congressman Mario Diaz-Balart in Miami, Medina was arrested, for no reason, and spent the day in jail. Upon his release, Medina tweeted:

"Went 2 Cong Diaz Balart re:CIR [Comprehensive Immigration Reform] moral crisis. Found clsd doors & arrest. Released 2nite& greeted by Lots ppl. Heart full."

Throughout 2014, immigrant-rights groups stepped up pressure on President Obama to take more decisive action without waiting for Congress. In March, Obama was reportedly stunned when he learned that Janet Murguía, president and CEO of the National Council of La Raza (NCLR), had called him "the deporter in chief." NCLR is the largest Latino civil rights and advocacy organization in the United States, and a key ally of Obama's. Murguía was speaking at NCLR's 2014 Capital Awards Dinner, and, after praising the bipartisan "Gang of Eight" senators who had crafted a comprehensive immigration bill (that was never taken up in the House), she said, "For us, this president has been the deporter in chief. Any day now, this administration will reach the two million mark for deportations. It is a staggering number that far outstrips any of his predecessors and leaves behind it a wake of devastation for families across America. Many groups, including NCLR, have long been calling on the president to mitigate the damage of these record deportations. But again we hear no. The president says his administration does not have the authority to act on its own. All we hear is no. No from Congress. No from the administration."

Later, in August, at a protest in front of the White House, 145 people laid red carnations over photos of deported loved ones and refused to leave. They were arrested, surrounded by crowds of supporters. Among the supporters was Jonathan Perez, who talked about why he was there:

"I'm an immigrant, and I achieved the DACA, so I can manage

to work legally now, but I'm the only one in my family, and it sad-
dens me to know that I earn [twice] what my mom makes in two
weeks. So, I want her to have the opportunity to make as much
money as I do, and no matter what kind of work she's doing. So,
you know, I feel like I need to be out here in support of everyone,
because I want everyone to have equal rights."

The prospects of a legislative solution dimmed in November
2014, when control of the US Senate shifted to the GOP. Now
there would be no compromise. The Republicans controlled both
the House and the Senate. So President Obama stepped in again
and enacted change using his executive authority. On November 20 and 21, 2014, the president and Department of Homeland
Security secretary Jeh Johnson issued several directives expanding
DACA and creating DAPA: Deferred Action for Parents of Americans and Lawful Permanent Residents. DACA was broadened to
remove the upper age cap, allowing people older than thirty years
of age as of June 15, 2012, to apply. The salient point that DACA
sought to address was to help those who were brought into the
United States when they were children, so the age cap seemed ar-
bitrary. Thus, as long as you were under sixteen when you entered
the country, regardless of what year you were born, you could potentially qualify for DACA. DAPA offered protection from deportation for parents of children who are legal residents or citizens.

The expansion was short lived. Twenty-six states, led by Texas,
filed suit, claiming the president had exceeded his constitutional authority. The case was filed in the US District Court in Brownsville,
Texas, presided over by conservative federal district judge Andrew
Hanen, who peppers his court opinions with the phrase "illegal
aliens" (language not used by *Democracy Now!* and later dropped
by news outlets, including the Associated Press, *USA Today*, the
Los Angeles Times, and the *San Francisco Chronicle*, following

protests by activists). On February 16, 2015, just two days before US Citizenship and Immigration Services was to begin accepting applications for expanded DACA and DAPA, Judge Hanen ruled against the Obama administration, barring the government from taking the applications. The Obama administration appealed, and asked for Hanen's injunction to be lifted until the appeals process was complete, but that was denied.

These political maneuvers have real-life consequences. We interviewed two people directly affected by the decision, in Houston, Texas: Oscar Hernandez and José Espinoza. Hernandez is a lead field organizer with United We Dream, a national, immigrant, youth-led organization fighting for relief and fair treatment for all undocumented immigrants. Hernandez was helping eligible immigrants prepare their applications for the expanded DACA program. He was undocumented, but qualified for DACA when it was first announced and was granted "deferred action."

I asked him about the judge's ruling. "This is something we expected," he said. "Deferred action was not given to us. This was something that was organized by undocumented immigrant youth in our community, and we were able to win this. And we will continue to prevail, and we will continue to fight for immigrant rights and make sure that we get the representation we deserve."

José Espinoza sat next to Hernandez in the Houston TV studio. He is a father of three and an undocumented immigrant who was too old to qualify for the first phase of DACA, but qualified for the expanded DACA. I asked him, "I know you drove an hour and a half to get to this interview, and it's your first TV interview. You're risking a lot to come out of the shadows and say you're an undocumented immigrant. You were planning to apply this week?"

"I came to the United States as a kid when I was fourteen years old, and I started working in different places. And right now, what

I've been doing the most of the last twelve years is, I've been working in the oil field industry." It was the first time he was "coming out"—telling the world about his status as an undocumented immigrant.

"When this new law came in place, I was very excited, and I was willing to move out of the shadows, to come out," Espinoza continued. "I had everything ready, but one day before, my dream came down." Judge Hanen shut down José's dream of living free from the fear of deportation. I asked him why he chose to declare his status so publicly.

"I just want to give an example and show [others] that, yes, we can do it, and there are people out there that can help us," he explained. "Many of the friends I have, they are afraid to come out. They are afraid to say something. They're afraid to show. They're afraid or insecure, because they don't have the resources."

DAPA and the expanded DACA were expected to give some measure of security to four to five million people in the United States. A single judge in Texas put a stop to that. United We Dream summarized the impacts of Judge Hanen's decision this way: "The path to justice is a long one, and we don't expect this lawsuit to be resolved overnight. But we need to continue organizing and building power within our community. And we can't do it without you."

While the number of undocumented in the United States has more or less stabilized, that doesn't mean that there is a stable status quo. There are still many people coming in, and there are many people going out and being deported. Hundreds die in transit, often from heat and dehydration in the desert. The Sonoran Desert, bisected by the US-Mexican border, is dry, hot, and very sparsely populated. Its vast expanse reaches from California all the way through Arizona, covering over a hundred thousand square miles. Thousands risk their lives to make the perilous journey north, through a section of the desert in Arizona that has been dubbed "the Corridor of Death."

A 2013 report from the Binational Migration Institute at the University of Arizona's Department of Mexican American Studies analyzed data from the Pima County Office of the Medical Examiner (PCOME), which, according to the report, "investigates the highest number of migrant deaths in the country, and as a consequence, now handles more unidentified remains per capita than any other medical examiner's office in the United States." Between 1990 and 2012, the PCOME examined the remains of 2,238 migrants, of whom 761 went unidentified. That is not the true number of migrants who perished in the desert but only those whose remains made it to the coroner. Some are buried where they fall, some are never found. Others surely die on the Mexican side of the border.

In 2004, in response to this humanitarian crisis, people in Tucson, Arizona, formed No More Deaths. They describe themselves as "people of conscience working openly and in community to uphold fundamental human rights." A central project they undertake is to provide direct aid to migrants in the desert, often by leaving caches of food and water. Dan Mills, a volunteer, told me how he found the body of a fourteen-year-old girl in the desert:

"We were actually walking along in the area of the migrant trails in order to leave out some water and some food and some medical supplies on the trails, like we normally do, and we just stumbled upon her—came around the corner, and there she was. And I can't tell you what a horrible experience that is to see a little fourteen-year-old girl who died in the desert by herself." Through coordination with activists on the Mexican side of the border, they were able to identify the remains as those of a young girl named Josseline, from El Salvador.

"She became sick, after probably drinking some dirty water or perhaps just running out of water and becoming dehydrated," Mills continued. "This is a very rugged area. She was down in the bottom of a canyon and had probably already crossed a mountain range or two before getting to that point, about fifteen to twenty miles north of the Mexico-US line. So, when she became ill, she fell behind the group. I'm told that she encouraged her little brother to keep going, because he needed to make it to meet their parents. And her little brother did make it, as did the rest of the group, to our knowledge. But Josseline did not."

This tragic tale has a very cruel twist. Two days after finding Josseline's corpse, Dan Mills was back in the desert, leaving food, water, and medical supplies to aid the migrants. He was accosted by agents of the US Fish and Wildlife Service and ticketed $175 for "littering." Leaving plastic water bottles could have earned him six months in prison and a $5,000 fine. Mills pled not guilty, asserting that delivering humanitarian aid is not a crime. He was found guilty, but the prison time, the fine, and even the ticket were all suspended. Mills described the absurdity of his predicament and of immigration laws generally: "The government is saying humanitarian aid is a crime for which no punishment is warranted. It's very hard to navigate the waters of border policies like that."

Migrant deaths aren't limited to Arizona. Journalist and filmmaker John Carlos Frey conducted investigative work and published a story in *Texas Observer* magazine called "Graves of Shame." Frey found that in rural Brooks County, Texas, where summer temperatures are well above 100 degrees Fahrenheit, local officials had been burying unidentified remains of migrants in mass graves. Between 2009 and 2013, 361 bodies were found there.

"The migrants mostly come from Central America and Mexico, and they find themselves crossing the US-Mexico border, trying to evade a checkpoint and walking about forty miles in what amounts to hundred-degree heat and hundred-percent humidity," Frey told *Democracy Now!* "Many of the individuals die. They don't have identification on them. The process by which the county and officials in the area try to identify them is pretty meaningless. And these individuals are buried in a county cemetery, basically dumped into a hole in the ground. Many of them don't have markers or proper burial techniques."

Official inquiries concluded that there was no wrongdoing. Frey, however, uncovered numerous violations of state law and standard practice. DNA was not collected and stored properly, and bodies became comingled in the mass grave, making identification and return of the bodies to loved ones virtually impossible.

While entry into the United States without documentation can be dangerous, conditions as people await deportation can be hellish too, or even fatal. The US immigration detention system is vast, decentralized, and increasingly privatized. People often disappear in a maze of complex administrative hearings and harsh conditions, largely beyond the reach of loved ones, advocates, or the media.

Violations of immigration laws are considered civil, not criminal, infractions, so jail time is not an appropriate penalty. Yet US Immigration and Customs Enforcement regularly confines people to long periods in conditions that are no different—or even worse—than prison. Immigration prisoners find themselves locked up and deprived of their rights to a court-appointed attorney and a speedy trial before a jury. Instead, they exist in legal limbo, awaiting a determination in an administrative hearing—and then likely deportation.

ICE maintains more than two hundred detention facilities, where, on any given day, thirty-four thousand people are locked up. Remarkably, this number is mandated by Congress. That's right: Congress has required the Department of Homeland Security (DHS) to increase the number of bed spaces ICE fills. So, regardless of the need, ICE must imprison thirty-four thousand men, women, and children per night.

The immigration detention might not be just, but it is highly profitable. Nine of the ten largest detention centers are privately run. Two private prison companies in the United States profit handsomely from the immigrant detention system: Corrections Corporation of America (CCA) and the GEO Group (known formerly as the Wackenhut Corrections Corporation, its current name is an acronym for Global Expertise in Outsourcing). Each company has enjoyed significant growth in the last decade, and each most recently posted annual net profits of between $150 million and $200 million. In addition to these giant for-profit corporate prison companies, hundreds of city and county jails are paid by the federal government to house people awaiting immigration hearings.

Conditions of detention are appalling. One seasoned social worker, Olivia López, took a job at what ICE calls the Karnes County Residential Center, in Karnes City, Texas. Don't be fooled: Karnes is a prison, not a residential center. It is owned by the GEO Group, and imprisons women and children at this facility. López started work there in October 2014 and left just six months later. She was deeply upset by what she saw there. She told *Democracy Now!*, "The most startling thing for me, once I got into the center and back to the medical department, was the clanging of the doors. I felt it really was a prison at that point. You know, the sally port doors and the clanging and monitors all over." A sally port is a two-step secure door system, wherein you walk through a door, which closes and locks behind you, and then a second door opens to allow you into the room you want to enter. It is used primarily in prisons and in secure military installations in war zones.

López continued: "There's a weekly monitoring that occurs at Karnes County, and it's a mental health check to make sure how women are doing and how their children are doing. At the bottom of that form there's a place to list concerns that women have. I was [told] not to write anything down on that." To further confirm that this is not a nurturing place for families to reside, she described the use of solitary confinement at Karnes: "It's not called that there, but what I came to understand is that when women were being reprimanded or punished, or GEO wanted some behavior modification, they and their children will be placed in a medical observation room. But truthfully, those rooms really were for punishment and behavior modification. They were not free to leave the rooms. They were in there for the duration of the time of their punishment."

These for-profit immigrant prisons are criticized consistently for inhumane conditions, poor sanitation, inadequate food and medical care, and overcrowding. They are often placed in rural communities, far from lawyers and advocacy groups. The small towns that ultimately host the prisons are typically desperate for jobs, pitting local wage earners against the imprisoned immigrants and their supporters. Meanwhile, corporations such as the GEO Group and CCA spend millions annually lobbying at the state and federal levels, ensuring that laws are passed that create additional demand for their prisons.

Sonia Hernández's story is all too typical. She fled violence in El Salvador, taking her three children to the United States. They were held at Karnes for 315 days. After she got out, she testified before a congressional committee:

When my children would get sick, like when they had a fever sometimes as high as 40 degrees C [104 degrees Fahrenheit], the only thing that I could do was to put them in the bath or in the shower in order to lower their fever. When they were hungry, I had to buy instant soup to be able to give them noodle soup. Sometimes immigration would see that I looked like I was doing really badly, like I wasn't doing well, and they would tell me that I should go to the psychiatrist. And I would respond to them, "The psychiatrist isn't going to resolve my problems. The only thing that will resolve my problems is to be freed from this place."

Resistance to abusive immigrant detention is widespread, but the flawed logic embraced by the federal authorities persists. Federal judge Dolly Gee of California ordered all mothers with children released from immigrant detention centers, citing evidence that conditions at Customs and Border Protection detention centers were "deplorable" and "overcrowded and unhygienic." Obama's Justice Department appealed her order.

The suffering and insecurity of these millions of our neighbors living without the safety of documentation was greatly exacerbated by political figures like Donald Trump. During the early months of Trump's bid for the 2016 Republican nomination for president, he constantly one-upped himself with a series of anti-immigrant statements. Using the presidential primary bully pulpit to bully the weakest, he targeted immigrants and Muslims. Speaking of Mexican immigrants, he said, "They are, in many cases, criminals, drug dealers, rapists, etc."

On the issue of deportations separating families, his answer was simple: deport them together. "We have to keep the families together, but they have to go. They have to go," he told NBC

News. He proposed rounding up and deporting over eleven million people, including the US citizens whose parents lack documentation. He advocated abolishing birthright citizenship for people born on US soil. He refused to offer specifics on how such a mass roundup of people would be managed. The United States still bears the shame of having interned approximately 115,000 Japanese Americans during World War II. Trump proposed rounding up a hundred times more people than that. Trump's motto was "making America great again," prompting protesters to carry signs at his rallies saying "making America hate again."

Trump's xenophobic messages resonated with the base of the Republican Party, the primary voters, so his competitors in the crowded Republican field began parroting him. Their fiercely anti-immigrant rhetoric brought to mind these words about US immigration policy:

"Illegal immigrants in considerable numbers have become productive members of our society and are a basic part of our workforce. Those who have established equities in the United States should be recognized and accorded legal status."

These were the words of President Ronald Reagan in 1981. Republicans frequently invoke Reagan's memory in an effort to burnish their conservative credentials. In truth, if Reagan were running for election today, he wouldn't stand a chance in the Republican primaries.

CHAPTER 4

STOPPING THE MACHINERY OF DEATH

On September 21, 2011, Troy Anthony Davis was scheduled to die. We were reporting live from the grounds outside Georgia's death row in the town of Jackson, awaiting news about whether the US Supreme Court would spare his life. "I am Troy Davis" had become the rallying cry of a growing international movement to stop his execution. The effort had grown, and now included not just traditional anti–death penalty activists but also prosecutors, prison wardens, exonerated death row prisoners, a former US president, and the pope.

This is the story of a struggle against death that refuses die.

Troy Anthony Davis grew up in a middle-class neighborhood in Savannah, Georgia. He lived in the same ranch house all his life with his parents, three sisters, and brother. His mother worked at a local hospital, and his father, a carpenter, was a veteran of the Korean War.

On the night of August 18, 1989, eighteen-year-old Troy, who is African American, went to Charlie Brown's Pool Hall with a friend. In the parking lot outside, Sylvester "Redd" Coles, a neighborhood tough, was arguing loudly with a homeless man named Larry Young. Several witnesses testified later that Coles pistol-whipped Young.[1]

Pool hall patrons came outside and joined other bystanders on Oglethorpe Drive to see what was going on. Troy Davis tried to intervene in the fight, but fled when Coles threatened him with a gun.

At a quarter after one in the morning, Mark MacPhail, a white off-duty Savannah police officer who was working as a security guard at a Greyhound bus station next door, came outside to break up the fight. Gunshots pierced the summer night. Moments later, MacPhail lay dying with a bullet wound to the head and another to the heart. He never drew his gun.

Redd Coles went to the police station, accompanied by a lawyer, and identified Davis as the shooter. But the day after the shooting, Davis was four hours away in Atlanta, job hunting with his cousin. While he was there, the police launched a high-profile manhunt, and splashed Troy Davis's picture across newspapers and TV.

Davis's panicked family alerted Troy that authorities were looking for him. His sister Martina picked up Troy in Atlanta a few days later, and Troy turned himself in to the Chatham County Sheriff's Office. The teenager thought it was a case of mistaken identity and that he would simply clear up the confusion.

Instead, Troy Anthony Davis was charged with murder. He was held in jail for two years before finally being tried in August

1991. A jury deliberated for two hours and returned a guilty verdict. On August 30, 1991, Troy Anthony Davis, age twenty, was sentenced to die.[2]

Davis would spend the next twenty years on death row. During that time, seven of the nine nonpolice witnesses recanted or changed their testimony, with some of them alleging police intimidation for their original false statements. One who did not recant was the man who many have named as the actual killer: Redd Coles. No physical evidence linked Davis to the shooting.

Jeffrey Sapp is typical of those in the case who recanted their eyewitness testimony. He said in an affidavit: "The police . . . put a lot of pressure on me to say 'Troy said this' or 'Troy said that.' They wanted me to tell them that Troy confessed to me about killing that officer . . . they made it clear that the only way they would leave me alone is if I told them what they wanted to hear." [3]

One of the jurors in the Davis case, Brenda Forrest, told CNN in 2009, "All of the witnesses—they were able to ID him as the person who actually did it." After the seven witnesses recanted, she said, "If I knew then what I know now, Troy Davis would not be on death row. The verdict would be not guilty." [4]

Despite the witness recantations, Georgia's parole commission refused to commute Davis's sentence. Courts declined to hear the new evidence, mostly on procedural grounds. Everywhere he turned, doors closed.

Davis was hamstrung by a federal law passed in 1996, the Antiterrorism and Effective Death Penalty Act, which was part of House Speaker Newt Gingrich's Contract with America that was signed by President Bill Clinton. The law was aimed at fast-tracking death penalty cases and eliminating avenues of appeal.

In 2004 Davis went to federal court to present the recanted

testimony and nine affidavits from people who insisted that Redd Coles was the real murderer of Mark MacPhail. The federal judge rejected the petition, claiming that such evidence must be presented in state court first. But Davis had been unable to present this evidence in state court, where he had been represented in his death penalty appeal by the Georgia Resource Center. In 1995, as part of speeding up death penalty cases, Congress slashed $20 million in funding to organizations specializing in postconviction defense. As a result, the Georgia Resource Center, which handles legal appeals for indigent death penalty prisoners, lost 70 percent of its budget, six of its eight lawyers, and three of its four investigators.

"The work conducted on Mr. Davis's case was akin to triage," wrote Georgia Resource Center executive director Beth Wells in an affidavit, "where we were simply trying to avert total disaster rather than provide any kind of active or effective representation . . . There were numerous witnesses that we knew should have been interviewed, but lacked the resources to do so."[5]

In a desperate effort to have the new evidence considered, Davis's lawyers appealed to the US Supreme Court. In a rare decision, the Supreme Court ordered a Georgia court to consider the new evidence from Davis. Justice John Paul Stevens wrote for the majority, "The substantial risk of putting an innocent man to death clearly provides an adequate justification for holding an evidentiary hearing." Yet conservative justice Antonin Scalia dissented (with Justice Clarence Thomas), writing that Davis's case "is a sure loser," and "[t]his Court has never held that the Constitution forbids the execution of a convicted defendant who has had a full and fair trial but is later able to convince a habeas court that he is 'actually' innocent."

In June 2010 a federal judge held a two-day hearing in Savannah to consider new evidence. Despite the recanted testimony of seven witnesses, Judge William Moore reaffirmed the original guilty verdict.

The serious discrepancies in Davis's case troubled even death penalty supporters. Conservatives such as former Georgia congressman and prosecutor Bob Barr and former FBI Director William Sessions called for Davis's life to be spared, along with Pope Benedict XVI, the NAACP, and Amnesty International.

Over the course of his legal odyssey through state and federal courts, Troy Davis was scheduled to be executed four different times. For his second execution date, on September 23, 2008, Davis was within two hours of receiving a lethal injection. The Davis family and anti–death penalty activists from around the country gathered at the prison to protest and pray. Less than two hours before Davis was to be put to death, the family received a call at the prison telling them that the US Supreme Court had granted a one-week stay of execution to consider Davis's appeal for a new trial.

As protesters and family celebrated the stay of execution, Troy called his sister Martina Davis-Correia. Troy asked her to relay a message to his supporters. "Have people pray for the MacPhail family. Tell them to keep working to dismantle this unjust system. Tell them I would not be fighting this hard for my life if I was guilty," he said.[6]

In March 2011 the US Supreme Court refused to hear Troy Anthony Davis's case. A series of appeals and applications for clemency were also denied. President Obama declined to intervene.

On September 7, 2011, Georgia set Troy Davis's fourth execution date for September 21.

WHEN "ACTUAL INNOCENCE" ISN'T ENOUGH

Following the Supreme Court decision, Martina told me, "We were really shocked and appalled yesterday when we received the news . . . No one wants to look at the actual innocence, and no one wants to look at the witness recantation as a real strong and viable part of this case, even though new witnesses have come forward. There needs to be a global mobilization about Troy's case, and the fact that in the United States it's not unconstitutional to execute an innocent person needs to be addressed once and for all by the US Supreme Court."

Davis-Correia raised a significant but little-known fact about death penalty law in the United states: current court precedent allows for the execution of innocent people. Remarkably, the Supreme Court, in a 1993 opinion, suggested that "actual innocence" is not a sufficient cause to be let free. The court cares only that the legal rules are followed, while acknowledging that innocent people could still be convicted and put to death. In such cases, a prisoner could appeal for executive clemency. It seems the court has not yet learned what many states have: the death penalty system is broken beyond repair.

Martina Davis-Correia was Troy Davis's biggest advocate. In addition to leading the fight for her brother, she was fighting for her own life. The day of the Supreme Court decision was the tenth anniversary of her battle against breast cancer. Her face adorned the mobile mammography van that helps save the lives of poor women in Savannah. The National Breast Cancer Coalition named her and former House Speaker Nancy Pelosi "Women Who Get It Right."

Davis-Correia, who was an army nurse and a veteran of the

Persian Gulf War, declared, "My battle is more than just for Troy. My battle is for everyone to fight injustice."

REPORTING FROM DEATH ROW

On September 21, 2011, the day he was scheduled to die, Davis's lawyers filed a request with the US Supreme Court for a stay of execution. The world watched to see whether Davis's final appeal would be granted.

Democracy Now! was the only news outlet to broadcast live continuously from the prison grounds in Jackson, Georgia. For six hours that day, I spoke with Davis's supporters and family members who held an all-day vigil.

With each of Davis's four execution dates, global awareness grew. Calls for clemency poured in, from Nobel Peace Prize laureate Archbishop Desmond Tutu to former president (and Georgia governor) Jimmy Carter. The Georgia State Board of Pardons and Paroles, in granting Davis a stay of execution in 2007, wrote that it "will not allow an execution to proceed in this state unless . . . there is no doubt as to the guilt of the accused."

But it is just that doubt that galvanized so much global outrage over this case. As we waited, the crowd swelled around the prison, holding signs reading "Too Much Doubt" and "I Am Troy Davis." Vigils were being held around the world, in countries such as Iceland, England, France, and Germany.

The chorus for clemency grew louder. Dr. Allen Ault, a former warden of Georgia's death row prison who oversaw five executions there, sent a letter to Governor Nathan Deal that was co-signed by five other retired wardens or directors of state prisons. They wrote: "While most of the prisoners whose executions we participated in accepted responsibility for the crimes for which they were punished, some of us have also executed prisoners who maintained their innocence until the end. It is those cases that are most haunting to an executioner."

Earlier in the day, prison authorities handed us a thin press kit. At three o'clock, it said that Davis would be given a "routine physical."

Routine? Physical? At a nearby church, Georgia's NAACP president, Edward DuBose, spoke, along with human rights leaders, clergy, and family members who had just left Davis. DuBose questioned the absurdity of having a physical. "So that they could make sure he's physically fit? So that they can strap him down? So that they could put the murder juice in his arm? Make no mistake: They call it an execution. We call it murder."

Not long before that, a Texas man had been scheduled to die, but he attempted suicide. Texas authorities rushed him to the hospital. They waited for him to get better. Then they executed him.

Davis turned down a special last meal. The press kit described the standard fare Davis would be offered: "grilled cheeseburgers, oven-browned potatoes, baked beans, coleslaw, cookies, and grape beverage."

Another page listed the lethal cocktail that would follow: "Pentobarbital. Pancuronium bromide. Potassium chloride. Ativan (a sedative)." The pentobarbital anesthetizes, the pancuronium bromide paralyzes, and the potassium chloride stops the heart. Davis refused the sedative and his last meal.

By 7:00 p.m., the US Supreme Court was reportedly reviewing Davis's plea for a stay. The case was referred to Supreme Court Justice Clarence Thomas, who hails from Pin Point, Georgia, a community founded by freed slaves that is near Savannah, where Davis had lived.

The Supreme Court denied the plea. Davis's execution began at 10:53 p.m. A prison spokesperson delivered the news to the reporters outside: time of death, 11:08 p.m.

The eyewitnesses to the execution stepped out. According to an Associated Press reporter who was there, these were Troy Davis's final words: "I'd like to address the MacPhail family. Let you know, despite the situation you are in, I'm not the one who personally killed your son, your father, your brother. I am innocent. The incident that happened that night is not my fault. I did not have a gun. All I can ask . . . is that you look deeper into this case so that you really can finally see the truth. I ask my family and friends to continue to fight this fight. For those about to take my life, God have mercy on your souls. And may God bless your souls."

The state of Georgia took Davis's body to Atlanta for an autopsy, charging his family for the transportation. On Troy Davis's death certificate, the cause of death is listed simply as "homicide."

As I stood on the grounds of the prison, just after Troy Davis was executed, the Georgia Department of Corrections threatened to pull the plug on our broadcast. The show was over.

I was reminded of what Mahatma Gandhi reportedly answered when asked what he thought of Western civilization: "I think it would be a good idea."

THE EXECUTIONERS

The United States is among the world's leading executioners, along with China, Iran, Saudi Arabia, and North Korea. But unlike countries such as Saudi Arabia (which conducts public beheadings), or China (which prefers firing squads for its more than one thousand executions per year), or Iran (which hangs people),[7] or Nigeria (which stones people convicted of rape or homosexuality), the "civilized" United States does its killing in private.[8] Since 1976, when the death penalty was reinstated in America after a brief moratorium, more than 1,400 people have been executed. Texas has been the most enthusiastic killer, with 531 executions since 1976 (as of December 2015), followed by Oklahoma (112), Virginia (111), and Florida (91). Georgia (60) is sixth on this list.[9]

Democracy Now! has covered death penalty cases extensively since we began. These cases go to the heart of why we exist: To give voice to the voiceless. To go to where the silence is. And there is nowhere more silent than America's death row, home to some three thousand people—overwhelmingly people of color, the poor, and others who have been marginalized.

The death penalty in America is reminiscent of another brutal injustice.

More than a century ago, the legendary muckraking African American journalist Ida B. Wells risked her life when she began reporting on the epidemic of lynchings in the Deep South. She was half owner of the anti-segregationist Memphis newspaper *Free Speech and Headlight*, which had its office burned down by angry whites in response to her editorials. Wells also published the pamphlet *Southern Horrors: Lynch Law in All Its Phases* in 1892, and followed up with *The Red Record* in 1895, detailing hundreds of lynchings. She wrote:

"In Brooks County, Georgia, 23 December, while this Christian country was preparing for Christmas celebration, seven Negroes were lynched in 24 hours because they refused, or were unable to tell the whereabouts of a colored man named Pike, who killed a white man . . . Georgia heads the list of lynching states."

Some things never change: the American Bar Association has singled out Georgia's racial disparities in capital-offense sentencing, saying that it has allowed inadequate defense counsel and been "virtually alone in not providing indigent defendants sentenced to death with counsel for state habeas proceedings."

Studies of racial bias in death penalty cases abound. The national nonprofit organization Death Penalty Information Center, citing a *Louisiana Law Review* study, reports that in Louisiana the odds of being sentenced to death were 97 percent higher for crimes in which the victim was white than those where the victim was African American. Nationally, 75 percent of the cases that resulted in execution had white victims. A study by Yale University revealed that African American defendants receive the death penalty at three times the rate of white defendants in cases where the victims are white.[10]

"The unjust execution of African American men thrives today on the same soil as the lynching trees, only now the noose has been replaced with the needle," wrote Angel Harris, a staff attorney with the ACLU Capital Punishment Project. "African American men are overrepresented on death row, in executions, and in exonerations. To boot, African American jurors are systematically excluded by prosecutors in jury service. Race is one of the most disturbing explanations for innocent men . . . ending up on death row for crimes they did not commit."[11]

Defendants charged in capital crimes are further disadvantaged by facing a jury that is "death qualified," meaning that each member has to be open to considering the death penalty; anyone who opposes it cannot serve.

Denny LeBoeuf, director of the ACLU's John Adams Project and former director of the Capital Punishment Project, has twenty-six years' experience as a capital defense attorney. She said on *Democracy Now!*, "Having picked some death-qualified juries in a very Catholic city, New Orleans, you watch as you lose a lot of Catholics, most of your African Americans and other people of color—you lose all the people who, even for nonreligious reasons, don't have a strong sense that the authorities, that the government, is always right and always tells the truth . . . You're instead picking a jury from a very small, unrepresentative, very conservative, conviction-prone pool. And it's the central unfairness of this process."

DEATH DRUGS

In an effort to stop the death machine, anti–death penalty activists have been choking off its lifeblood: the killing drugs.

Hospira, the last US-based company to make sodium thiopental, one of the three drugs used in the lethal "cocktail" administered in most executions in this country, quit making the controlled drug, creating a national shortage. States began scrambling to keep their death chambers well stocked. When California borrowed a similar drug from Arizona, its undersecretary of corrections and rehabilitation, Scott Kernan, wrote in an email, "You guys in AZ are life savers."

An exposé by Katie Fretland in the *Colorado Independent* reported that assistant Oklahoma attorney general Seth Branham joked in an email with a Texas colleague in 2011 that he might be able to help Texas get the drugs in exchange for fifty-yard-line tickets for a top college football game between the University of Oklahoma and the University of Texas.

Branham went on to propose in an email that Oklahoma officials, who he dubbed "Team Pentobarbital," be rewarded with "an on-field presentation of a commemorative plaque at halftime recognizing Oklahoma's on-going contributions to propping up the Texas system of capital punishment." [12]

European drug companies are refusing to supply the drugs if they are used in lethal injections. The death penalty has been abolished in all of Europe except Belarus and Kazakhstan. The ban against capital punishment is enshrined in the Charter of Fundamental Rights of the European Union (EU).

The American Pharmacists Association (APhA) has now joined national organizations of physicians and anesthesiologists in discouraging their members from participating in executions. In 2015, APhA delegates approved a declaration that "discourages pharmacist participation in executions on the basis that such activities are fundamentally contrary to the role of pharmacists as providers of health care."

Dr. Leonard Edloe is an African American pharmacist with the APhA who led the movement to stop pharmacists from participating in executions. He said on *Democracy Now!*: "We just don't want our pharmacists being involved either in the dispensing of the drugs or the use because, really, the prescriptions are illegal. They aren't prescriptions, they're purchase orders."

Louisiana Department of Corrections secretary James LeBlanc lamented in 2014, "It's become almost impossible to execute someone." [13]

Because of the shortage of lethal-injection drugs, Utah reinstated the firing squad in 2015. After Oklahoma used untested drug combinations that caused botched executions with painful, protracted deaths in 2014, the state announced in 2015 that it would introduce a nitrogen gas chamber—another untried execution method. (Previous gas chambers used hydrogen cyanide, which was considered inhumane.) [14] But when it was revealed that Oklahoma used the wrong drugs in a botched execution in January 2015—and had mixed up the drugs again nine months later as it prepared to execute death row prisoner Richard Glossip—the

Oklahoma attorney general announced a ban on executions at least until mid-2016.

Richard Glossip's case dates back to 1997, when he was working as a manager at the Best Budget Inn in Oklahoma City and his boss, Barry Van Treese, was murdered. A maintenance worker, Justin Sneed, admitted he beat Van Treese to death with a baseball bat, but claimed Glossip offered him money for the killing. The case rested almost solely on Sneed's claims. No physical evidence ever tied Glossip to the crime. And Sneed, in exchange for his testimony, did not get the death penalty.

Steven Hawkins, executive director of Amnesty International USA, observed, "Glossip's assertion that he did not commit the crime isn't what saved him. It was the state's own incompetence. Just minutes before the execution, Oklahoma Governor Mary Fallin issued a temporary stay of execution because state officials suddenly realized they had failed to procure the right mixture of drugs to kill him. The following day, the Oklahoma attorney general requested an indefinite stay on executions while his office investigated what went wrong. The reality is that just about everything went wrong. Glossip's case shows, yet again, how fundamentally flawed the capital punishment system is."[15]

The list of states having to suspend executions continues to grow. Ohio announced in 2015 that due to a lack of execution drugs, it would put a hold on executions until at least 2017, forcing Ohio Governor John Kasich to issue temporary reprieves to about a dozen prisoners who were slated to die. And in October 2015 an Arkansas judge temporarily halted the executions of eight death row prisoners while they challenged the state's protocols for lethal injection.

The state of Georgia planned to kill Troy Davis by administering a lethal dose of pentobarbital. Georgia was using this new execution drug because the federal Drug Enforcement Administration

(DEA) seized its supply of sodium thiopental in early 2011, accusing the state of illegally importing the poison.

"This is our justice system at its very worst," said Ben Jealous, then president of the NAACP.

THE STRUGGLE CONTINUES

For as long as there has been a death penalty, there has been a movement to abolish it. In the United States, early death penalty opponents included Pennsylvania Attorney General William Bradford, and signers of the Declaration of Independence Ben Franklin and Dr. Benjamin Rush, who was also founder of the Pennsylvania Prison Society. In 1794 Pennsylvania became the first state to repeal the death penalty for all offenses except first-degree murder.[16]

Following World War II, international efforts to abolish the death penalty gained ground. Today 71 percent of countries have ended the death penalty for most crimes, either de facto or by law.[17]

In the United States, the exoneration of numerous death row prisoners has moved a number of states to ban or suspend executions. Since 1973, over 150 death row prisoners have been exonerated.[18] Illinois Governor George Ryan, a conservative Republican, commuted the death sentences of 120 prisoners in 2000. He described his reason for changing his position on the death penalty in a powerful speech to the New York City Bar Association:

> I was looking at a pretty shameful record in the state of Illinois. The scorecard wasn't good. Since the death penalty had been reinstated back in 1977, out of the twenty-five people that were on death row, twelve of them had been executed and thirteen had been exonerated. That's a terrible record. And up until then,

with each remarkable complex and sometimes confusing development, I had resisted a lot of calls from some to declare a moratorium on executions.

So I asked myself, "How can I go forward when we've got so many questions about all of this, when we, out of twenty-five people, we exonerate thirteen that we almost kill? How can we proceed with a system like this?" There were a lot of unanswerable questions. There were questions about the fairness of the administration of the death penalty in Illinois. And in my heart, I just knew I couldn't go forward. I couldn't live with myself.

It was clear to me that when it came to the death penalty in Illinois, there was no justice in the justice system.

So on January the thirty-first, I told the citizens of Illinois that I was going to impose a moratorium, because of the grave concerns I had about the state's shameful record of convicting innocent people and putting them on death row. I can't support that system. And its administration, it's proven to be very fraught with error, and it's come awful close to the ultimate nightmare.

It's easy to be an ardent death penalty supporter when you don't have to make the decision. When you don't have to throw the switch, when you don't have to decide who's going to live or die—it's pretty easy to say, "Kill him. An eye for an eye." But when you sit in judgment, when you have the power to decide who's going to live or die, it's an awesome responsibility.[19]

DEAD MAN WALKING

One of the world's leading organizers against the death penalty is a Catholic nun. Sister Helen Prejean was working in a poor neighborhood of New Orleans when she was asked if she would be a pen pal to a death row prisoner. Sister Helen agreed, forever changing her life, as well as the debate on capital punishment.

Her experiences inspired her first book, *Dead Man Walking: An Eyewitness Account of the Death Penalty in the United States*, which in 2013 was republished on its twentieth anniversary. Sister Helen was a pen pal with Patrick Sonnier, a convicted murderer on death row in Louisiana's notorious Angola prison. In her distinctive southern accent, she told me of her first visit to Sonnier: "It was scary as all get-out. I had never been in a prison before . . . I was scared to meet him personally. When I saw his face, it was so human, it blew me away. I got a realization then, no matter what he had done . . . he is worth more than the worst thing he ever did. And the journey began from there."

Sister Helen became Sonnier's spiritual advisor, conversing with him as his execution approached. She spent his final hours with him, and witnessed his execution on April 5, 1984. She also was a spiritual advisor to another Angola death row prisoner, Robert Lee Willie, who was executed the same year.

Dead Man Walking was made into a film, directed by Tim Robbins and starring Susan Sarandon as Prejean and Sean Penn as the character Matthew Poncelet, an amalgam of Sonnier and Willie. In 1995 Sarandon won the Oscar for Best Actress, and the film's success further intensified the national debate on the death penalty.

Prejean said one of her greatest regrets was that she failed to reach out to the families of the murder victims while she was spiritual advisor to Sonnier and Willie. She went on to found Survive, an organization to support families of murder victims.

Prejean concluded one of my many conversations with her by saying, "I've accompanied six human beings and watched them be killed. I have a dedication to them to do this. I can't walk away from this. I'm going to be doing this until I die."

NO MORE TROY DAVISES

At Troy Davis's funeral in October 2011, I spoke with his sister Martina Davis-Correia, who by then was in a wheelchair. She had lost the fight to save her brother, but she was steadfast in her commitment to the larger fight. She told me: "I know we will be able to abolish the death penalty, because people all over the world are asking the question 'Why kill when there's doubt?' And I want people to know that we're no longer going to accept that, not in our names."

Martina died three months after her brother's execution, ending her ten-year battle with cancer. But her sister Kimberly Davis has continued the fight. "Troy gave each of us a charge, and he told us that he wanted us to continue to fight to end the death penalty," she told me. She said that Martina told her before she died, "It's time for you to be my voice."

"And that's what I'm doing," she declared, "continuing to be the voice of Martina, continuing to be the voice of Troy."

A year after the execution of Troy Davis, former NAACP President Ben Jealous, who was deeply involved in Davis's case, reflected on the legacy of Troy Davis. "The really remarkable thing—and you heard it in Troy's words—was that this was somebody who ultimately had an understanding of movements. His mom had been active in the civil rights movement. [He] really understood that there were multiple types of victory that could be accomplished here. And we've started to see some of that. We abolished the death penalty in Connecticut . . . And we just abolished it below the Mason-Dixon Line for the first time, in Maryland." Without this case, he emphasized, "neither one of those things would have happened."

Jealous said that the death penalty abolition movement is aiming to abolish the death penalty in twenty-six states. Once a majority of states ban capital punishment, it will meet the threshold for "cruel and unusual punishment" and the US Supreme Court can rule that the death penalty is illegal.

"We are getting to a place where, quite frankly, more and more people are sort of openly conflicted about the death penalty," Jealous continued. "And that's a good thing."

Death penalty opponents continue to make progress. In 2013 Maryland abolished capital punishment. After passage of the law, Maryland Governor Martin O'Malley wrote: "Evidence shows that the death penalty is not a deterrent, it cannot be administered without racial bias, and it costs three times as much as life in prison without parole. What's more, there is no way to reverse a mistake if an innocent person is put to death."

It's not just traditionally liberal states that are revolting against the death penalty. In May 2015 the Nebraska legislature overrode a governor's veto to become "the first predominantly Republican state to abolish the death penalty since North Dakota abolished the death penalty in 1973," said Robert Dunham, executive director of the Death Penalty Information Center. Nebraska is the nineteenth state, plus the District of Columbia, to abolish the death penalty as of 2015.

"I believe the state shouldn't kill anybody. I don't think anybody should kill anybody," declared Nebraska State Senator Ernie Chambers, who introduced legislation to ban the death penalty for thirty-seven consecutive years before it finally succeeded.[20] He is one of only two African American members of the Nebraska legislature.

But Nebraska Governor Pete Ricketts is fighting hard to keep the death penalty alive in his state. He and his father, TD Ameritrade founder Joe Ricketts, invested a combined $300,000 to back a successful petition drive demanding that the repeal of the death penalty be suspended and then put to a state referendum in November 2016, in the hopes that the state's conservative electorate would reinstate it. Ricketts also directed state corrections officials to spend over $50,000 to purchase execution drugs from a dealer in India, in apparent violation of US law. Nebraska purchased enough drugs to kill hundreds of people—the day before the Nebraska legislature overrode the governor's veto and barred the death penalty, at least temporarily.[21]

THE EXONERATED

A steady stream of exonerations continues to expose the racism and unfairness that fuel the death penalty—and the risk that innocent people are being put to death.

Anthony Ray Hinton is alive today, a free man. But in early 2015 he was on death row in Alabama. Hinton was the 152nd person in the United States to be exonerated from death row, where he spent three decades for a crime he did not commit. He was accused of killing two fast-food restaurant managers in 1985. There were no eyewitnesses, nor fingerprints. Prosecutors alleged that bullets found matched a revolver belonging to Hinton's mother. Hinton had ineffective counsel, and no money to mount a credible defense or to hire a genuine expert witness to challenge the ballistics.

"The American criminal justice system . . . treats you better if you're rich and guilty than if you're poor and innocent," Bryan Stevenson told *Democracy Now!* He is the founder and executive director of the Equal Justice Initiative, and the attorney who eventually freed Anthony Ray Hinton.

Hinton's unfair trial was just the beginning. "We developed the evidence that showed that these bullets could not be matched to a single gun and that it wasn't Mr. Hinton's gun," Stevenson explained. "The state then refused for sixteen years to even retest the evidence . . . It was really unconscionable that they chose to risk executing an innocent person over risking the perception that they were somehow making a mistake or not being tough on crime."

In a remarkable and, according to Stevenson, extremely unlikely turn of events, the US Supreme Court agreed to look at Hinton's case and unanimously overturned his conviction. "Had they not intervened, I think the risk of a wrongful execution would have been very, very high," Stevenson said.

During the interview on *Democracy Now!*, Stevenson paused to observe, "I just have to say how extraordinary it is to be sitting next to my friend and my client. We've spent so many hours together . . . but we've never been able to sit together in suits in a place like this." He and Hinton were sitting in a television studio in Montgomery, Alabama, just across the street from the first White House of the Confederacy—the home of Confederate President Jefferson Davis.

Glenn Ford was another recent exoneree. He was released in March 2014 after three decades on Louisiana's death row. Evidence cleared him of the 1983 fatal shooting of a jewelry store owner. As a free man, he faced a death sentence of a different kind: stage four lung cancer that had spread to his bones, lymph nodes, and spine.

Ford wasn't strong enough to speak on *Democracy Now!* But Marty Stroud was. He is the man who prosecuted Glenn Ford thirty years ago, and today regrets that he did so. He now says that Ford had an unfair trial in which key evidence was suppressed by police and the prosecutors, and that Ford lacked the money to mount a proper defense. Ford's lawyers might have been trying their first case—with life-and-death stakes. Moreover, Stroud says, if he had done his job properly at the time, and all the evidence was collected, they would not have even been able to arrest Glenn Ford, let alone try him for the crime.

Now, thirty years later, prosecutor Marty Stroud feels differently about capital punishment: "I am one hundred percent against the death penalty," he said. "It is barbaric. And the reason it is barbaric is that it is administered by human beings, and we make mistakes. We are not infallible."

Stroud apologized to Ford in a 2014 editorial in which he wrote, "In 1984, I was 33 years old. I was arrogant, judgmental, narcissistic, and very full of myself. I was not as interested in justice as I was in winning."

In the last weeks of Ford's life, when he was in hospice care, Stroud met with Ford to apologize in person.

"I'm sorry I can't forgive you. I really am," Ford responded. The emotional encounter was filmed and aired on ABC's *Nightline*.

"I understand," said Stroud. After the men parted, Ford wept softly as he was comforted by his hospice caregivers. Two months after this apology, Glenn Ford died.

The movement to abolish state-sanctioned killing is finding unlikely allies as it continues to gain momentum. Troy Davis died, but his fight continues.

CHAPTER 5

THE RISE OF THE 99 PERCENT

No business which depends for existence on paying less than living wages to its workers has any right to continue in this country.
—President Franklin Roosevelt, 1933

A global movement is challenging the grotesque levels of economic inequality that are the hallmark of the modern age. From the Arab Spring, to Occupy Wall Street, to antiausterity campaigns in Europe, to low-wage workers in the United States fighting and winning a livable wage, each part of the movement inspires the other. This is the story of the rise of the 99 percent.

A worldwide rebellion against inequality is under way. Oxfam America, a global organization that works to overcome poverty, hunger, and injustice, reports that as of 2015, the world's richest sixty-two billionaires now own as much wealth as half the world. This figure is down from 388 individuals in 2010.

This bears repeating: the sixty-two wealthiest people—a group that could fit on a bus—control more wealth than three and a half billion people.

The wealthy are not only accumulating more wealth but also are getting it faster. Between 2010 and 2015, Oxfam states in its report, *An Economy for the 1 Percent*, the wealth of those sixty-two richest people rose by a half trillion dollars, while the bottom half of humanity lost over a trillion dollars. This, while the rest of the world was mired in the Great Recession, with rampant unemployment and people's life savings wiped out. The richest 1 percent of the world's population now controls more wealth than the rest of the world combined.

Despite the economic noose that is tightening around the 99 percent, governments and financial institutions around the globe are insisting that the solution to economic inequality is austerity: shrinking the public sector, slashing pensions, and privatizing public assets. One after another, countries such as Spain and Greece, states such as Wisconsin, Michigan, and Kansas, and American colonies such as Puerto Rico—are becoming laboratories for how much pain can be inflicted on a population for the purpose of satisfying creditors and ideologues.

Pablo Iglesias is the secretary general of Podemos, an anti-austerity party in Spain. A month after establishing itself in 2014, Podemos won five seats in the European Parliament. In December 2015, Podemos shocked the establishment in the Spanish general elections, winning 21 percent of the vote and becoming the third largest party in parliament, winning 69 of 350 seats. I spoke with the thirty-six-year-old political science professor and longtime activist in June 2015 when he came to New York. I asked him to talk about what austerity has meant in Spain.

"Austerity means that people are evicted from their homes," he replied. "Austerity means that the social services don't work anymore. Austerity means that public schools do not have the means to [operate]. Austerity means that the countries do not have sovereignty anymore, and we become a colony of the financial powers and a colony of Germany. Austerity probably means the end of democracy. I think if we don't have democratic control of the economy, we don't have democracy. It's impossible to separate economy and democracy, in my opinion."

Another political leader, Ada Colau, gained fame as a housing activist in Barcelona. A photo of her being arrested and dragged by police at an antieviction demonstration in 2013 went viral after she was elected as the first woman mayor of Barcelona in May 2015. Colau and others founded Barcelona en Comú ("Barcelona in Common"), a movement to build grassroots power and win the municipal elections.

"We have serious political problems here in Barcelona and in the entire country, and so there was a need for change, which you could see in the streets," she told me on *Democracy Now!* "What is happening in Spain and in Barcelona is not an isolated event; rather, there is a crisis in the way we do politics. There is a political elite, which has become corrupt and has ended up as accomplices of a financial power which only thinks to speculate and to make money even at the expense of rising inequality and the impoverishment of the majority of the people. Fortunately, there has been a popular reaction, here and in other parts of the Mediterranean—for example, in Greece—to confront the neoliberal economic policies." One of her first actions as mayor was to stop all evictions.

As Colau won in Barcelona, another woman, Manuela Carmena, won the mayor's race in Madrid. Neither woman was a member of the Podemos party, but ran antiausterity campaigns against financial corruption, against evictions with the support of Podemos. Colau explained, "In this movement of democratic revolution from below, there are different political parties, different acronyms, which must be a tool in this process of empowerment and democratic revolution. So this is why Podemos, Pablo Iglesias, Ada Colau, and other parties that are emerging right now are just instruments at the service of a wide people's process that has decided to take back the institutions for the people."

REBELLION

In a remote town in central Tunisia, a young man named Mohamed Bouazizi had been pushed to the limit. He had grown up in poverty and quit school to work after his father died. Like so many of his generation around the world, opportunities were scarce. He made his living selling fruit and vegetables, and suffered frequent harassment from local authorities. On December 17, 2010, Bouazizi had another conflict with one of these petty bureaucrats, who confiscated his scale and made it impossible for him to sell produce. Utterly frustrated, he set himself on fire, lighting a spark that ignited the protests that spread revolution across the Middle East and North Africa. For decades in the region, people have lived under dictatorships—many that receive US military aid—suffering human rights abuses along with low income, high unemployment, and almost no freedom of speech. All this, while the elites amassed fortunes.

Bouazizi died after eighteen days in a coma. The protests that followed led to the overthrow of long-reigning Tunisian dictator Zine El Abidine Ben Ali. The furor over Bouazizi's self-immolation was intensified when WikiLeaks released hundreds of thousands of classified US diplomatic cables. (See chapter 2, "The Whistleblowers.") The cables proved not only what Tunisians already knew—that the ruling family was profoundly corrupt—but that American leaders knew it too and nevertheless continued to prop up the dictatorship with tens of millions of dollars of aid money each year. Several people in Egypt also set fire to themselves.

As these acts of protest mounted, a courageous young woman took a very dangerous step in authoritarian Egypt. Asmaa Mahfouz was twenty-five years old and part of the April 6 Youth Movement, which included thousands of young people who engaged in online debate about the future of their country. The April 6 Youth Movement formed in 2008 to demonstrate solidarity with workers in the industrial city of El-Mahalla El-Kubra, Egypt. Workers there, primarily in the state-owned textile industry, were planning a general strike to protest against low wages and rising food costs. Government forces brutally suppressed the strike. Several workers were killed.

On January 18, 2011, Asmaa Mahfouz posted a video online, staring directly into the camera, her head covered, but not her face. She identified herself and called for people to join her on January 25 in Tahrir Square in downtown Cairo. She said (translated from Arabic): "I'm making this video to give you one simple message: we want to go down to Tahrir Square on January 25. If we still have honor and want to live in dignity on this land, we have to go down on January 25. We'll go down and demand our rights, our fundamental human rights . . . I won't even talk about any political rights. We just want our human rights and nothing else. This entire government is corrupt—a corrupt president and a corrupt security force. These self-immolators were not afraid of death but were afraid of security forces. Can you imagine that?"

As history would show, many Egyptians could imagine that. Over fifty thousand protesters poured into Tahrir Square to protest the thirty-year rule of the US-backed dictator Hosni Mubarak. Crowds of students and unionists soon grew to over a million

Egyptians from every walk of life. Government forces cracked down, killing and arresting protesters. *Democracy Now!* correspondent Sharif Abdel Kouddous reported on the uprising in vivid dispatches as it was unfolding. The unprecedented demonstrations succeeded in toppling Mubarak. Other Arab strongmen fell soon after, as the uprising spread like a brush fire through the Middle East.

UPRISINGS, FROM THE MIDDLE EAST TO THE MIDWEST

As Mubarak was falling, halfway across the world workers in Wisconsin were rising up.

In February 2011, Wisconsin's Republican governor, Scott Walker, tried to break the state's public employee unions, provoking massive protests at the capitol in Madison. A sign held by one university student, an Iraq War vet, read, "I went to Iraq and came home to Egypt?" Another read, "Walker: Mubarak of the Midwest." A photo circulated in Madison of a young man at a rally in Cairo, with a sign reading "Egypt supports Wisconsin workers: One world, one pain."

Economist Dean Baker wrote at the time that, due to the financial crisis, "many political figures have argued the need to drastically reduce the generosity of public sector pensions, and possibly to default on pension obligations already incurred. Most of the pension shortfall . . . is attributable to the plunge in the stock market in the years 2007–2009."

In other words, Wall Street hucksters, selling the complex mortgage-backed securities that provoked the collapse, were the ones who caused the pension shortfalls. Pulitzer Prize–winning journalist David Cay Johnston added: "The average Wisconsin state employee gets $24,500 a year. That's not a very big pension . . . 15 percent of the money going into it each year is being paid out to Wall Street to manage the money. That's a really huge, high percentage."

So, while investment bankers skim a huge percentage off pension funds, it's the workers who are being demonized and asked to make the sacrifices. Those who caused the problem—the bankers who got lavish bailouts, huge salaries, and bonuses—were not held accountable.

Governor Walker's campaign was funded by the billionaire Koch brothers, major backers of scores of right-wing "think tanks," policy advocates, climate deniers, and Tea Party organizations. They also gave $1 million to the Republican Governors Association, which gave substantial support to Walker's campaign. Is it any surprise that Walker supported corporations with tax breaks and launched a massive attack on unionized, public-sector employees? Interestingly, Wisconsin is home to a number of historic organizations. The Koch brothers' father, Fred Koch, was the cofounder of the John Birch Society, the staunchly anti-Communist, antiunion, and fiercely segregationist group that came to reside in Appleton. Journalist Jane Mayer reported that Fred Koch helped build an oil refinery in Nazi Germany—a project personally approved by Adolf Hitler.

One of the unions targeted by Walker is AFSCME, the American Federation of State, County and Municipal Employees. The union was founded in 1932, in the midst of the Great Depression, in Madison. Its 1.6 million members include nurses, corrections officers, child-care providers, EMTs, and sanitation workers. It was the struggle of the sanitation workers of AFSCME Local 1733 that brought Dr. Martin Luther King Jr. to Memphis in April 1968. As

Jesse Jackson told me as he marched with students and their union-ized teachers in Madison during the Wisconsin uprising of 2011: "Dr. King's last act on Earth, marching in Memphis, Tennessee, was about workers' rights to collective bargaining . . . You cannot re-move the roof for the wealthy and remove the floor for the poor."

Three months later, on May 15, 2011, demonstrators in Spain, dubbed the *indignados*—the outraged—took to the streets to pro-test Spain's 20 percent unemployment and the government's solu-tion of austerity for all. As thousands of *indignados* flooded the streets in cities around Spain and occupied iconic squares such as Madrid's Puerta del Sol, polls showed that 80 percent of Spaniards agreed with their demands.[1]

American activists took note of the power and tactics of this movement. A global uprising was spreading. It arrived in the United States on September 17, 2011, the first day of Occupy Wall Street.

Democracy Now! covered the story before the protests began. Justin Wedes, one of the organizers, told our team the day before Occupy Wall Street moved into Zuccotti Park, a small park around the corner from the New York Stock Exchange, "More than having any specific demand per se, I think the purpose of September 17, for many of us who are helping to organize it and for people who are coming out, is to begin a conversation, as citizens, as people affected by this financial system in collapse, as to how we're going to fix it, as to what we're going to do in order to make it work for us again."

As the protest unfolded, organizer Lorenzo Serna told *Democ-racy Now!*, "The idea is to have an encampment . . . This isn't a one-day event. We're hoping that people come prepared to stay as long as they can and that we're there to support each other."

Another participant explained, "I came because I'm upset with the fact that the bailout of Wall Street didn't help any of the people holding mortgages. All of the money went to Wall Street, and none of it went to Main Street."

The protests radiated out, in cities and towns across the country. People labeled the movement "Occupy."

The gross disparity in coverage between independent, non-commercial news organizations such as *Democracy Now!* and most of the corporate media entities was part of the problem that drove the Occupy movement in the first place. Among the grievances against corporations detailed in the protesters' first major statement, the Declaration of the Occupation of New York City, on September 29, 2011, was: "They purposely keep people misinformed and fearful through their control of the media."

When corporate media finally deigned to visit Zuccotti Park, the reporters usually complained that the movement had no identifiable leaders and no clear, concise list of demands. Freshly hired by CNN, Erin Burnett, who had previously worked for the investment firms Goldman Sachs and Citigroup and was known for her fawning interviews with corporate CEOs as a host on the financial channel CNBC, produced, for her first show on CNN, a mocking segment called "Seriously?!" She opened with a clichéd video montage mischaracterizing protesters as dirty, unemployed layabouts seeking handouts who were universally ignorant of the very financial industry they were protesting:

ERIN BURNETT: Seriously, it's a mixed bag. But they were happy to take some time from their books, banjos, bongos, sports drinks, catered lunch. Yes, there was catered lunch, designer yoga clothing—that's a Lululemon logo—computers, lots of MacBooks, and phones to help us get to the bottom of it. This is unemployed software developer Dan . . . So do you know that taxpayers actually made money on the Wall Street bailout?

DAN: I was unaware of that.

ERIN BURNETT: They did. They made—not on GM, but they did on the Wall Street part of the bailout.

DAN: Okay.

ERIN BURNETT: Does that make you feel any differently?

DAN: Well, I would have to do more research about it, but um—

ERIN BURNETT: If I were right, it might?

DAN: Oh, Sure.

[*End video clip.*]

ERIN BURNETT: Seriously?! That's all it would take to put an end to the unrest?

Well, as promised we did go double-check the numbers on the bank bailout, and this is what we found. Yes, the bank bailouts made money for American taxpayers—right now to the tune of ten billion dollars, anticipated that it will be twenty billion. Those are seriously the numbers. This was the big issue, so we solved it.

Contrary to Burnett's summary of the bank bailout and her claim that US taxpayers made money off the disaster, the nonprofit investigative news organization ProPublica's detailed reporting on the bailout showed clearly that the $10 billion to $20 billion in reported revenue was dwarfed by the hundreds of billions of still-outstanding debt, likely never to be recovered. Burnett's pro-corporate coverage was biased, inaccurate, and, sadly, all too typical.

If two thousand Tea Party activists descended on Wall Street, you would probably have an equal number of reporters there covering them. Yet two thousand people did occupy Wall Street on September 17. They weren't carrying the banner of the Tea Party: the Gadsden flag with its coiled snake and the threat "Don't Tread on Me." Yet their message was clear: "We are the ninety-nine percent that will no longer tolerate the greed and corruption of the one percent." They were there, mostly young, protesting the virtually unregulated speculation of Wall Street that caused the global financial meltdown of 2008.

One of New York's better-known billionaires, then-Mayor Michael Bloomberg, commented on the protests: "You have a lot of kids graduating college, can't find jobs. That's what happened in Cairo. That's what happened in Madrid. You don't want those kinds of riots here."

Riots? Is that really what the Arab Spring and the European protests were about?

Perhaps to the chagrin of Mayor Bloomberg, that is exactly what inspired many who occupied Wall Street. In another of its early communiqués, the Wall Street protest umbrella group said: "On Saturday we held a general assembly, 2,000 strong . . . By 8 p.m. on Monday we still held the plaza, despite constant police presence . . . We are building the world that we want to see, based on human need and sustainability, not corporate greed."

I interviewed David Graeber, one of the Occupy Wall Street protest organizers. Graeber, an American who now teaches at the London School of Economics, has authored several books, including *Debt: The First 5,000 Years*. He points out that in the midst of the financial crash of 2008, enormous debts between banks were renegotiated. Yet only a fraction of troubled mortgages have gotten the same treatment. Graeber said, "Debts between the very wealthy or between governments can always be renegotiated and always have been throughout world history . . . It's when you have debts owed by the poor to the rich that suddenly debts become a sacred obligation, more important than anything else. The idea of renegotiating them becomes unthinkable."

President Barack Obama proposed a so-called millionaire's

tax, which was endorsed by billionaire Warren Buffett. The Republicans called the proposed tax "class warfare."

Graeber responded: "For the last thirty years, we've seen a political battle being waged by the superrich against everyone else, and this is the latest move in the shadow dance, which is completely dysfunctional economically and politically. It's the reason why young people have just abandoned any thought of appealing to politicians. We all know what's going to happen. The tax proposals are a sort of mock populist gesture, which everyone knows will be shot down. What will actually probably happen would be more cuts to social services."

Outside in the cold on Wall Street, the demonstrators continued their protest amid a heavy police presence and the ringing of an opening bell at nine thirty in the morning for a "people's exchange," just as the opening bell of the New York Stock Exchange was rung. While the bankers remained secure and reaped unprecedented profits in their bailed-out banks, outside, the police arrested protesters.

In a just world, with a just economy, we have to wonder, who would be out in the cold? Who would be getting arrested?

CALL OF DUTY

Occupy Wall Street happened as the United States was entering its second decade of war in Afghanistan, the longest war in the nation's history. US veterans of the Iraq and Afghanistan wars were appearing more and more on the front lines—of the Occupy Wall Street protests, that is.

Video from the Occupy Oakland march on October 25, 2011, looked and sounded like a war zone. Tear-gas projectiles were being fired into the crowd, when suddenly the cry of "Medic!" rang out. Civilians raced toward an unconscious protester lying on his back on the pavement, mere steps from a throng of black-clad police in full riot gear, pointing guns as the civilians attempted to administer first aid.

The critically injured man was Scott Olsen, a twenty-four-year-old former US Marine who had served two tours of duty in Iraq. While he was not injured overseas, it was at home, on a different battlefield, where he was struck down. The publicly available video showed Olsen standing calmly alongside a navy veteran holding an upraised Veterans for Peace flag. Olsen was wearing a desert camouflage jacket and sun hat, and his Iraq Veterans Against the War (IVAW) T-shirt. Suddenly, he was on the ground, bleeding from the head. Oakland police in riot gear had fired on the lance corporal with a shotgun that shoots lead-pellet "bean bags." Olsen was shot in the head from twenty feet away, fracturing his skull as well as a vertebrae in his neck. As the small group of people gathered around him to help, a police officer lobbed a flashbang grenade directly into the huddle and it exploded. Flashbangs are used as "distraction devices" for dispersing crowds, but when they explode close to people, they can cause permanent hearing loss and even dismemberment.

Four or five people lifted Olsen and raced him away from the police line. He was admitted to the hospital in critical condition and put into a medically induced coma to relieve brain swelling. When he regained consciousness, Scott was unable to speak and had to communicate using a notepad.

I interviewed one of Olsen's friends, Aaron Hinde, also an Iraq War veteran. He was at Occupy San Francisco when he started getting a series of frenzied tweets about a vet down in Oakland.

Hinde raced to the hospital to see his friend. He later told me a little about him: "Scott came to San Francisco about three months ago from Wisconsin, where he actually participated in the holding of the state capitol over there. Scott's probably one of the warmest, kindest guys I know. He's just one of those people who always has a smile on his face and never has anything negative to say . . . And he believed in the Occupy movement, because it's very obvious what's happening in this country, especially to us veterans. We've had our eyes opened by serving and going to war overseas. So, there's a small contingent of us out here, and we're all very motivated and dedicated."

As I was covering one of the Occupy Wall Street rallies in Times Square, Manhattan, on October 15, I saw another veteran, Shamar Thomas, become deeply upset. Police on horseback had moved in on protesters, only to be stopped by a horse that went down on its knees. Other officers had picked up metal barricades, squeezing the frightened crowd against steam pipes. Thomas, a former sergeant in the US Marines, was wearing his desert camouflage, his chest covered with medals from his combat tour in Iraq. He shouted at the police, denouncing their violent treatment of the protesters. Later, Thomas wrote of the incident: "There is an obvious problem in the country, and *peaceful people* should be allowed to *protest* without Brutality. I was involved in a *riot* in Rutbah, Iraq, 2004, and we did *not* treat the Iraqi citizens like they are treating the unarmed civilians in our *own* Country."

A group calling itself Veterans of the 99 Percent formed, and, with the New York City chapter of Iraq Veterans Against the War, they marched to Zuccotti Park to formally join and support the movement. Their announcement read: " 'Veterans of the 99 Percent' hope to draw attention to the ways veterans have been impacted by the economic and social issues raised by Occupy Wall Street. They hope to help make veterans' and service members' participation in this movement more visible and deliberate."

When I stopped by Occupy Louisville in Kentucky a few weeks later, the first two people I met there were veterans. One of them, Gary James Johnson, told me, "I served in Iraq for about a year and a half. I joined the military because I thought it was my obligation to help protect this country . . . And right here, right now, this is another way I can help."

In 2014 the city of Oakland agreed to pay Iraq War veteran Scott Olsen $4.5 million to settle a federal lawsuit that he filed. He nearly died from the police attack and lives with permanent brain damage.

These stories gave new meaning to the sign at Zuccotti Park, held by yet another veteran: "2nd time I've fought for my country. 1st time I've known my enemy."

DESTROYING THE PEOPLE'S LIBRARY

At around one in the morning on November 15, 2011, we got word that New York City police were raiding the Occupy Wall Street encampment. I raced down with the *Democracy Now!* news team to Zuccotti Park, which had been renamed by the occupiers as Liberty Square. Hundreds of riot police had already surrounded the area. As they ripped down the tents, city sanitation workers were throwing the protesters' belongings into dump trucks. Beyond the barricades, back in the heart of the park, two hundred to three hundred people locked arms, refusing to cede the space they had occupied for almost two months. They were being handcuffed and arrested, one by one.

The few of us members of the press who managed to get through all the police lines were sent to a designated area across the street. As our cameras started rolling, they placed two police buses in front of us, blocking our view. My colleagues and I managed to slip between them and into the park, climbing over the trashed mounds of tents, tarps, and sleeping bags. The police had almost succeeded in enforcing a complete media blackout of the destruction.

We saw a broken bookcase in one pile. Deeper in the park, I spotted a single book on the ground. It was marked "OWSL," for Occupy Wall Street Library, also known as the People's Library, one of the key institutions that had sprung up in the organic democracy of the movement. By the latest count, it had accumulated five thousand donated books. The one I found amid the debris of democracy that was being hauled off to the dump was *Brave New World Revisited*, by Aldous Huxley. He wrote it in 1958, almost thirty years after his famous dystopian novel *Brave New World*. The original work described a society in the future where people had been stratified into haves and have-nots. The *Brave New World* denizens were plied with pleasure, distraction, advertisements, and intoxicating drugs to lull them into complacency, a world of perfect consumerism, with the lower classes doing all the work for the elite.

Brave New World Revisited was Huxley's nonfiction response to the speed with which he saw modern society careening toward that bleak future. It seemed relevant, though, as the encampment—motivated in large part by the opposition to the supremacy of commerce and globalization—was being destroyed.

Huxley wrote, "Big Business, made possible by advancing technology and the consequent ruin of Little Business, is controlled by the State—that is to say, by a small group of party leaders and the soldiers, policemen, and civil servants who carry out their orders.

In a capitalist democracy, such as the United States, it is controlled by what Professor C. Wright Mills has called the Power Elite."

Huxley continued, "This Power Elite directly employs several millions of the country's working force in its factories, offices, and stores, controls many millions more by lending them the money to buy its products, and, through its ownership of the media of mass communication, influences the thoughts, the feelings, and the actions of virtually everybody."

One of the People's Library volunteers, Stephen Boyer, was there during the police raid. After avoiding arrest and helping others with first aid, he wrote: "Everything we brought to the park is gone. The beautiful library is gone. Our collection of 5,000 books is gone. Our tent that was donated is gone. All the work we've put into making it is gone."

Mayor Michael Bloomberg's office later released a photo of a table with some books stacked on it, claiming the books had been preserved. As the People's Library tweeted: "We're glad to see some books are OK. Now, where are the rest of the books and our shelter and our boxes?" The shelter, by the way, was donated to the library by National Book Award winner Patti Smith, the rock 'n' roll legend.

New York City was later forced to admit that its destruction of the People's Library violated the law. In 2013 the city agreed to pay more than $365,000 to settle a lawsuit brought by Occupy activists over the illegal destruction of their property.[2]

Many other Occupy protest sites were also raided. Oakland Mayor Jean Quan, whose police were particularly brutal, admitted to the British Broadcasting Corporation (BBC) that she had been on a conference call with eighteen cities discussing the situation. Another report noted that the FBI and Homeland Security had been advising the cities.

A New York State judge ruled that protesters could not return to Zuccotti Park with sleeping bags or tents. After the ruling, constitutional attorney Michael Ratner sent me a text message: "Just remember: the movement is in the streets. Courts are always last resorts."

Or as Patti Smith sings famously, "People have the power."

OCCUPY EVERYWHERE

I met Gabriel Johnson the day after the eviction. As he scanned the piles of debris that was the former encampment, including the remains of the library and the communal kitchen, he told me, "One of the huge misconceptions is that all the movement is in this park. The movement is in our head: it's an idea. It's what happens while we're here, the conversations we have that we take with us everywhere."

Occupy has now occupied our language. The word *occupy* was the most commonly used word on the internet and in print in the English language in 2011.[3] When you occupy the language, you change the world.

Occupy Wall Street morphed from being an encampment of public space to a movement with countless offshoots.

Shortly after Zuccotti Park was cleared by police, about a thousand students marched outside a meeting where City University of New York trustees voted to authorize tuition increases. The protests were part of a long-running battle against tuition hikes and education cuts that originated on University of California campuses in 2009 and quickly spread across the country.

Pamela Brown, a doctoral student at The New School, helped launch the Occupy Student Debt Campaign, which asked students to sign a "Pledge of Refusal" to pay their student loan debt until a number of education reforms are implemented, including free public education. She explained, "Occupy Wall Street has attacked the inequality in our social system and student loans are a critical juncture where that inequality is developed. . . . This debt carries with [students] an entire lifetime."

Brown talked about the link between inequality, racism, and student debt. "City University of New York actually graduates more African American students than all of the historically black colleges combined. So, when you increase tuition at a location like CUNY, what actually occurs long term is increased inequality. This is part and parcel with the shifting burden that we've seen over the last thirty years, where the costs of education are now [borne] by individuals, rather than the public, which is how the system used to be."

The protest born in the rubble of Zuccotti Park has continued to gather momentum. A group called Rolling Jubilee, named for the ancient practice of forgiving all debts every fifty years, started buying debt from lenders, for pennies on the dollar, and canceling it. This discounted debt market exists primarily because collection agencies and "vulture capitalists" acquire bad loans that people have stopped paying for two to three cents on the dollar, and still make a profit by hounding people to pay back some or all of that debt. Rolling Jubilee, according to its website, "believes people should not go into debt for basic necessities like education, healthcare, and housing. Rolling Jubilee intervenes by buying debt, keeping it out of the hands of collectors, and then abolishing it . . . to help each other out and highlight how the predatory debt system affects our families and communities."

In February 2015, more than one hundred former students of the for-profit Corinthian Colleges system joined what they said was the nation's first student debt strike. The students refused to pay back loans they took out to attend Corinthian, which was sued by the federal government for its predatory lending. Meanwhile, Rolling Jubilee announced it erased over $13 million of debt owed by students of Everest College, a Corinthian subsidary.

"Think of it as a bailout of the ninety-nine percent by the ninety-nine percent," declared Rolling Jubilee.

POLICING THE PROPHETS OF WALL STREET

The response by police departments nationwide to the Occupy Wall Street protests was violent and oppressive. That includes their abusive treatment of the media. In the midst of the Occupy protests, two of my colleagues and I settled a lawsuit we had filed years earlier against the police departments of Minneapolis and Saint Paul, as well as the US Secret Service, for arresting us while reporting in 2008 at the Republican National Convention in St. Paul (see Introduction, pp. 14–17). When organizing a press conference to announce the legal victory, we decided it would be appropriate to hold it at Zuccotti Park, the center of Occupy, to serve as a reminder to the police that journalism is not a crime. Perhaps the settlement would be a warning to police departments around the country to stop arresting and intimidating journalists, or engaging in any unlawful arrests. We shouldn't have to get a record while trying to put things on the record.

But do police actually pay the price? Before the 2008 Republican and Democratic conventions, each of the political parties bought insurance policies to indemnify the convention cities from any damages resulting from lawsuits. Bruce Nestor, president of the Minnesota chapter of the National Lawyers Guild, told me: "Saint Paul actually negotiated a special insurance provision with the Republican host committee so that the first ten million dollars in liability for lawsuits arising from the convention will be covered by the host committee . . . It basically means we [the city] can commit wrongdoing, and we won't have to pay for it."

In 2011 the bailed-out Wall Street megabank JPMorgan Chase & Co. gave a tax-deductible $4.6 million donation to the New York City Police Foundation. It left protesters asking, Who was the NYPD paid to protect, the public or the corporations? The 99 percent or the 1 percent?

According to an undated press release on JPMorgan Chase's website, in response to the $4.6 million donation: "New York City Police Commissioner Raymond Kelly sent CEO and Chairman Jamie Dimon a note expressing 'profound gratitude' for the company's donation." Given the size of the donation, and the police harassment and violence against the protesters, it made us wonder if this was how Kelly showed his gratitude.

The 2008 financial crisis radiated out from Wall Street and engulfed the globe. The crisis was the product of unregulated markets, fed upon by unrestrained greed that was encouraged and rewarded at banks like JP Morgan Chase and Goldman Sachs. "The mortgage bubble," journalist Matt Taibbi told me, "was essentially a gigantic criminal fraud scheme where all the banks were taking mismarked mortgage-backed securities, very, very dangerous, toxic subprime loans, they were chopping them up and then packaging them as AAA-rated investments, and then selling them to state pension funds, to insurance companies, to Chinese banks and Dutch banks and Icelandic banks. And, of course, these things were blowing up, and all those funds were going broke." By "mismarked" Taibbi means fraudulently overvalued. The details of the alleged financial crimes are complex, involving things like "CDOs" or collateralized debt obligations, and credit default swaps. But in the final analysis, it is about an army of financiers creating high-risk investments and selling them as low risk. When they collapsed, they brought down the entire house of cards with them, stripping millions of their life savings and plunging the world into a recession.

After the Great Recession and Occupy Wall Street, the question many Americans have is this: How could millions lose their homes to foreclosure, millions more lose their jobs, people around the world have their lives destroyed, and none of the elite financiers who manipulated the market, crashed the economy, and were enriched by their schemes go to jail?[4]

Vermont Independent senator and presidential candidate Bernie Sanders described this sorry state of affairs in the last Democratic debate before the Iowa Caucus in January 2016. "Let me give you an example of how corrupt this system is," he said. "Goldman Sachs was recently fined $5 billion. Goldman Sachs has given this country two secretaries of treasury, one under Republicans, one under Democrats. The leader of Goldman Sachs is a billionaire who comes to Congress and tells us we should cut Social Security, Medicare, and Medicaid. . . . I find it very strange that a major financial institution that pays $5 billion in fines for breaking the law, not one of their executives is prosecuted, while kids who smoke marijuana get a jail sentence."

TAKING IT TO WALMART

Many workers in the United States are demanding better working conditions and better pay. Among them are the workers at Walmart, the largest private employer in the world, with 1.4 million employees in the United States and 2.1 million workers globally. The company amassed over $16 billion in annual profits in both 2014 and 2015. Yet, despite the multinational corporation's vast wealth, it pays the bulk of its workers poverty wages.

According to a May 2013 study by the Democratic staff of the US House Committee on Education and the Workforce, US taxpayers pay $6.2 billion in public assistance, including food stamps, Medicaid, and subsidized housing, to subsidize Walmart's low-wage workers.[5] Meanwhile, Americans for Tax Fairness, a diverse campaign of national, state, and local organizations working for comprehensive, progressive tax reform, found in a 2015 study, "The four primary Walton heirs saw their [collective] fortune increase by $20.9 billion between March 2014 and March 2015. For about half this money—$10.8 billion—the Waltons could give every one of Walmart's 1.3 million US employees a $5 per hour raise and still pocket $10 billion."[6]

One year after Occupy Wall Street, on the day after Thanksgiving 2012—Black Friday, the biggest retail shopping day of the year—Walmart workers launched the first strike against the giant retailer in its fifty-year history, with protests and picket lines across the United States. Strikes took place at over one hundred Walmart locations involving about five hundred workers, and solidarity protests without worker participation were held at over one thousand of Walmart's roughly five thousand US stores. In late May and early June 2013, a series of events and protests took place, leading up to a mass protest outside Walmart's annual meeting in Bentonville, Arkansas.

By Black Friday 2013, the number of protests outside Walmarts grew to 1,500. The strikers carried the banner of OUR Walmart: Organization United for Respect at Walmart, started with support from the United Food and Commercial Workers (UFCW) union. OUR Walmart is not a union, per se, but, as the group states on its website, helps "Walmart employees as individuals or groups in their dealings with Walmart over labor rights and standards and their efforts to have Walmart publicly commit to adhere to labor rights and standards." We interviewed OUR Walmart organizer Barbara Collins, who joined *Democracy Now!* via satellite from outside Walmart's headquarters, where she had traveled for the 2013 Black Friday protests. The recently fired Walmart worker told us, "I participated in the Black Friday strike last year, and then I also participated with the two-week-long strike in June. And in June is when I was terminated for speaking out."

She and several other workers who were fired in alleged retaliation for their organizing appealed to the National Labor Relations Board (NLRB). Just before we interviewed her, she got the news that the NLRB had determined that Walmart's firing was unfair. "The NLRB ruling is just overwhelming. We are really excited that they found that we're telling the truth, that they broke the law. And we want to be reinstated. So we are here in Bentonville, and it's very cold. And we've been out in front of the home office every day, Friday, Saturday, and then yesterday, and we'll be out there today."

Among the demands supported by the OUR Walmart campaign are minimum annual wages of $25,000, and more consistent work hours. Walmart has long been criticized for keeping many of its workers on erratic schedules, working far less than a full forty-hour week. While that goal has yet to be achieved, the organizing and the pressure has had some effect. In February 2015, Walmart announced an increase in the starting pay to $9 per hour, with an increase to $10 per hour in February 2016.

Another ploy Walmart has mastered is to engage a web of subcontractors to perform tasks such as warehousing and delivery. Walmart has a massive warehouse in Elwood, Illinois, that is run by a subcontractor called Schneider Logistics which, in turn, hires warehouse workers from four separate temporary labor companies. Workers employed by one of those subcontractors, RoadLink Workforce Solutions, went out on strike immediately after a similar strike in California. The Elwood workers were supported by Warehouse Workers for Justice (WWJ), a Chicago-based worker center that aims "to win stable, living wage jobs with dignity for the hundreds of thousands of workers in Illinois' logistics and distribution industry." WWJ reports, "Warehouse workers labor under extreme temperatures, lifting thousands of boxes that can weigh up to 250 lbs. each. Workplace injuries are common; workers rarely earn a living wage or have any benefits."

After twenty-one days on strike in Elwood, the workers won their principal demand for an end to retaliation for protesting poor conditions. They returned to work with full pay for the time they'd been on strike.

I spoke with one of the Elwood strikers, Mike Compton, who described just one of the awful conditions they endured at their low-wage job:

> We have a big problem with dust. You know, all our containers that we unload come from China, and they're just filled with black dust. It's horrible, breathing the stuff in all day, you know, and we'd have to ask seven, eight times to get a dust mask. We'd just be pointed in different directions, to a different manager, to a different department. And half the time, we'd walk away empty-handed at the end of it anyway. We've actually had trailers that were labeled "defumigated in Mexico." We don't know why. People have had trouble breathing in the trailers. You know, dust—something as simple and as cheap as a dust mask should just be readily available to anyone, in my opinion, especially a company as wealthy as Walmart.

As Walmart's operations are global, so too is the organizing among its workers. Kalpona Akter, a workers' rights activist from Bangladesh, was at the same Walmart annual meeting in June 2013 that Barbara Collins attended before being illegally fired. Akter was a garment worker from the age of twelve, and is now executive director of the Bangladesh Center for Worker Solidarity. She came to the Walmart meeting less than two months after the Rana Plaza building disaster in Dhaka, Bangladesh, on April 24, 2013, when a massive building containing multiple garment factories, employing five thousand people, collapsed. Over 1,100 people were killed. It was the worst accident in the history of the garment industry, anywhere in the world. Walmart was one of the buyers of garments from the Rana Plaza building. At the shareholders meeting, Akter was able to directly appeal to Walmart chairman of the Board Rob Walton:

"Mr. Rob Walton, I'm sure you know that fixing these buildings would cost just a tiny fraction of your family wealth. So I implore to you, please, help us. You have the power to do this very easily. Don't you agree that the factories where Walmart products are made should be safe for the workers? For years, every time there is an accident, Walmart officials have made promises to improve the terrible conditions in my country's garment factories, but the tragedies continue. With all due respect, the time for empty promises is over."

The Rana Plaza disaster happened six months to the day after the Tazreen garment factory fire in Dhaka. It was the worst fatal fire in Bangladesh's history, leaving at least 117 people dead, with more than 200 injured. The factory held over 1,600 workers, and when the fire broke out, fabric and yarn ignited into a massive conflagration. Exits were too narrow, trapping people on the upper floors. Twelve people reportedly died leaping from upper stories.

As with Rana Plaza, Walmart had garments produced at the Tazreen factory at the time of the fire. Less than a month after the catastrophe at Rana Plaza, and seven months after Tazreen, activists and labor organizations managed to bring together manufacturers, unions, and related groups to draft the Accord on Fire and Building Safety in Bangladesh. The signatories, as noted on its website, included "over 200 apparel brands, retailers and importers from over twenty countries in Europe, North America, Asia and Australia; two global trade unions; and eight Bangladesh trade unions and four NGO witnesses." But not Walmart.

THE FIGHT FOR FAIR FOOD

The work of harvesting much of our food is done just as it was over a hundred years ago: toiling in the fields, by hand. This is certainly true for those who pick tomatoes. Generations of immigrant farmworkers have labored under brutal conditions harvesting tomatoes around the rural town of Immokalee, Florida. In 1993 a group of migrant farmworkers formed the Coalition of Immokalee Workers (CIW). Although the group is largely composed of Central American immigrants today, at its founding the majority were Haitians who had fled the violence that followed the US-backed coup d'état against the democratically-elected Haitian president, Jean-Bertrand Aristide. Many of these Haitians who fled for their lives did so after being targeted for their political activism. Thus, when they arrived in Immokalee, Florida, they brought with them the grassroots organizing skills they had developed in Haiti.

The Coalition of Immokalee Workers is a farmworker-led human rights organization, demanding not only better pay—one penny more per pound of tomatoes picked—but also breaks, safe working conditions, access to clean water and sanitation, and zero tolerance for sexual harassment on farms. It has an impressive list of victories against some of the largest food companies in the world.

When they first started, CIW tried to pressure the farm owners for whom they worked. The farm owners countered that they had no choice but to keep wages low, since their major buyers, the large restaurant and supermarket chains, insisted on low wholesale prices for tomatoes. If the growers didn't keep wholesale prices low, the large institutional buyers would go elsewhere. So, instead, the coalition decided to pressure the restaurant chains. They began with Taco Bell, and its parent company, Yum Brands. To be most effective, they knew they needed consumer support, so they reached out to students on campuses across the nation. Together, their "Boot the Bell" campaign succeeded in booting Taco Bell off of twenty-three campuses. In March 2005, Yum Brands relented, and agreed to buy tomatoes only from suppliers who could guarantee that the workers were paid the higher wage demanded by the CIW as part of their "Fair Food Program" (FFP).

More victories followed for the workers. In April 2007, McDonald's signed on, followed by the supermarket chain Whole Foods Market, then, by the end of 2008, Burger King and the sandwich chain Subway. In 2009 and 2010, the CIW sought, and gained, agreements from large corporate food service providers Bon Appétit Management Co., Compass Group, Aramark, and Sodexo. By 2012, the grocery chain Trader Joe's signed the FFP as well.

We interviewed farmworker and CIW organizer Gerardo Reyes-Chavez on *Democracy Now!* in the fall of 2012. He was in Denver, where the fast-food outlet Chipotle Mexican Grill is based. CIW had been working on Chipotle for ten years. It was just days before the restaurant chain was hosting a high-profile, public "Cultivate Food, Ideas & Music Festival." Their press release promised that the free, one-day festival "will include cooking demonstrations by celebrity chefs, live music, food artisans and other activities emphasizing fresh and affordable food made with sustainable ingredients." Mark Crumpacker, Chipotle's chief marketing officer, added, "These events give our customers an opportunity . . . to learn something about issues in food, develop a deeper appreciation for farmers and food artisans who are changing food culture for the better."

Reyes-Chavez told us: "We have been able to create a Fair Food Program, addressing abuses in the tomato industry. We created a whole new system . . . to identify where abuses are going on and uproot them from the system. This is an opportunity for Chipotle to do the right thing. They claim that they sell food with integrity, and they are really focused on sustainability . . . What we are saying is this is an opportunity for them to make it a reality." The CIW had announced they, along with hundreds of their student and labor supporters, would protest the festival to highlight Chipotle's refusal to join the Fair Food Program. The day after we spoke with Reyes-Chavez, Chipotle signed the agreement.

In 2014, the coalition focused its attention on some of the largest supermarkets in that $550 billion industry. Within two years, CIW signed Fair Food agreements with Walmart, the Fresh Market, and the owner of Stop & Shop and Giant supermarkets. The work of this small, worker-led coalition is seemingly never done, however. In March 2016, they ratcheted up two ongoing campaigns, challenging Wendy's, the third-largest burger chain in the United States, and Publix, a major grocery chain, to finally sign the FFP.

SEA CHANGE IN SEATTLE

Kshama Sawant never expected to become one of the most visible leaders of the economic justice movement in the United States. In November 2013 Sawant was elected to the Seattle City Council as the country's only declared Socialist in city government.

Why Socialism? "I was born in India, and I was basically obsessed with questions of poverty," she tells me. "I was looking for real explanations for why there is so much poverty in the world even though it was clear that there is enough wealth and resources to solve the problems of humanity."

Her passion for answers led her to pursue a PhD in economics at North Carolina State University. In 2006 she moved to Seattle with her husband, who is an engineer at Microsoft, and she taught economics at local colleges. When Sawant attended a talk by a member of the organization Socialist Alternative, she found her political home. "We had a vision of a world beyond capitalism," she says.

In 2011 Sawant became involved in Occupy Seattle, an offshoot of Occupy Wall Street. "After Occupy was winding down, we thought it would be a really excellent way of demonstrating the need of where the movement should go by running our own independent left-wing working-class candidate to show how necessary it was for young people and working people to break from the Democratic Party establishment. So that's how we decided to run an electoral campaign . . . I was chosen to represent that campaign as the candidate."

In 2012 Sawant ran and lost a race for the Washington State House of Representatives. Undeterred, she ran for Seattle City Council the following year. "There was no prospect of winning," she concedes. "We were doing it to demonstrate what a real independent campaign looks like. Halfway through that campaign, we realized we had a chance of winning. And we went for it. And the rest is history."

The idea of championing a $15-per-hour minimum wage grew out of a hard-fought labor battle in 2012. Workers in the city of SeaTac, home to Seattle's international airport, were demanding a 66 percent increase in the minimum wage in their city, raising it from Washington's statewide minimum wage of $9.04 to $15.

Sawant attended some of the SeaTac rallies and was deeply moved by what she saw. At one demonstration, a woman in her early twenties approached Sawant. "This woman had no training in public speaking, and she had no experience as an activist. She was simply a worker who obviously grew up with a lot of disadvantages . . . I was struck by her intense confidence."

"We're going to win," the young woman declared flatly to Sawant. She continued, "I have worked full-time for four years. I have never been able to put a roof over my head. I am homeless. And I have experienced all the ravages that one experiences not only as a homeless person but as a woman who is homeless."

Sawant was startled. "That made the hairs stand up on the back of my neck. You know there were days that it was really hard, when we faced a lot of resistance from the Democratic Party establishment, who did everything they could to stab the movement in the back. But these people [in SeaTac] were able to sustain themselves and their activism. One way that I sustain myself is to keep in mind that there were people who were making far more sacrifices than I was."

The SeaTac effort was led by the SEIU. It organized a ballot measure in 2013 asking voters to approve raising SeaTac's minimum wage to $15. The measure won narrowly. In the aftermath of Occupy Wall Street, issues of economic justice resonated with ordinary people. The movements were building on one another.

Sawant and other Seattle activists saw an opportunity.

"What Occupy did was it ended the silence on the state of rage that everyone has been feeling not only at the endemic inequality, but at the banks and hedge fund donors and billionaires who were responsible for participating in the global financial collapse and very nearly bringing the global economy into the abyss," she says. "And these people were actually being rewarded: There was more deregulation, more wealth concentration, more stashing their money in offshore accounts. Meanwhile, the rest of us in America were being subjected to a major unemployment crisis which ushered in a low-wage economy and the first generation to be subjected to severe cuts in education funding and financial aid and major tuition hikes around the nation."

Seattle activists also took note of the 2012 strikes by fast-food workers in New York City. One week after Walmart workers staged their Black Friday strike in 2012, hundreds of fast-food workers in New York City walked off their jobs to demand a $15 hourly wage and a union. This action was organized by the grassroots group New York Communities for Change, along with the powerful Service Employees International Union (SEIU).

Saavedra Jantuah, a minimum-wage employee at Burger King, told *Democracy Now!* why she walked out: "Managers tell us we can't do it, we don't have no power, we don't have no right—it's what they say goes. And it's *not* what they say goes. They're acting like they're our masters and we're slaves. Those days are over."

Sawant told us, "It was at that time that we in Socialist Alternative thought that that might be something that a mass of workers would feel passionate about and join a movement for the Fight for Fifteen Dollars," recalls Sawant. "When we launched our city council campaign and made the fifteen-dollar minimum wage a central demand of our campaign platform, that really illustrates what movements need to do: have our finger on the pulse of the majority of the working class and get a sense of what the next step might be. We don't have a crystal ball to tell us that, but the more we engage in actual movements, the more you get a sense for that. We were sure at that time that the fight for fifteen dollars an hour would be a central part of our coming struggle."

Sawant's crusade gained momentum and picked up an unlikely ally late in the campaign: Seattle mayoral candidate Ed Murray also endorsed the $15 minimum wage. On election night, both Sawant and Murray were elected.

"A candidate who had declared herself openly as a Socialist with meager resources compared to her sixteen-year incumbent opponent wasn't supposed to win with nearly ninety-five thousand votes," says Sawant. "It was a sign that people are looking for a real alternative. They hunger for it."

Soon after Sawant's election, Mayor Ed Murray convened a twenty-four-member committee comprised of business, labor, and nonprofit groups to determine how the minimum-wage hike would occur. As the committee struggled to find a compromise acceptable to all, Sawant held a trump card: following the model of SeaTac, she threatened to take the issue to voters and seek a more aggressive minimum-wage hike. Her fellow activists, wearing red T-shirts that read "15 Now," would pack city council hearings.

"We are not interested in a measure that is fifteen in name only and has more holes than Swiss cheese," Sawant declared to 15 Now activists.[7]

The referendum threat forced the issue. Finally, on May 1, 2014, the Seattle City Council approved the $15 minimum wage, to be phased in over several years.

David Rolf, president of the SEIU Seattle local, said that the combination of fast-food strikes nationally and in Seattle, passage of the $15 SeaTac minimum wage, and the elections of Murray and Sawant were the three keys to victory for the $15 wage in Seattle.

"It took a perfect storm," he said.[8]

MOVEMENTS UNITE

Inspired by Occupy and championed by fast-food workers, the victory in Seattle was the first major national win of the Fight for $15 campaign. It is now one of the most potent and successful economic justice campaigns of the last twenty years. This movement has risen from the grassroots and is forcing powerful politicians and corporations to change course.

On April 15, 2015—Tax Day—low-wage workers across the country staged what organizers called the "largest-ever mobilization of underpaid workers," with some sixty thousand workers walking off the job in more than two hundred cities. The Fight for $15 campaign brought together fast-food workers, home-care aides, child-care providers, Walmart clerks, adjunct professors, airport workers, and other low-wage earners. The Service Employees International Union helped organize the campaign. Organizers said the action was held on Tax Day to highlight the taxpayer funds needed to support underpaid workers. A 2015 study from the University of California at Berkeley showed that low wages are forcing working families to rely on more than $150 billion in public assistance.

In Chicago, demonstrators held signs that read "We are worth more!," while in New York, dozens of protesters temporarily halted business at a McDonald's by staging a die-in, lying on the ground in front of the franchise. Several New York protesters carried signs reading "We work hard" and "We see wage slavery." Protesters included Jemere Calhoun, who works at two McDonald's restaurants.

"We're fighting for fifteen dollars and a union," he said. "We need benefits. We need health care. We need sick days. We need maternity leaves. These things are really important to families."

Katherine Cruz worked at McDonald's. She explained to *Democracy Now!*, "We've been working for $8.75, and it's not enough to live off of. And we work really hard to make $8.75 and not be able to live . . . Everyone that lives off minimum wage should make more, so we can all support our families, support ourselves."

Clergy leaders backed the call by low-wage workers to raise the minimum wage. "It's a righteous demand," Rabbi Michael Feinberg told *Democracy Now!* "It's right that workers are paid their fair due, are given a living wage, and shown the respect and dignity on the job that they deserve."

On April 1, 2015, McDonald's announced that it was raising the minimum wage at company-owned stores to $1 more an hour than the local minimum wage, or an average of $9 an hour. But there was a catch: the wage hike applied only to 10 percent of McDonald's workers. The raise was only slated for the 1,500 restaurants that the McDonald's corporation owned itself. Most of the McDonald's restaurants are owned by franchisees. These account for 90 percent of all the McDonald's stores and employ most of its workers. The raise was not mandatory at the franchises. The move backfired. Former *New York Times* labor reporter Steven Greenhouse told *Democracy Now!*, "One of the weird things is McDonald's said, 'Look, we're doing this great thing to help workers,' but many workers in the franchise restaurants got really pissed off, and I think it really jazzed them up."

Greenhouse cited the UC Berkeley study: "Three-quarters of the money nationwide spent on public assistance—whether food stamps, Medicaid—goes to families who have at least one person working . . . This is an indirect subsidy to companies like Wendy's and Burger King and McDonald's and Taco Bell and Walmart and Target, which often pay $7.25, $8, $9 an hour . . . Should taxpayers be subsidizing the Walmarts and McDonald's? And Walmart and McDonald's respond that, 'Well, thanks in part to our low wages, we're able to give consumers low-cost products.' "

But the real beneficiary of McDonald's low wages are the company executives, who reward themselves lavishly while their workers struggle. A 2014 study from the public-policy organization Demos found that fast-food CEOs make 1,200 times as much money as the average fast-food worker, a disparity that maximizes short-term profit while harming worker security and the overall economy.

In July 2015 New York Governor Andrew Cuomo—who has opposed numerous progressive initiatives—responded to the relentless protests by low-wage workers and by progressive New York City Mayor Bill de Blasio by announcing that fast-food workers throughout New York State should be paid $15 per hour— a 70 percent increase over the state minimum wage.

This represented an about-face for the man dubbed "Governor 1 percent" by activists. In March 2015 Cuomo had dismissed a plan by New York State Assembly Democrats to raise the state minimum wage to $15 by 2018. "God bless them—shoot for the stars," Cuomo said sarcastically during a speech in Rochester, suggesting that their goal was unrealistic. He later told reporters the figure was "too high," reported the New York *Daily News*.[9]

On May 6, 2015, Governor Cuomo published an op-ed piece

in the *New York Times*, "Fast-Food Workers Deserve a Raise." He wrote:

> Nowhere is the income gap more extreme and obnoxious than in the fast-food industry. Fast-food CEOs are among the highest-paid corporate executives. The average fast-food CEO made $23.8 million in 2013, more than quadruple the average from 2000 (adjusting for inflation). Meanwhile, entry-level food-service workers in New York State earn, on average, $16,920 per year, which at a 40-hour week amounts to $8.50 an hour. Nationally, wages for fast-food workers have increased 0.3 percent since 2000 (again, adjusting for inflation) . . .
>
> New York State ranks first in public assistance spending per fast-food workers, $6,800 a year. That's a $700 million annual cost to taxpayers.[10]

You would think Cuomo's op-ed was written by grassroots activists. In a way, it was.

"There is not a price tag you can put on how this movement has changed the conversation in this country," declared Mary Kay Henry, international president of the SEIU. "It's raised wages for 8 million workers. I believe we are forcing a real conversation about how to solve the grossest inequality in our generation. People are sick of wealth at the top and no accountability for corporations."[11]

The fight by low-wage workers is also a fight for immigrants, Henry told *Democracy Now!*:

> There's an incredible intersection of the immigrant-rights movement and the fast-food workers' movement . . . We've seen it across this country as the city organizations get built in local coalition with the immigrant-justice movement. We still hope the

president will take swift and bold action, but we understand that we have to grow a powerful movement that is not subject to the bad politics of this nation but makes the case where everybody in this nation understands that we have to get the Republican House to act on common-sense immigration reform, so eleven million people can enter our democracy and join in the fullness of our economy. And we are not going to stop our movement building on immigrant justice or economic justice until we win.

When Seattle activists won the victory to raise the minimum wage to $15, they made the impossible possible. It is no longer considered radical to demand a doubling of the federal minimum wage. As the *New York Times* editorialized in July 2015, "$15 is a minimally decent wage, not a symbol or an extravagance." [12] A new normal has been established.

Even as antiunion governors in states such as Wisconsin, Kansas, and Michigan have been winning elections, citizens have been demanding and winning livable wages.

Defying partisan trends, voters in Alaska, Arkansas, Nebraska, and South Dakota approved ballot initiatives in 2014 to raise the minimum wage, as they did in San Francisco and Oakland. In Illinois and several Wisconsin counties—both states that elected Republican governors—significant majorities passed nonbinding ballot proposals to increasethe minimum wage. Since Republicans and some Democrats in Congress have consistently blocked an increase in the national minimum wage, people are taking control of the issue in their communities and finding resounding support across the political spectrum.

In May 2015 Los Angeles became the nation's largest city to approve a significant increase in the minimum wage. The Los Angeles City Council voted to raise the minimum from $9 to $15 an hour by 2020. The move will impact as many as eight hundred thousand workers, or almost 50 percent of the workforce. It is expected to spark wage hikes across Southern California and boost similar efforts nationwide.

Kshama Sawant—who was reelected to Seattle City Council in November 2015—reflects on the process that led to victory:

> Without movements, we get nothing. We don't win victories against economic inequality because the CEO of Walmart wakes up one morning and decides he's going to be nice and out of his largess give something to workers. We see big business making concessions when they recognize that making concessions is going to be less expensive politically and financially than allowing the movement to take on bigger proportions.
>
> So there is a twofold lesson for us from this experience. One is that we can win . . . But the second lesson is that we cannot stop at these victories . . . What we are looking for is not just fifteen dollars an hour. We are looking for a fundamental transformation away from a system that results in so much misery for so many of us. So we have to take these victories and raise everybody's vision to bigger victories.

CHAPTER 6

CLIMATE JUSTICE

The satellite phone reception was poor, but we could still make out our guest's words as we interviewed him live on *Democracy Now!* It was Kumi Naidoo, the executive director of Greenpeace International, but he wasn't in his office. He was being pummeled by water cannons as he and a fellow activist dangled off the side of a Russian oil rig in the Arctic Ocean. It was August 24, 2012. Here's the transcript of the interview:

KUMI NAIDOO: We are being sprayed by a high-pressure hose. We've been holding on for the last three hours. But you probably can hear the hose, a heavy [inaudible] spray. We are in a tent. We simply want to make the point that drilling in the Arctic is completely reckless and will accelerate catastrophic climate change. But we are terribly anxious now because they are spraying us heavily with water hoses. And it's really hard to hang on to the little tent where we are taking refuge.

JUAN GONZÁLEZ: And, Kumi, who precisely is spraying you with the water hoses?

KUMI NAIDOO: The employees and the security of Gazprom. Gazprom is the oil company that is probably going to be, if we don't stop them, the first company to start drilling oil in the Arctic. And they've been at us now for over an hour, so we're really struggling to stay up here on the rig at the moment.

AMY GOODMAN: So, you're on the deck of the Gazprom oil drilling rig, where they're shooting you with water cannons?

KUMI NAIDOO: Gazprom doesn't actually have a license to drill at the moment. It expired twelve days ago. They do not have an oil spill response plan. In fact, what they have is even worse than Shell, and that's saying a lot. And in the next couple of days, the Arctic sea minimum ice figure will be released, and that will show that protecting the Arctic North is seriously important. And that is why we are campaigning to declare the Upper Arctic a global sanctuary as a global commons. And we are working together with the indigenous peoples of northern Russia, who agree that they should not be drilling in the Arctic.

AMY GOODMAN: How long do you plan to stay there?

KUMI NAIDOO: Well, it looks like they're going to drive us down pretty soon. We're pretty much hanging on with the heavy, heavy cannon water being sprayed on us. We're going to try and stick around as long as possible, but at this rate, I can't say whether it will be an hour or more. But our action is peaceful. We want to draw global attention to what is the defining environmental struggle of our time, and time is running out for us to avert catastrophic climate change. And that's why we are here.

AMY GOODMAN: Kumi Naidoo, please be safe.

The direct action by Kumi Naidoo and others from Greenpeace was extraordinarily dangerous. Climbing any industrial structure has inherent risks; doing so a hundred feet above the Arctic ocean, the waters of which can kill a person within twenty minutes, while being hit with water cannons, is beyond perilous. That Kumi Naidoo could do that, while participating in a live interview in the midst of it, says a lot about what kind of activist he is.

As a postscript to help explain the power of independent media, Kumi Naidoo would later recount on *Democracy Now!* an experience he had two weeks after his action on the oil rig: "I was in Washington, DC, and I was in a cab. And I get in, and the taxi driver kindly, you know, turned down the volume on the radio, because he didn't want to disturb me. And then I recognized it was Amy's voice. And then I said, 'Oh, please, turn it up.' And then he said, 'Oh, do you know Amy Goodman and this program?' I said, 'Yes, yes, I know it, and actually I was speaking to her recently.' He says, 'Oh, you were speaking to her? When?' I said, 'Oh, it was rather weird circumstances.' And then he turned around and said, 'You're not that crazy dude from Africa that was hanging off the rig in the Arctic!' And he refused to take a payment for my trip."

Kumi Naidoo is from Durban, South Africa. In 1980, at the age of fifteen, he was one of millions of South Africans fighting against the racist apartheid regime. He was thrown out of high school and eventually had to go underground. He emerged in England, living in exile, and went on to become a Rhodes scholar. Naidoo has long struggled for human rights, against poverty, and for action to combat climate change.

In September 2013, the year after he was arrested in the Arctic, thirty more Greenpeace activists attempted to block drilling by the same Gazprom rig. This time, the Russians were even more prepared. The Greenpeace vessel, the Arctic Sunrise, was trailed, then boarded, by the Russian coast guard. The coast guard fired warning shots with their cannon. Later, as the activists approached the rig in the rough, frigid sea, their small boats were rammed by Russian security forces. Russian commandos swooped in, rappelling off helicopters, and took control of the Arctic Sunrise. The activists, along with two independent journalists who were documenting the action, were arrested, and they and their vessel were hauled off to the Russian port city of Murmansk. They were jailed and charged with piracy, a serious felony carrying a potential sentence of fifteen years in prison (their charges were later lowered to "hooliganism," which has a seven year maximum). They became known as the "Arctic Thirty," and a global campaign grew to free them. They spent two months jailed in Russia, and eventually were freed on bail, and left the country. The Kremlin ultimately granted them amnesty, although the activists maintain they were not guilty of the charges and vowed to continue the fight against Arctic drilling.

"It is only civil disobedience and mass mobilization that actually sends a message for the urgency," Kumi Naidoo reflected, appearing again on *Democracy Now!* in 2014, two years after his Arctic protest and one year after the Arctic Thirty were arrested. Naidoo sees parallels in the struggle against South African apartheid and the growing movement for climate justice. "One of the things we succeeded in doing in South Africa is building an alliance of faith leaders, trade union leaders, women's movement, youth organizations and so on," he continued. "For far too long climate change was seen as an environmental issue. Actually, it is much bigger. It's a cross-cutting issue. It's an issue of survival."

Survival. Central to our reporting on climate change is the reality that global warming is real, is happening now, and is killing tens of thousands of people and displacing millions more. The warming planet presents an existential crisis for humanity. The problem could be solved, were it not for large institutions with vested interests in maintaining this highly polluting status quo: the fossil fuel corporations and petrostates that have grown immeasurably wealthy by drilling, refining, and selling oil and gas. Other corporations continue to mine coal, one of the dirtiest fuels, which major energy companies then burn to generate electricity. All these interest groups invest huge sums to block not only meaningful action to halt climate change, but to block public awareness about this disaster that is happening around us. They sow confusion and deny the science that says with increasing clarity and certainty: the world is burning.

The year 2015 will be remembered as a pivotal one for the climate. It was the hottest year on record, by far, and also the year that, for the first time in three- to four million years, the concentration of carbon dioxide (CO_2) in the atmosphere averaged 400 parts per million (ppm), far above the 350 ppm threshold for a safe, livable planet (hence the name of the global grassroots climate-justice group 350.org).

In 2015, an unusually fierce storm raced toward the North Pole, increasing temperatures there to about 50 degrees Fahrenheit above average. A drought in South America fueled wildfires in Colombia, which issued a red alert for more than 80 percent of the country. Record rains around the world swelled rivers, causing disastrous floods. In the UK, river flow broke all records. December was the wettest month in England in more than a century, and the hottest December since recording began in 1659. The United States experienced the hottest December on record, during which fifty people were killed by two severe weather events: the worst flooding in two decades in Missouri and a series of rare December tornados in Texas. The combined economic toll of these events is expected to surpass $3 billion. While December 2015 was the hottest December in the United States, February 2015 was the coldest February on record in many northeastern cities, with record snowfall. Add to these disasters the ongoing record drought in California, extensive wildfires in the Pacific Northwest and Alaska, a summer of severe weather and tornadoes in the Midwest and extensive flooding in South Carolina, 2015 saw ten weather- or climate-related events with costs that exceeded one billion dollars.

A study was released predicting that in the Persian Gulf, in cities such as Doha in Qatar and Dubai in the United Arab Emirates, the daily high temperatures by the end of the century will simply be too hot for people to survive outside for more than a few hours at a time. In the polar regions, ice is melting at unprecedented rates, and the ocean is warming, causing the water to expand. Both phenomena, the melting ice and the warming seas, are causing sea levels to rise, already impacting small island nations like Tuvalu, Kiribati, and the Marshall Islands in the Pacific, and the Maldives in the Indian Ocean. Scientists predict that hundreds of millions of people will eventually have to flee the world's coastal cities.

The year 2015 will also be remembered for the Paris Agreement, the culmination of over twenty years of United Nations negotiations to reach a binding, global agreement to confront, and solve, the problem of human-induced global warming.

Democracy Now! has long covered the negotiations, the climate-related natural disasters, and the growing movement for climate justice. We have reported from the streets outside the UN climate summits to the front lines of impacted communities, from the Arctic, where Kumi Naidoo and his allies were scaling oil rigs, to Africa, the continent that he comes from, to his ancestors' homeland in India. We have followed the unrelenting efforts by corporations to extract resources from the planet's remaining rain forests, and the resistance to that by the indigenous people who have lived in harmony with the forests from time immemorial.

IF ONLY INFORMATION FLOWED AS FREELY AS OIL

Television stations pour millions of dollars into building flashy "Weather Centers" to grab their audience's attention. As they flash the words "Severe Weather" and "Extreme Weather," why not also flash the words, "Climate Change" or "Global Warming"? The public depends on broadcasters for most of their news and information, even in this internet age. The daily deluge of sensational weather reporting must include explanations of the deeper changes occurring on our planet.

How else will people understand the connection between disparate weather events, from dust-bowl conditions in the Midwest, to epic wildfires in the Northwest, and record-breaking cold in the Northeast? Scientists tell us that climate change played a role in at least half of the droughts, floods, and storms in 2014. The National Aeronautics and Space Administration (NASA), on its global climate change website, states that "multiple studies published in peer-reviewed scientific journals show that 97 percent or more of actively publishing climate scientists agree: Climate-warming trends over the past century are very likely due to human activities. In addition, most of the leading scientific organizations worldwide have issued public statements endorsing this position."[1] In Europe and other parts of the world there are debates on what to do about climate change. But in the United States, we have debates on whether it exists at all, or if humans have contributed to it. It's as if every time we talked about the Earth being round, we interviewed a member of the Flat Earth Society for "balance."

Why does the climate change debate continue in the United States? Because oil barons, such as the Koch brothers, pour billions of dollars into foundations and corporations that obfuscate the issue or deny the problem exists at all. The oil companies have knowingly deceived the public: In 2015, exposés by the Pulitzer Prize–winning nonprofit news organization InsideClimate News (ICN) and the *Los Angeles Times* revealed that, for decades, Exxon concealed its own findings that burning fossil fuels causes global warming, alters the climate, and melts the Arctic ice. Exxon scientists knew about climate change as early as 1977. But beginning in the 1980s, the company openly embraced climate denial and spent millions of dollars funding outside groups and politicians who sought to undermine climate science. The news prompted New York State Attorney General Eric Schneiderman and California Attorney General Kamala Harris to open investigations into whether Exxon (now ExxonMobil) misled investors and the public.

Further documents obtained by InsideClimate News revealed that the conspiracy was even deeper. Neela Banerjee of ICN reported in late 2015 that from 1979 to 1983, the American Petroleum Institute, a fossil fuel industry lobbying organization, ran a CO_2 task force that included "senior scientists and engineers from nearly every major US and multinational oil and gas company, including Exxon, Mobil, Amoco, Phillips, Texaco, Shell, Sunoco, Sohio as well as Standard Oil of California and Gulf Oil, the predecessors to Chevron."[2] Investors and legal experts have compared the activities of the big oil corporations in undermining public confidence in climate science to similar efforts famously waged by Big Tobacco. Activists are pressuring the Justice Department to launch an investigation similar to the ones in New York and California. Whether or not the tobacco comparison is borne out,

ExxonMobil and the other participants in climate denial could eventually face enormous liabilities.

In 1997, *Democracy Now!* followed the efforts in Kyoto to forge a binding climate agreement. We covered efforts by Canadian and US government climate scientists to fight censorship, and reported on the struggles of the First Nations people in Canada to halt exploitation of the tar sands of Alberta. We chronicled the movement that stopped the proposed 1,200-mile-long Keystone XL oil pipeline, and followed the "fracktivists" who have pushed US municipalities and states to ban toxic drilling for natural gas. We spoke with indigenous leaders in Ecuador, Peru, and Brazil who are fighting off multinational companies that are intent on exploiting their resources.

Bill McKibben, founder of the climate-justice group 350.org, says, "The only question now is whether the relentless rise in carbon can be matched by a relentless rise in the activism needed to stop it."

With the fate of the Earth on the line, the stakes could not be higher.

DRILLING AND KILLING

In 1998 *Democracy Now!* producer Jeremy Scahill and I traveled to Nigeria, Africa's most populous country and largest oil producer. I had wanted to go there since late 1994, when I interviewed the Nigerian writer and activist Ken Saro-Wiwa at WBAI radio. Bernard White and I were hosting *Wakeup Call*, the popular morning community radio show. A Nigerian activist walked in and said, "I have Ken Saro-Wiwa here, and we'd like to do the interview."

What interview? We were already in the midst of a live broadcast, the show fully booked. I am embarrassed to say I had never
heard of Ken Saro-Wiwa. We said we could give him two minutes.
We ended up spending the rest of the show with him. Saro-Wiwa
told us, "I am a marked man." He was traveling the world to let
people know what the oil company Royal Dutch Shell was doing
to the half million Ogoni people of the Niger Delta. Ken was a
poet, journalist, novelist, and the screenwriter for a popular television soap opera in Nigeria. He served for three years as the national president of the Association of Nigerian Authors, stepping
down to devote himself to the struggle of his people, the Ogoni. He
said pipelines crisscrossed their land, and petroleum flares the size
of apartment buildings lit up the sky around the clock. Ogoni children never knew a dark night, living in the shadow of the flame. Yet
they didn't have oil or gas for themselves. They breathed in the pollution from these flares—a cheap method of burning off methane
waste that is rarely allowed in the United States. Ken Saro-Wiwa
said when he returned to Nigeria he would most likely be arrested.

And that is exactly what happened. Back in Nigeria, he was
arrested with eight other environmental and human rights activists
and went through a sham trial. Shell representatives monitored the
kangaroo court proceedings. According to Ken's brother, Dr. Owens
Wiwa, the head of Shell's Nigerian operations, Brian Anderson,
promised "to get Ken and the others freed if we stopped the protest
campaign abroad." Wiwa continued, "Even if I had wanted to, I
didn't have the power to control the international environmental
protests." In Nigeria, it was Shell that had the power. Ken Saro-
Wiwa and his eight compatriots refused to stop speaking out. The
Nigerian military dictatorship hanged them on November 10, 1995.

Three years later, Jeremy Scahill and I would go to Ogoniland.
We were greeted by Ken Saro-Wiwa's parents, and his whole

community. One man came forward and read Ken's last statement in his trial:

> My lord, we all stand before history. I am a man of peace, of ideas, appalled by the denigrating poverty of my people, who live on a richly endowed land, distressed by their political marginalization and economic strangulation, angered by the devastation of their land, their ultimate heritage, anxious to preserve their right to life and to a decent living, and determined to usher to this country as a whole, a fair and just democratic system which protects everyone in every ethnic group, and gives us all a valid claim to human civilization.
>
> I have devoted my intellectual and material resources, my very life, to a cause in which I have total belief, and from which I cannot be blackmailed or intimidated. I have no doubt at all about the ultimate success of my cause no matter the trials and tribulations which I and those who believe with me may encounter on our journey. Neither imprisonment nor death can stop our ultimate victory.

Nigeria earns 90 percent of its export revenue from oil sales, but it comes at a high human cost. While we were there, we investigated the practices of another oil giant working in the Niger Delta: Chevron. Headquartered in California, it is one of the largest companies operating in Nigeria.

The Niger Delta was on fire. Leaky gas pipelines frequently exploded. An October 2000 explosion killed more than seven hundred people and a 2006 pipeline explosion killed two hundred, causing another fire to burn: the rage of millions of people kept in desperate poverty, providing power to the most powerful countries in the world while being kept powerless themselves.

The oil companies would always say that they were working with the Nigerian government. It was true: the oil companies shored up dictatorships and corrupt governments, which in turn kept the oil flowing and the people pacified. Ken Saro-Wiwa exposed those links between military, corporate, and government power.

In May 1998 the people of another Delta region, Ilajeland, were fed up with yet another oil spill. In this case, they were dealing with Chevron. Toxic spills killed their fish and livestock and destroyed their mangrove forest. Among the people's demands: clean drinking water, electricity, environmental reparations, employment, and scholarships for young people. So a group of about a hundred villagers rode to Chevron's offshore drilling rig and said they would not leave until they could negotiate with the top man at Chevron. They knew the Americans were ultimately in control. They wanted to talk with George Kirkland, then the head of Chevron Nigeria Ltd., a wholly owned subsidiary of Chevron in California. Chevron flew in a Nigerian spokesperson to negotiate. Community elders met with him while others stayed on the oil rig. The protesters waited to learn if there would be compensation for the oil spills, and jobs for the local youth. They wanted to know if the communities would finally get something back from these corporations that were draining the wealth from their country.

As the young people on the barge waited to get word about the negotiations, Chevron helicopters flew in. But instead of Chevron negotiators emerging, out came the Nigerian military and Mobile Police, known as the "Kill 'n' Go." They opened fire on the protesters, killing two of them and critically wounding a third. They then rounded up the remaining people and transported them to Nigerian jails, where some of them were tortured.

After hearing this story, we headed back to the Chevron

compound in Lagos. Here in the middle of Africa, we found what looked like an American suburb. There were lush green lawns with swimming pools in a picture-perfect gated community. The only hint that they might not be so welcome here is that the whole compound was surrounded by a moat and security guards.

Once we negotiated our way into the compound, I asked Chevron spokesperson Sola Omole about the killings in Ilajeland. Specifically, who flew in the Nigerian military?

"We did. Chevron did. We took them there," he replied, by "helicopters, yes, we took them in."

I asked who authorized bringing in the military.

"That's Chevron's management," he answered confidently.

We later requested further comment from Chevron's headquarters in San Francisco. Michael Libbey, the company's manager of media relations, wrote us a letter stating that Sola Omole's comments "fully represent the views of both our Nigerian business unit and of Chevron."

Chevron's acting head of security in Nigeria, James Neku, admitted he flew in with the military the day of the attack. He further revealed that the naval attack force included members of the Kill 'n' Go. As the late Oronto Douglas, an environmentalist who exposed the brutal record of the Kill 'n' Go in Ogoniland, described them, "The Kill 'n' Go shoot without question, they kill, they maim, they rape, they destroy."

After Jeremy and I returned to New York, we produced a radio documentary called *Drilling and Killing: Chevron and Nigeria's Oil Dictatorship*. While it won a number of awards, we continued to pursue the story further. In April 1999, I went to a Chevron shareholders meeting in California to question CEO Kenneth Derr. I don't make a habit of wearing habits, but I did use the proxy of the Ursuline Sisters of Tildonk, an order of Belgian nuns. I got up during the question-and-answer period when shareholders are allowed to address the well-protected CEO. I asked Derr if he would stop Chevron's practice of allowing the Nigerian military to kill protesters on company sites.

"No, that's a ridiculous question," he replied. And he moved on. Derr was confident that Chevron would never be held accountable for its actions.

As for Shell, in 2009—fourteen years after the execution of Ken Saro-Wiwa—Royal Dutch Shell agreed to pay a $15.5 million settlement to avoid a trial over its alleged involvement in human rights violations in the Niger Delta. The case was brought by the Center for Constitutional Rights and EarthRights International on behalf of ten plaintiffs who accused Shell of complicity in the 1995 executions of Saro-Wiwa and the eight other human rights activists. Part of the settlement money was used to establish a trust for the benefit of the Ogoni people.

Ken Wiwa, the son of Ken Saro-Wiwa, spoke about the landmark settlement on *Democracy Now!*: "For us, it's a moral victory . . . my father always said that they'll have their day in court. It shows that corporations cannot act with impunity in places like Nigeria." [3]

DISPATCHES FROM THE SUMMITS

The United Nations began holding high-level conferences about climate change at the Earth Summit in Rio de Janeiro in 1992. The summit led to the Kyoto Protocol in 1997, a treaty that committed nations to reducing greenhouse gas emissions. While that was a binding treaty, some countries refused to ratify it, most notably the country that was historically the world's largest polluter: the United States.

In 1995 the UN started holding annual climate conferences, known as conference of parties, or COP. The 2009 COP in Copenhagen, Denmark, was especially significant, since governments were supposed to agree there on a successor to the Kyoto Protocol.

Democracy Now! has gone to every UN Climate Summit since the one in Copenhagen, from Cancún to Durban to Doha, from Poland and Peru to Paris.

All of these major gatherings involve thousands of delegates, observers, and journalists, each who wear the UN credentials to access the secure summit sites. Outside the gates, though, thousands more come: people who are uninvited and uncredentialed, but who care deeply about climate change. They may not get into these sessions, but these are the people who feel the effects of climate change. They are on the front lines, whether they live in sub-Saharan Africa, which is turning into a desert, or if they live on one of the world's many small island states, like the Maldives in the Indian Ocean, which could soon be submerged. The protests of thousands who gather outside at these summits are the real hope. Our responsibility in independent media is to cover the entire discussion, from the suites to the streets.

Democracy Now! reported live from Copenhagen in 2009. We were especially eager to hear from people who came to press world leaders to commit to significant measures to stop climate change. Hopes were high that a meaningful successor to the Kyoto Protocol could result from the conference.

"Politicians talk, leaders act," read the sign outside the Bella Center in Copenhagen on the opening day of the United Nations climate summit. Inside the convention center, the official delegations from 192 countries, hundreds of nongovernmental organizations—an estimated fifteen thousand people in all—were engaging in two weeks of meetings aiming for a global agreement to stave off catastrophic global climate change. Five thousand journalists covered the event.

Outside, Copenhagen was transformed into a vibrant, global hub of climate-change activism, forums, and protest planning. In one square, an ice sculpture of a polar bear melted day by day, and an open-air exhibit of towering photos displayed "one hundred places to remember that will disappear."

But just as the US Environmental Protection Agency (EPA) designated carbon dioxide as a threat to health, President Barack Obama announced that there would not be a binding agreement from this summit. In fact, the United States emerged as a key obstacle to an agreement in what environmental writer and activist Bill McKibben has described as "the most important diplomatic gathering in the world's history." At stake were not only the rules that will govern entire economies, driven for well more than a century by fossil fuels, but also the very existence of some nations and cultures, from the tropics to the Arctic.

The Republic of Maldives, sent fifteen-year-old Mohamed Axam Maumoon as a climate ambassador. After attending the Children's Climate Forum he told me, "We are living at the very edge . . . because our country is so fragile, only protected by the natural barriers, such as the coral reefs and the white sandy beaches."

Most of the two hundred inhabited islands of the Maldives are at most three feet above sea level, and projected sea-level rises would inundate his country. Even at his age, Axam comprehended the enormity of the threat that he and his country face.

He starkly framed the question to people in the industrialized world: "Would you commit murder, even while we are begging for mercy and begging for you to stop what you're doing, change your ways, and let our children see the future that we want to build for them?"

Farther north, in Arctic Village, Alaska, indigenous people are fighting to survive. Sarah James is an elder of the Gwich'in people, who live in the far northwest of North America. She is also a member of the Gwich'in Steering Committee, which has fought to stop oil drilling on native lands in and around the Arctic National Wildlife Refuge. I met her at Copenhagen's Klimaforum09, dubbed the People's Summit, where she told me, "Climate change, global warming is real in the Arctic. There's a lot of erosion, because permafrost is melting . . . And last summer, there was a fire all summer long, no visibility. Last spring, twenty villages got flooded along the Yukon [River]. Sixty villages within the Yukon area never got their fish."

With just 5 percent of the world's population, the US produces about a quarter of the world's greenhouse gases. The model for the past century has been clear: if you want to grow your economy, industrialize with fossil fuels as your main source of energy. Yet the wealthy nations have not been willing to pay for the environmental damage they have caused, or significantly change the way they operate.

Ross Gelbspan, author of *The Heat Is On* and *Boiling Point*, insists that poverty is at the root of the problem: Take care of poverty, and humanity can solve the climate crisis. He says that retooling the planet for a green economy can be the largest jobs program in history, can create more equality among nations, and is necessary—immediately—to avoid catastrophe.

Between sessions at the Bella Center, in the crowded café area, a group of activists walked in dressed as space aliens, in white spacesuits and with green skin and goggles. "Take us to your climate leaders!" they demanded. "Show us your binding treaty!" In the rarified diplomatic atmosphere of the summit, such antics stood out.

But the calls from the developing world, both inside and outside the summit, to cut emissions and to compensate countries, from Africa, to Asia, to Latin America, for the devastating effects of global warming that they did not cause are no laughing matter.

Barack Obama said, minutes before racing out of the Copenhagen Climate Summit, "We will not be legally bound by anything that took place here today."

These were among his remarks made to his own small White House press corps, excluding the thousands of credentialed journalists covering the talks. It was late on December 18, 2009, the last day of the Copenhagen summit, and reports were that the negotiations had failed.

Copenhagen, which had been cobranded for the talks on billboards with Coke and the tech company Siemens as "Hopenhagen," was looking more like "Nopenhagen."

That morning, as I entered the Bella Center (which we had started referring to as "the Bella of the beast"), I saw several dozen people sitting on the cold stone plaza outside the police line. Throughout the summit, people had filled this area, hoping to pick up credentials. Thousands from nongovernmental organizations and the press waited hours in the cold, only to be denied. On the final days of the summit, the area was empty.

Most groups had been stripped of their credentials so that the summit could meet the security and space needs for traveling heads of state, the UN claimed. These people sitting in the cold were engaged in a somber protest: they were shaving their heads.

One woman told me, "I am shaving my head to show how really deeply touched I feel about what is happening in there. . . . There are six billion people out there, and inside they don't seem to be talking about them." She held a white sign, with just a pair of quotation marks but no words.

"What does the sign say?" I asked her.

She had tears in her eyes. "It says nothing, because I don't know what to say anymore."

Obama reportedly heard of a meeting taking place between the heads of state of China, India, Brazil, and South Africa, and burst into the room, leading the group to consensus on the Copenhagen Accord. One hundred ninety-three countries were represented at the summit, most of them by their head of state. Obama and his small group defied UN procedure, resulting in the nonbinding, take-it-or-leave-it document.

The accord at least acknowledged that countries "agree that deep cuts in global emissions are required according to science . . . so as to hold the increase in global temperature below 2 degrees Celsius." For some, after eight years with President George W. Bush, just having a US president who accepted science as a basis for policy might be considered a huge victory. The accord pledged "a goal of mobilizing jointly $100 billion a year by 2020" for developing countries. This was less than many say is needed to solve the problem of adapting to climate change and building green economies in developing countries, and was only a nonbinding goal. Secretary of State Hillary Clinton refused to specify the US share, saying only that if countries didn't come to an agreement, it would not be on the table anymore.

James Hansen, formerly the top climate scientist at NASA, told me, "The wealthy countries are trying to basically buy off these countries that will, in effect, disappear." He added, "Based on our contribution to the carbon in the atmosphere, [the US share] would be twenty-seven percent, or twenty-seven billion dollars per year."

I asked Bolivian President Evo Morales for his solution. He recommended that "all war spending be directed toward climate change, instead of spending it on troops in Iraq, in Afghanistan, or the military bases in Latin America." According to the Stockholm International Peace Research Institute, in 2008 the fifteen countries with the highest military budgets spent close to $1.2 trillion on armed forces.

Erich Pica, president of Friends of the Earth (FOE), one of the major NGOs stripped of credentials, criticized the outcome of the Copenhagen talks, writing: "The United States slammed through a flimsy agreement that was negotiated behind closed doors. The so-called Copenhagen Accord is full of empty pledges." But he also applauded "concerned citizens who marched, held vigils, and sent messages to their leaders, [who] helped to create unstoppable momentum in the global movement for climate justice."

Many felt that Obama's disruption of the process in Copenhagen might have derailed twenty years of climate talks. But Pica had it right. The summit failed to reach a fair, ambitious, and binding agreement, but it inspired a new generation of activists to join what has emerged as a sophisticated global movement for climate justice.

"GET IT DONE"

Anjali Appadurai strode confidently from the back of the conference room at the UN's Seventeenth Conference of Parties, or COP17, the official title of the United Nations Climate Change Conference held in Durban, South Africa, in December 2011.

Appadurai, a student at the ecologically focused College of the Atlantic in Bar Harbor, Maine, was about to address the plenary as part of the youth delegation. The youth attendees were keenly aware that it was their generation that would have to deal with the greatest impacts of climate change.

This was the official closing plenary session of the Durban summit. The negotiations were extended for two extra days in hopes of avoiding complete failure. At issue were arguments over words and phrases: for instance, the replacement of "legal agreement" with "an agreed outcome with legal force," which is said to have won over India to the Durban Platform.

The countries in attendance agreed to a schedule that would lead to an accord by 2015, which would commit all countries to reduce emissions starting no sooner than 2020, eight years into the future.

The young people at these climate summits have always amazed me with their eloquence and bravery. Anjali Appadurai faced the international delegates and said:

> I speak for more than half the world's population. We are the silent majority. You've given us a seat in this hall, but our interests are not on the table. What does it take to get a stake in this game? Lobbyists? Corporate influence? Money?
>
> You've been negotiating all my life. You've failed to meet pledges, you've missed targets, and you've broken promises. But you've heard this all before.
>
> We're in Africa, home to communities on the front line of climate change . . . The International Energy Agency tells us we have five years until the window to avoid irreversible climate change closes. The science tells us that we have five years maximum. You're saying, "Give us ten."

The starkest betrayal of your generation's responsibility to ours is that you call this "ambition." Where is the courage in these rooms? Now is not the time for incremental action. In the long run, these will be seen as the defining moments of an era in which narrow self-interest prevailed over science, reason, and common compassion.

There is real ambition in this room, but it's been dismissed as radical, deemed not politically possible. Stand with Africa. Long-term thinking is not radical. What's radical is to completely alter the planet's climate, to betray the future of my generation, and to condemn millions to death by climate change. What's radical is to write off the fact that change is within our reach. Two thousand eleven was the year in which the silent majority found their voice; the year when the bottom shook the top. Two thousand eleven was the year when the radical became reality . . .

Respect the integral values of humanity. Respect the future of your descendants.

[Nelson] Mandela said, "It always seems impossible, until it's done." So, distinguished delegates and governments around the world, governments of the developed world: deep cuts now. Get it done.

When Appadurai finished, acting COP President Artur Runge-Metzger spoke. "On a purely personal note," he said, "I wonder why we let not speak half of the world's population first in this conference, but only last."

The following year at the climate conference in Doha, I bumped into Anjali Appadurai. I asked her why she wasn't inside.

"They banned me," she replied. After her actions at the previous year's conference, her credentials were pulled, and the UN initially wouldn't allow her in.

Meanwhile, just before the Doha conference, Christiana Figueres, the executive secretary of the UN Framework Convention on Climate Change, addressed the Conference of Youth. She told the young people, "Keep on going. Don't let your impatience move you into inaction or into cynicism."

Yet when Appadurai acted, she was barred.

We need to hear these silenced voices. That is the power of independent media: to give voice to the voiceless; to those who have been shut out of the debate.

Appadurai was right about 2011 having been a banner year of activism. It began with the Arab Spring, continued with mass protests in Wisconsin to defend labor rights, and included Occupy Wall Street in the fall. Environmental activists were in the thick of the protests.

RING AROUND THE ROSE GARDEN

On November 5, 2011, more than ten thousand people gathered in Washington, DC, with a simple goal: encircle the White House. They succeeded, just over two months after 1,253 people were arrested in a series of protests at the same spot. These thousands, as well as those arrested, were unified in their opposition to the planned Keystone XL pipeline.

The primary function of the Keystone XL pipeline was to move oil from the tar sands region of Alberta to port facilities on the South Texas coast for shipping to overseas customers. It would enable expanded extraction of the tar sands, a form of oil that is much more environmentally destructive than other types.

Climate scientist James Hansen, former director of the NASA Goddard Institute for Space Studies, wrote in the *New York Times*,

"If Canada proceeds, and we do nothing, it will be game over for the climate." Hansen, America's leading climate scientist, was among those arrested in front of the White House while protesting Keystone XL.

Another person arrested outside 1600 Pennsylvania Avenue was Julian Bond, former chair of the NAACP, civil rights activist, and previously a member of the Georgia legislature. Bond (who died in 2015) said, "The threat to our planet's climate is both grave and urgent . . . I am proud today to stand before my fellow citizens and declare, 'I am willing to go to jail to stop this wrong.' The environmental crisis we face today demands nothing less."

Encircled by activism, President Obama announced that he would delay a decision about Keystone until after the 2012 election. Later he granted permission to build the southern leg of the pipeline, from Oklahoma through Texas. That decision sparked protests from landowners and environmentalists, including a nonviolent direct-action blockade campaign in Texas, with people chaining themselves to pipeline equipment, occupying land, and sitting in trees to block construction.

Early in the permit process, Secretary of State Hillary Clinton said she was inclined to approve the pipeline, even though the State Department's mandatory review was incomplete. Controversy erupted when the *Washington Post* reported that the lobbyist for TransCanada, the Canadian company that wanted to build the pipeline, was Paul Elliott, who'd been a senior staffer on Hillary Clinton's 2008 presidential campaign. He also worked on Bill Clinton's campaign in 1996 and Hillary Clinton's Senate campaign in 2000.

Friends of the Earth obtained emails from 2010 between Elliott and Marja Verloop, whom FOE described as a "member of the senior diplomatic staff at the US Embassy in Ottawa." In one email, Verloop cheers Elliott for obtaining the buy-in on Keystone XL from conservative Democratic Senator Max Baucus, writing: "Go Paul! Baucus support holds clout."

Another one of the people arrested at the White House during the 2011 protests was Canadian author and activist Naomi Klein. Of the cozy email exchange, she said, "The response of the State Department was, 'Well, we meet with environmentalists, too.' But just imagine them writing an email to Bill McKibben, when he says, 'We got more than 1,200 people arrested.' Would they write back, 'Go Bill!'? The day that happens, I'll stop worrying."

Klein explained the environmental impact of the project: "Tar sands oil emits three times as much greenhouse gases as a regular barrel of Canadian crude, because, of course, it is in solid form. So you have to use all of this energy to get it out and to liquefy it."

Adding to the controversy, the *New York Times* revealed that the State Department chose an environmental services company called Cardno Entrix as an outside consultant to run the environmental impact study of Keystone XL. It turned out that Cardno Entrix listed as one of its major clients none other than Trans-Canada. The Obama campaign also drew fire for hiring Broderick Johnson, a lobbyist who formerly represented TransCanada.

The environmental impacts were potentially extreme, with, first, the potential for a catastrophic leak of the toxic tar sands extract, and second, but no less significant, the potential long-term impacts on the global climate.

A PEOPLE'S CLIMATE MOVEMENT

On September 24, 2014, the People's Climate March was held in New York City, with other marches taking place in cities around the world. The march coincided with a one-day UN climate summit. Organizers expected about a hundred thousand people to show up. Instead, four hundred thousand flooded the streets of New York City to demand action on climate change.

"There hasn't been a political gathering about anything that's this large in this country for many years," march organizer Bill McKibben told me during a three-hour live broadcast of *Democracy Now!* from the streets of Manhattan. "And I think what it demonstrates is climate change is at the absolute tip now of people's consciousness."

Naomi Klein, who was at the march, observed, "I think it's really significant that this is happening in post–Hurricane Sandy New York, because there's the connection between the need, the imperative, to fight inequality, to have economic and racial justice, and to fight climate change. The connections between these projects and these values were so clear in the midst and in the aftermath of Hurricane Sandy, because you saw how different the experience of the storm was if you were wealthy and had private resources, or if you were relying on the state or if you were in public housing." Hurricane Sandy, which slammed into the East Coast and caused widespread flooding and other damage in New York and New Jersey in November 2012, is the second costliest hurricane in US history.

Klein, the author of the bestseller *This Changes Everything: Capitalism vs. the Climate*, characterizes evolving climate-justice activism as "blockadia":

"Blockadia is really this transnational space, roving space, where regular people are stepping in where our leaders are failing," she explained. "And they are trying to stop this era of extreme extraction with their bodies or in the courts, particularly indigenous people, First Nations people, using their traditional land rights, their treaties, their aboriginal title, to take on massive corporations and to take on the Canadian government, the US government— and winning some really significant victories."

Klein said the climate-justice movement is about more than stopping a few bad polluters. "It's a resistance movement against the whole logic of extractivism, the whole idea that we need to create sacrifice zones in order to have a healthy economy. And the shift is toward a regenerative economy, an economy that takes care of the land, in which no one, no people, and no place needs to be sacrificed in the name of progress."

The fossil fuel divestment movement is one way that activists are rejecting an extractive economy. Klein's husband, filmmaker Avi Lewis, who made *This Changes Everything* into a documentary film, observed, "The divestment movement has exploded in three years—$2.6 trillion in capital now which is committed to divesting from fossil fuel investments. But it's not just the 'No' to the fossil fuel stocks and bonds. It's the 'Yes' in terms of redirecting and reinvesting that money in community cooperatives, in renewable energy."

Fossil fuel divestment has become mainstream, as states, universities, and foundations respond to enormous pressure and protest. In October 2015, Governor Jerry Brown signed a bill forcing California's pension system, comprised of the nation's two largest public funds, to divest from coal. Among the institutions that are divesting all or part of their portfolios from fossil fuels are Stanford University, the University of California system (which in 2015 sold off $200 million in investments in coal and oil sands companies), the Norway Pension Fund, the World Council of Churches, and the British Medical Association. Even the Rockefeller family, which made its vast fortune on oil, has begun divesting from fossil fuel companies.

Stephen Heintz, an heir of Standard Oil tycoon John D. Rockefeller, said, "We are quite convinced that if he were alive today, as an astute businessman looking out to the future, he would be moving out of fossil fuels and investing in clean, renewable energy."

GLOBAL WARMING AND GLOBAL WARRING

Hours after four hundred thousand people joined in the largest climate march in history in September 2014, the United States began bombing Syria. The Pentagon claimed that the targets were military installations of the Islamic State, in Syria and Iraq, as well as newly revealed terrorist outfit, the Khorasan Group, made up of former members of Al Qaeda.

The world is beset with twin crises, inextricably linked: global warming and global warring. Solutions to both exist but won't be achieved by bombing.

"In today's wars, many more civilians are killed than soldiers; the seeds of future conflict are sown, economies are wrecked, civil societies torn asunder, refugees amassed, children scarred."

These words were spoken on December 10, 2009, by that year's Nobel Peace Prize winner, President Barack Obama. His pronouncement still reads like a daily headline.

"The world must come together to confront climate change," Obama said in his Nobel Prize acceptance speech. "There is little scientific dispute that if we do nothing, we will face more drought, more famine, more mass displacement—all of which will fuel more conflict for decades." Obama even made the key point that "it is not merely scientists and environmental activists who call for swift and forceful action—it's military leaders in my own country and others who understand our common security hangs in the balance."

Indeed, the Pentagon has long considered climate change to be a major threat to the national security of the United States. In its 2014 Quadrennial Defense Review, the Pentagon noted that the many impacts of climate change "will aggravate stressors abroad such as poverty, environmental degradation, political instability, and social tensions—conditions that can enable terrorist activity and other forms of violence."

So it is fair to ask: Why not address the threat of climate change when it is still possible?

Asad Rehman, of Friends of the Earth, who was in New York for the climate march, told me, "If we can find the trillions [of dollars] we're finding for conflict—whether there's been the invasion in Iraq or Afghanistan or now the conflict in Syria—then we can find the kind of money that's required for the transformation that will deliver clean, renewable energy."

Rehman spent years as an antiwar organizer, and sees the deep connection between warring and warming. "Oil has been a curse on the people of the Middle East," he added. "It has been a harbinger of conflict and violence and of destruction of ancient civilizations in communities and the lives of millions of people."

Codepink cofounder Medea Benjamin echoed the words of Rehman. She participated in the historic climate march, and joined thousands more the next day to "Flood Wall Street," where a hundred people were arrested. Before heading to the White House to protest the bombing of Syria, she told me: "Oil is the basis of US policy in the Middle East. Were it not for Iraq's oil, the US would have never invaded."

Or as Vermont Senator Bernie Sanders tweeted during his 2016 presidential bid, "If the environment were a bank, it would have been saved by now."

Before the 2003 invasion of Iraq, General Anthony Zinni predicted success only with an invading force of four hundred thousand. Secretary of Defense Donald Rumsfeld went in with less than half. A year after the invasion, he quipped famously, "You go to war with the army you have—not the army you might want or wish to have at a later time."

Well, four hundred thousand people turned out for the climate march in September 2014—an army of hope for a sustainable future.

"A MOVEMENT OF MILLIONS"

Climate-justice momentum has continued to build as people take on the fossil fuel industry in their own communities. As fossil fuel corporations intensify their exploitation of the world's oil, protesters are weighing in as never before about the catastrophic effects of climate change.

In 2015 a broad coalition came together in Seattle to challenge a multinational corporate behemoth, Shell Oil Company. Citizens and elected officials alike, concerned about Shell's plans to drill for oil in the Arctic, swarmed the waters around Seattle, trying to block the massive oil-drilling platform Polar Pioneer from leaving on its journey to the Arctic.

This confrontation evoked the famous Battle of Seattle that

raged in 1999, when tens of thousands protested the meeting of the World Trade Organization, or WTO. Grassroots organizers successfully blocked world leaders, government trade ministers, and corporate executives from meeting to sign a global trade deal that many called deeply undemocratic, harming workers' rights, the environment, and indigenous people globally.

Fast forward to May 2015. The Polar Pioneer arrived in Puget Sound in preparation for its trip to the Chukchi Sea in the Arctic Ocean. Royal Dutch Shell had the vessel under contract from Transocean, the same company whose Deepwater Horizon oil rig caused the 2010 blowout and oil spill disaster in the Gulf of Mexico. As the platform of the Polar Pioneer was tugged into the Port of Seattle's Terminal 5, the first wave of the "Mosquito Fleet" paddled out to block it. The protest flotilla was made up of "kayaktivists," people in small kayaks who establish a blockade, much like the protesters in 1999 linked arms on the rainy streets of Seattle to block the delegates attempting to attend the WTO Ministerial Conference.

Even legendary musician Paul McCartney weighed in. In his foreword to a new book against Arctic drilling by Greenpeace activist Ben Stewart, McCartney wrote, "As the ice retreats, the oil giants are moving in. Instead of seeing the melting as a grave warning to humanity, they are eyeing the previously inaccessible oil beneath the seabed at the top of the world. They're exploiting the disappearance of the ice to drill for the very same fuel that caused the melting in the first place."

Ultimately, the Polar Pioneer escaped Puget Sound. As the rig entered the open sea off the coast of Vancouver Island in Canada, Greenpeace Canada dispatched inflatable boats. Indigenous activist Audrey Siegl of the Musqueam First Nation stood on the bow of one small boat, holding her hands in a defiant order to stop.

Meanwhile, two more people were swimming in the open ocean, in front of the gargantuan Shell vessel, treading water while holding a sign reading "People Vs. Oil."

In early September, Obama became the first sitting president ever to visit the Arctic. While there, he gave some of the strongest speeches on climate change of any world leader. Many wondered why, just a few weeks before, his administration granted a permit to Shell to drill for oil in the environmentally fragile region. This conflicting message soon took yet another dramatic twist.

In late September 2015, in the face of mounting opposition and after what became a futile search for oil, Shell announced that it was abandoning its $7 billion Arctic oil drilling operation. Greenpeace UK executive director John Sauven responded, "Big oil has sustained an unmitigated defeat. They had a budget of billions, we had a movement of millions. For three years, we faced them down, and the people won . . . Now President Obama should use his remaining months in office to say that no other oil company will be licensed to drill in the American Arctic."

Several weeks after Shell's announcement, the Obama administration canceled plans to sell new drilling leases and refused to extend leases that had been sold previously, thus ending the possibility of oil drilling in the Arctic for the rest of President Obama's tenure. In the same week, Canadian voters unseated three-term prime minister Stephen Harper, a major backer of carbon-intensive oil extraction and a foe of global climate regulation.

"What a victory for brave activists, especially in the Northwest, those kayaktivists," Bill McKibben told me on *Democracy Now!* "Shell claimed that they didn't find much oil in the Arctic. What they really found was way more trouble than they bargained for."

Other leaders were finding that backing climate polluters was nothing but trouble. In September 2015 Hillary Clinton, while campaigning for president, reversed her position that she held as secretary of state and announced that she opposed the Keystone XL pipeline.

On November 6, 2015, President Obama announced that he was rejecting TransCanada's application to build the pipeline.

"America is now a global leader when it comes to taking serious action to fight climate change. And frankly, approving this project would have undercut that global leadership," said Obama. "And that's the biggest risk we face: not acting. Today we're continuing to lead by example, because, ultimately, if we're going to prevent large parts of this Earth from becoming not only inhospitable but uninhabitable in our lifetimes, we're going to have to keep some fossil fuels in the ground rather than burn them and release more dangerous pollution into the sky."

McKibben responded, "President Obama is the first world leader to reject a project because of its effect on the climate. It eloquently confirms the five years and millions of hours of work that people of every kind put into this fight."

Clayton Thomas-Müller, a leading environmental justice and indigenous-rights organizer, and a member of the Cree Nation in Northern Manitoba, Canada, reacted on *Democracy Now!* "What this victory represents to the climate-justice movement, to the indigenous-rights movement, is . . . the incredible power of social movements here in North America."

WITH GOD ON THEIR SIDE

In 2015 fossil fuel resistance gained a powerful new ally: Pope Francis. He declared, in the first-ever papal encyclical on the environment and climate change, "The idea of infinite or unlimited growth, which proves so attractive to economists, financiers, and experts in technology . . . is based on the lie that there is an infinite supply of the Earth's goods, and this leads to the planet being squeezed dry at every limit."

Pope Francis has called for swift action to save the planet from environmental ruin, urging world leaders to hear "the cry of the Earth and the cry of the poor." The pope said that protecting the planet is a moral and ethical "imperative" for believers and nonbelievers alike that should supersede political and economic interests.

While touring South America, the pope said, "The goods of the Earth are meant for everyone. And however much someone may parade his property, it has a social mortgage. In this way, we move beyond purely economic justice, based on commerce, toward social justice, which upholds the fundamental human right to a dignified life. The tapping of natural resources . . . must not be concerned with short-term benefits."

A major theme of the encyclical is the disparity between rich and poor. "We fail to see that some are mired in desperate and degrading poverty, with no way out, while others have not the faintest idea of what to do with their possessions, vainly showing off their supposed superiority and leaving behind them so much waste, which, if it were the case everywhere, would destroy the planet," he said.

Woven throughout the pope's clarion call to action to confront climate change is a harsh critique of capitalism. Take just one paragraph from the forty-thousand-word encyclical:

"The economy accepts every advance in technology with a view to profit, without concern for its potentially negative impact on human beings. Finance overwhelms the real economy. The lessons of the global financial crisis have not been assimilated, and we are learning all too slowly the lessons of environmental deterioration."

Later in Bolivia, the pope would say, "An unfettered pursuit of money rules." Quoting an early Catholic theologian, he added, "This is the 'dung of the devil.'"

THE ROAD THROUGH PARIS

The culmination of more than two decades' worth of negotiations on how to tackle the collective problem of climate change was long slated to take place in Paris in December 2015. This was to be the moment when nations came together to confront a common foe, to take bold and decisive action and save the planet for future generations.

At least, that was the plan.

The Paris summit of the United Nations Framework Convention on Climate Change (UNFCCC), COP21, was scheduled for November 30 to December 11, 2015. It would include the largest gathering of heads of state on a single day in world history. Thousands of journalists would be there to cover the high-stakes event. More than twenty thousand people were expected each day at the highly secure conference venue, Le Bourget, the suburb of Paris where Charles Lindbergh landed his famous transatlantic flight in 1925. Outside of the official proceedings, civil society had organized with students, labor unions, environmentalists, grassroots social justice organizations, indigenous nations, and concerned citizens planning vibrant events, from a march through Paris with up to half a million people, to a weekend-long "Citizens Summit for the Climate," to a rolling series of protests and direct actions to challenge the corporate influence over the UN climate negotiations. Paris was buzzing, and the eyes of the world would be on the City of Light.

Then, on Friday, November 13, a small group of men launched a brutal attack on civilians in Paris. The first target was the Stade de France, the national stadium, where a soccer match was happening, with French President François Hollande in attendance. Three suicide bombers exploded their vests outside the stadium, killing themselves and one victim. Another group attacked several cafés, calmly firing machine guns into crowds sitting at the sidewalk terraces. Then, three more gunmen entered the Bataclan nightclub, where 1,500 people were enjoying a rock show. Here the gunmen slaughtered 89 people, before blowing themselves up or being shot during the eventual police raid. Ultimately, 130 people were murdered by the assailants that night, and over 350 were injured. President Hollande declared the first state of emergency in France since World War II, and banned all public protests. The mood in France was somber and tense as a massive dragnet took place, seeking those who planned and participated in the attacks. ISIS took responsibility for the attacks, and France immediately expanded its bombing of Syria. This as hundreds of thousands of refugees from wars and climate disruption were making arduous journeys, seeking refuge in Europe.

It was in this difficult context, with large public gatherings banned and militarized streets, that the most important climate summit in history was convened.

November 29 was scheduled to be what could have been the largest ever mass march for climate justice. With the ban on protests in place, the organizers agreed to cancel the march. Instead, a human chain was formed, with thousands of people lining the Champs Élysées, hand in hand, in a show of solidarity with those on the front line of the climate crisis. After the chain disbanded, hundreds marched to the Place de la République, the main memorial where people had been gathering to mourn the victims of the recent attacks, just blocks from the Bataclan theater. Tens of thousands of shoes had been carefully laid out in the large plaza, including a pair from Pope Francis, to represent the people who had been denied the right to march. Riot police moved in, attacking the marchers with tear gas, pepper spray, and concussion grenades, arresting two hundred people. Mainstream media parroted official reports that the protesters trampled the large, makeshift memorial at the Place de la République. *Democracy Now!*'s video showed just the opposite: protesters locked arms and tried to protect the memorial of flowers, candles, and signs placed in memory of the November 13 attack victims; it was the riot police who trampled it.

The Paris summit started with a meeting of 130 heads of state. They were there to give "momentum" to the talks, but also, reportedly, to limit their involvement at the end of the summit, to avoid the type of closed-door meetings that helped the process collapse at the Copenhagen summit in 2009. President Obama, in his address, said, "I've come here personally, as the leader of the world's largest economy and the second-largest emitter, to say that the United States of America not only recognizes our role in creating this problem, we embrace our responsibility to do something about it."

Inside the summit site, we bumped into the former head climate negotiator for the Philippines, a soft-spoken man named Naderev "Yeb" Saño. We hardly recognized him in his T-shirt, cargo pants, and sneakers. We last saw him in 2013 at the UN climate summit in Warsaw, while Typhoon Haiyan, one of the strongest cyclones in recorded history, devastated his country, killing thousands of people. At the time, Yeb Saño made headlines with an emotional plea to the world body to take immediate action on climate change:

"Typhoons such as Haiyan and its impacts represent a sobering reminder to the international community that we cannot afford to delay climate action. . . . It must be poetic justice that Typhoon Haiyan was so big that its diameter spanned the distance between Warsaw and Paris." He implored his fellow negotiators in 2013, "If not us, then who? If not now, then when? If not here, then where?" After days of not knowing, he had just learned that his brother, A. G. Saño, had narrowly survived the typhoon in his devastated town of Tacloban.

The following year, as yet another deadly storm battered the Philippines, Yeb Saño was unexpectedly absent from the UN climate summit in Lima, Peru, shocking many. He had been pulled from the delegation at the last minute, leading to speculation that he had been targeted for his outspokenness following pressure from wealthier countries, like the United States. At the time, he tweeted: "They can silence my mouth. But they cannot silence my soul."

In Paris, Yeb Saño was back at the UN climate summit, not as the chief negotiator for the Philippines, but as a grassroots activist. He had just walked nine hundred miles over sixty days from Rome to Paris on a People's Pilgrimage for Climate Action. At his side was A. G., who is a street artist. Along the way A. G. painted six beautiful murals, with the help of locals, depicting pilgrims from around the world walking to Paris. Since he had no official credentials to access the summit, I interviewed him outside the secure zone. A. G. Saño offered a tribute to a friend of his, killed in Typhoon Haiyan:

I came here to bring the voice of my dead friend. I'd just like to tell the world the name of my friend, Agit Sustento. Climate change is as real as Agit Sustento. I was with him the night before, and the last thing that I told him was to take care of himself and his family because that's the strongest typhoon in recorded history that we're about to face, and that was the last time that I ever talked to him. He lost his wife, his little boy, his mom and dad. My promise to him is that I'll tell the world about his name. His name is Agit Sustento, and he will never get to see the sun rise again.

To understand what COP21 was all about, what the UNFCCC was created to address, one must hear the stories of people like Yeb and A. G. Saño, in order to grasp the incredible, often violent, life-altering, or life-ending, impacts that the changing climate is imposing on people everywhere. Inside the secure summit, where diplomatic decorum prevails, and negotiators argue over small differences between competing versions of the official text being negotiated, it is easy to forget that lives hang in the balance.

Another lens through which to understand the negotiations—perhaps the most important lens—is through science. Three numbers to know in reference to COP21 are 1.5, 2, and 2.7 degrees. These represent targets for the maximum average increase in global surface temperature, in Celsius, above preindustrial levels. In degrees Fahrenheit, the numbers are 2.7, 3.6, and 4.9 degrees, respectively. Since Copenhagen, the agreed upon—but not binding—goal of the UNFCCC process was to limit the increase to "no more than 2 degrees C."

When this goal was announced in 2009 at Copenhagen, blocs of nations from the small island states and impacted regions like sub-Saharan Africa were defiant. They were fighting for an ambitious goal of 1.5 degrees Celsius. "If the Copenhagen Accord stands, we're going to have global temperature increase of more than four degrees," Nnimmo Bassey told me after the Copenhagen summit. He is a Nigerian environmental activist and former chairperson of the large and influential environmental NGO, Friends of the Earth International. He went on, "That will mean roasting Africa, destroying African people, destroying African environment, and simply, possibly, just having a continent on the map with nobody in it."

In a speech shortly after the conclusion of the 2015 Paris summit, Naomi Klein recalled the moment six years earlier in Copenhagen when the target of 1.5 degrees was abandoned:

> The African delegates marched through the conference center in Copenhagen and called it a death sentence for Africa. Some of them described it as "genocide" and they said that Africa would burn with warming of two degrees Celsius, particularly Sub-Saharan Africa. Island nations, low-lying island nations, like Tuvalu, the Marshall Islands, held their own demonstrations and their chant was, "1.5 to survive." Because the sea level rise that's projected with two degrees warming would mean the end of their countries. Despite what these countries were saying, they were ignored and two degrees was enshrined in the text. Witnessing it was one of the most emotional moments of my life.

At the Cancún climate summit in 2010 (COP16), Johnson Toribiong, who was then president of Palau, one of the small island states in the Pacific Ocean, described his country's situation:

"Our livelihood, indeed our very existence, depends upon the oceans. The ebb and flow of the oceans are as much a part of our life as the air we breathe. But today we find ourselves on the front lines of climate change. The oceans, which once sustained us, are now threatening to swallow us. While Palau is safe for the time being, the ocean's warming, the rise in acidification, threaten everyone's existence. The world cannot continue to treat climate change as a subject of negotiation. Climate change is not negotiable. It is a crisis."

Two degrees Celsius has become the official maximum allowable temperature increase. The goal can only be achieved by reducing greenhouse gas emissions. The process that the nations agreed to at the previous summits was that, just prior to Paris, each country would announce its plan to reduce emissions. In the jargon of the climate summits, these pledges are called "INDCs," or Intended Nationally Determined Contributions. These are promises that countries make to reduce carbon emissions, which are entirely voluntary, and unenforceable.

When the bulk of the INDCs were pledged, Christiana Figueres, executive secretary of the UNFCCC, said, "The INDCs have the capability of limiting the forecast temperature rise to around 2.7 degrees Celsius by 2100, by no means enough but a lot lower than the estimated four, five, or more degrees of warming projected by many prior to the INDCs." This is the third number to note, 2.7. The voluntary contributions from all the nations only amount to enough reduction in emissions to limit the global temperature rise to 2.7 degrees C, far above the stated goal of 2 degrees C.

What is the big deal? I asked Kevin Anderson, deputy director of the Tyndall Centre for Climate Change Research at the University of Manchester in Britain, who attended COP21. "When you add up all of the commitments that the countries are making in terms of their reductions in emissions, then actually it's far, far above that, nearer 3 or 4 degrees C temperature rise, which is a huge increase," he told me. "Remember, that is a global average. And most of the globe is covered in water, so on land that's an average of, if we carry on like we're going now, 4, 5, possibly even as high as 6 degrees C temperature rise."

I asked him what would happen if temperatures were allowed

to rise like that: "We'd see dramatic reductions in the staple food crops. So that's a really big issue, if we have big 40 percent or so reductions in rice, maize, wheat, sorghum, those sorts of crops. Huge changes in sea level rise by the end of the century, but also locking in very large sea level rise changes going forward beyond that. And we'd see increase in droughts and in flooding, increase in severity of typhoons."

The Intergovernmental Panel on Climate Change (IPCC), the group of over 1,800 scientists who collect and analyze all the science on climate change and interpret it for policymakers, summed up in their most recent report, "Stabilizing temperature increase to below 2°C relative to pre-industrial levels will require an urgent and fundamental departure from business as usual. Moreover, the longer we wait to take action, the more it will cost and the greater the technological, economic, social, and institutional challenges we will face."

On December 12, 2015, official delegates and observers gathered in the plenary hall of COP21. It was there that the Paris Agreement was announced. The end result of decades of work, world leaders hailed it as a great success. "The Paris Agreement is a monumental triumph for people and our planet," UN secretary general Ban Ki-Moon tweeted immediately after the closing gavel fell.

Many environmental groups praised the outcome as well. "We do think it's a turning point," Michael Brune, executive director of the Sierra Club, told us on *Democracy Now!* "The best news that I think we saw from COP is that every country has realized this is a problem, we need to do a lot more. But even better is that the climate movement, that helped to secure all of these victories, is showing up to work today. And we're not going to let up until we get an economy, a just society, that is powered by 100 percent clean energy."

Not everyone agreed. Joining Brune on *Democracy Now!*, British journalist and author George Monbiot countered, "What I see is an agreement with no timetables, no targets, with vague, wild aspirations. It's almost as if it's now safe to adopt 1.5 degrees centigrade as their aspirational target now that it is pretty well impossible to reach. I see a lot of backslapping, a lot of self-congratulation, and I see very little in terms of the actual substance that is required to avert climate breakdown." Monbiot, who is a columnist with the *Guardian* newspaper, wrote, "By comparison to what it could have been, it's a miracle. By comparison to what it should have been, it's a disaster."

"This is really a total fraud," esteemed climate scientist James Hansen told me inside COP21—the first climate summit he had attended. He gave the first official warning about climate change to the US Congress in 1988 and has become one of the most outspoken critics of the UN process. His solution: a carbon fee. "We're not going to reduce emissions as long as we let fossil fuels be the cheapest form of energy."

He explained how it would work: "It should be an across-the-board carbon fee. And in a democracy, the money should be given to the public. You collect the money from the fossil fuel companies. The rate would go up over time, but the money should be distributed 100 percent to the public, an equal amount to every legal resident."

The fee would, he says, make the cost of fossil fuels "honest," embedding, with the fee, their true cost to society. With the increased costs at the gas pump, people would have an incentive to shift away from, for example, gasoline-powered cars. The same goes for industry. "An economic study shows that in the United States, after ten years, emissions would be reduced 30 percent, because you've got the economy forcing you in the right direction.

But as long as you just leave fossil fuels cheap, you're not going to fundamentally change things."

One result of the Paris Agreement is clear: it will take a movement to ensure that the voluntary targets are pursued, made more ambitious, and that climate change does not advance to the point at which human society cannot survive. James Hansen coauthored a scientific paper recently, showing the two degrees Celsius target could cause major ice sheets in Antarctica and Greenland to melt much more quickly than the IPCC currently believes. I asked what would happen if the West Antarctic ice sheet melted. He said, "That would mean several meters of sea level rise. That's the biggest threat that climate change has in store for us, because it would mean that all coastal cities would become dysfunctional. And the economic consequences of that are incalculable. And the number of refugees that you would have—a hundred million people in Bangladesh—have to find someplace to go. So, it's something—it's hard to imagine how we can have a governable world if we let the Antarctic ice sheet collapse."

As COP21 was coming to a close, Greenpeace's Kumi Naidoo told me, "Most of us in civil society never said 'the road to Paris,' we always said 'the road through Paris.' " The night the Paris Agreement was announced, Naidoo was there:

This is neither a moment for triumphalism or for despair. We cannot be triumphalistic of the deal that is done here when tens of thousands of lives have been lost already as a result of climate impacts and where, furthermore, tens of thousands of lives are on the precipice of survival—indigenous peoples, people in low-lying states and so on. Neither should it be a message of despair for us in the climate movement. We have won the core argument that the climate crisis is serious, it requires urgent action. And we will continue to mobilize from tomorrow to make sure that the end of the fossil fuel era starts today and that we see the transition to a 100 percent renewable energy future by no later than 2050.

Thousands of people had planned to rally that day in Paris, in defiance of President Hollande's state of emergency, which was cynically scheduled to end with the closing of COP21. Given the prospect of more violent police crackdowns on peaceful protesters as the diplomats were nearing their agreement, Hollande lifted the protest ban. More than ten thousand people marched from the Arc de Triomphe to the Eiffel Tower, wearing red to signify the red line that civil society was drawing, against the fossil fuel industry, against the failure of the world's governments to achieve a fair, ambitious, and binding agreement, and against the calamity that is assured if the agreement's stated aspirational goal of no more than 1.5 degrees C temperature increase is not achieved.

CHAPTER 7

THE LGBTQ REVOLUTION

In the early-morning hours of Saturday, June 28, 1969, eight New York City police officers entered a gay bar in Greenwich Village called the Stonewall Inn. "We're taking the place!" the officers shouted.

It was supposed to be just another routine indignity inflicted on gay men and lesbians. But the ones who took power that night were not the cops; it was the nascent gay and lesbian movement (now referred to as lesbian, gay, bisexual, transgender, and queer, or LGBTQ). As the police began dragging some of the patrons out of the bar, gay men and lesbians fought back, sparking three days of rioting. This act of defiance was "the shot heard round the world . . . crucial because it sounded the rally for that movement," wrote historian Lillian Faderman.[1]

The officers were from New York City's public morals squad.

They came in four unmarked police cars and headed to the Stonewall at Seventh Avenue and Christopher Street. This was one of a series of raids on gay bars initiated by the new commanding officer at the local precinct.

The Stonewall was a dance bar that was operated by the Gambino crime family without a liquor license. Drag queens, hustlers, and minors were the regular clientele. Many of the bar's patrons had attended the funeral of actress Judy Garland hours earlier.

The morals squad pulled up to the Stonewall Inn at midnight. Deputy Inspector Seymour Pine was in charge. What happened next was captured on the remarkable radio documentary *Remembering Stonewall*, which was produced in 1989 by Dave Isay, a gifted documentarian who got his start in radio when he walked into our newsroom at New York's Pacifica Radio station, WBAI. He would go on to found StoryCorps, the largest oral history project in the United States. The documentary later aired on *Democracy Now!*

Officer Pine, interviewed for the documentary, recounted, "For some reason, things were different this night. As we were bringing the prisoners out, they were resisting. One drag queen, as we put her in the car, opened the door on the other side and jumped out, at which time we had to chase that person. And he was caught, put back into the car. He made another attempt to get out . . . the other door. And at that point, we had to handcuff the person. From this point on, things really began to get crazy."

Sylvia Rivera, a pioneering LGBTQ activist, said in *Remembering Stonewall*, "People started gathering in front of the Sheridan Square Park right across the street from Stonewall. People were upset—'No, we're not going to go!'—and people started screaming and hollering."

Robert Rivera (no relation to Sylvia) was at the bar that night. He described himself as a man who dressed as a woman for many years. "The police were escorting the queens out of the bar and into the paddy wagon. And there was this one particularly outrageously beautiful queen with stacks and stacks of Elizabeth Taylor–style hair, and she was asking them not to push her. And they continued to push her, and she turned around, and she mashed the cop with her high heel. She knocked him down, and then she proceeded to frisk him for the keys to the handcuffs that were on her. She got them, and she undid herself and passed them to another queen that was behind her."

"That's when all hell broke loose," said Pine. "And then we had to get back into the Stonewall."

Pine and the other police officers retreated inside the bar and barricaded the doors. The crowd outside had swelled, and they began throwing things. Garbage cans, cobblestones, trash—anything—went crashing through the windows. Pine, who'd written the US Army's manual on hand-to-hand combat for World War II and survived a mine explosion at the Battle of the Bulge, said later, "There was never any time that I felt more scared than I felt that night."[2] It took the arrival of a police tactical team to free the cops from inside the bar.

Years of pent-up rage at being humiliated, arrested, and abused at the hands of police and the larger society poured out that night on the streets of Greenwich Village, as LGBTQ people revolted and fought back.

Mama Jean was emerging from a lesbian bar called Cookies. "We were coming out of the gay bar going toward Eighth Street, and that's when we saw everything happening, blasting away—people getting beat up; police coming from every direction, hitting women as well as men with their nightsticks; gay men running down the street with blood all over their face. We decided right then and there—whether we're scared or not, we didn't think about it—we just jumped in," she recounted in *Remembering Stonewall.*

> I remember one cop coming at me, hitting me with the nightstick on the back of my legs. I broke loose, and I went after him. I grabbed his nightstick. My girlfriend went behind him. She was a strong son of a gun. I wanted him to feel the same pain I felt. And I kept on saying to him, "How do you like the pain? Do you like it?"
>
> It's like just when you see a man protecting his own life. They weren't the "queens" that people call them; they were men fighting for their lives. And I'd fight alongside them any day, no matter how old I was.

Sylvia Rivera said, "I wanted to do every destructive thing that I could think of at that time to hurt anyone that had hurt us through the years." Rivera described "this queen is going completely bananas, you know, jumping on [a taxi], hitting the windshield. The next thing you know, the taxicab was being turned over, the cars were being turned over, windows were shattering all over the place, fires were burning around the place. It was beautiful. It really was. It was really beautiful."

The running street battles with police continued intermittently for two more nights as LGBTQ people poured into the streets of Greenwich Village to revel in their newfound freedom.

"A lot of heads were bashed, people were hurt. But it didn't hurt their true feelings," said Rivera. "They all came back for more and more. That's when you could tell that nothing could stop us at that time—or at any time in the future."

Beat poet Allen Ginsberg observed famously during the

uprising, "The guys there were so beautiful—they've lost that wounded look that fags all had ten years ago."

The Stonewall uprising had an immediate and far-reaching impact. Gay and lesbian groups soon sprung up around the country. At the time of Stonewall, there were fifty to sixty gay rights groups in the United States. A year later, there were at least 1,500. Within two years, there were 2,500. One of the most significant groups, the Gay Liberation Front, was formed immediately after Stonewall.

The uprising emboldened and inspired countless LGBTQ people. Henry Baird was a soldier in Vietnam when he heard about the uprising. "I remember I was having lunch in the army mess, reading the armed forces news summary of the day, and there was a short paragraph describing a riot led by homosexuals in Greenwich Village against the police," he recalled in *Remembering Stonewall*. "And my heart was filled with joy . . . Secretly within myself, I decided that . . . if I should survive to come back stateside, I would come out as a gay person. And I did."

The activism inspired by Stonewall cross-pollinated other movements. Sylvia Rivera was also a central player in the Young Lords, a radical group founded by Puerto Ricans in 1968 that was modeled on the Black Panther Party; *Democracy Now!* cohost Juan González was one of the cofounders of the Young Lords and its minister of information. In late July 1969, the group staged their first action in an effort to force the City of New York to increase garbage pickup in East Harlem. The Young Lords would go on to inspire activists around the country as they occupied churches and hospitals in an attempt to open the spaces to community projects, and provide services such as a free breakfast program, free health care, and cultural events for working-class Latino communities. The group also called for self-determination for all Puerto Ricans; independence for the island of Puerto Rico; community control of institutions and land;

freedom for all political prisoners; and the withdrawal of US troops from Vietnam, Puerto Rico, and other areas.

In 1970 the Young Lords formed both a gay caucus and a women's caucus to address gender discrimination and discrimination against gays and lesbians. Johanna Fernández, professor of history at Baruch College–CUNY and author of *When the World Was Their Stage: A History of the Young Lords Party, 1968–1976,* said on *Democracy Now!*, "One of the least-written-about aspects of the gay and lesbian liberation movement is that it was people of color who rioted against their oppression in the Lower East Side. And Sylvia Rivera was part of that movement, and she was a member of the Young Lords."

DEATH-DEFYING ACTIVISM

In 1981 the US Centers for Disease Control's weekly update reported five unrelated cases of pneumonia in gay men in the Los Angeles area. Two of them had already died. The report generated little interest. This was the silent, deadly start of the AIDS epidemic. The scourge gave LGBTQ activism new urgency and demanded creative new tactics.

As the death toll mounted, people with AIDS, or acquired immune deficiency syndrome, and their allies found themselves up against incredible odds: a government that refused to acknowledge the disease (President Reagan never mentioned AIDS publicly for more than six years); government bureaucrats who dragged their feet on drug approval; right-wing and religious leaders who called the disease "God's revenge on gays"; brutal police who wore rubber gloves while beating up activists; and a homophobic general population that stood by watching silently.

AIDS activists needed a way to break through this deadly complacency. Taking inspiration from the civil rights movement, their creative confrontations brought unprecedented attention to this hidden plague:

- October 11, 1988: the newly formed AIDS Coalition to Unleash Power—ACT UP—shuts down the US Food and Drug Administration building in Washington. Its members demanded increased funding for and easier access to promising AIDS drugs.
- September 14, 1989: ACT UP members stage a demonstration on the floor of the New York Stock Exchange, stopping trading for the first time in history. The activists demanded that traders sell stock in Burroughs Wellcome (now GlaxoSmithKline), which was the only maker of the AIDS drug AZT, for which it charged exorbitant prices.
- December 1989: ACT UP members lay down in the center aisle of St. Patrick's Cathedral in New York City to protest the role of the Catholic Church interfering with AIDS education in the public schools.

As AIDS continued its deadly course, activists grew increasingly frustrated at how little the media covered the disease and at the misplaced priorities of the government. The two issues converged in January 1991, when President George H. W. Bush launched the Persian Gulf War. John Weir, a member of ACT UP in New York City, was planning for a protest dubbed "Day of Desperation" in New York City, which aimed to protest both the war and the inadequate response to AIDS.

Weir and two other activists decided to make a surprise appearance on *CBS Evening News* with Dan Rather the night before the Day of Desperation. Another ACT UP member, Ann Northrup, was a former CBS producer. She provided them with directions to Rather's studio and an old CBS ID tag to gain entrance to the building.

On January 22, 1991, Dan Rather began his broadcast in the usual fashion: "This is the *CBS Evening News*, Dan Rather reporting. Good evening—"

Suddenly John Weir's head popped into the frame in front of Rather. "Fight AIDS not Arabs! Fight AIDS not Arabs!" he shouted with two others.

Rather stared straight ahead but appeared startled. He announced urgently, "We're going to go to take a quick break for a commercial now." Studio technicians grabbed the men, hauled them off the set, and they were later taken to jail.

A grim-faced Rather appeared after the break. "I want to apologize to you for the way the broadcast came on the air tonight. There were some rude people here. They tried to stage a demonstration. They've been ejected from the studio, but our apologies for the way we began our coverage of the Gulf War. We will continue after these messages."

Meanwhile, another ACT UP group was staging an action a few blocks away at PBS on the set of *The MacNeil/Lehrer News-Hour*. Activists sat down during the live broadcast and chained themselves to chairs and a desk. The action prompted a discussion between the hosts. Robin MacNeil explained to the viewing audience what had happened:

"There's been a demonstration in our studio. It was a group of nonviolent demonstrators from ACT UP who complained that we and the media are spending too much time and attention on the war in the Middle East, which they say will never kill as many people as are dying of AIDS. And I told them that this program has spent a lot of time on the AIDS matter and will be covering it more in the future."

A reporter questioned the disrupters afterward: "Don't you think this is an immature and silly way to get your point across to the country?"

The activists responded, "No, we think spending hundreds of billions of dollars bombing people in another continent is a silly and immature way to get a point across." [3]

As Ann Northrup recounted later on *Democracy Now!*, "I thought it was fantastic because this interruption of the CBS News was seen all over the world. CNN ran it as a story, and I remember the columnist Jimmy Breslin told me that he was in Israel at the time trying to cover the Gulf War, and he saw it on CNN. This did make an impact everywhere.

"The whole point of all these actions was to get AIDS into the news, to get it talked about, to get it recognized and looked at as an issue," she explained. "Because what happens is these issues we care about get ignored by the mainstream media. What we've learned as activists is that we have to do things that will grab attention to get the issue covered. Our aim has always been not being liked personally, but simply do whatever we need to do to get these things covered."

She says of ACT UP: "We do not defer to authority. And I think that's what has made us so effective. We are willing to speak the truth under any circumstances."

Out of tragedy, a new direction emerged for those fighting for LGBTQ rights. "AIDS changed our movement from a movement fighting just to be let alone—don't harass us, don't attack us, don't beat us up, don't blackmail us—into a movement [to be] let in," said Evan Wolfson, an attorney who founded Freedom to Marry in 2003 and is a pioneer of the marriage equality movement. "Let us into the protection and safety net of marriage, of family. That really set the stage for the robust, rich marriage conversation that we've been pursuing." [4]

EDIE WINDSOR'S DAY IN COURT

In March 2013 the US Supreme Court heard several arguments about same-sex marriage. One case was about the controversial California ballot initiative known as Proposition 8, which banned same-sex marriages in that state. Another case challenged the constitutionality of the federal Defense of Marriage Act, or DOMA, the legal travesty that defined marriage in federal law as only between a man and a woman. That case was called *United States v. Windsor*. Edie Windsor, then eighty-three years old, was married to a woman, Thea Spyer. They were a couple for forty-four years.

Edie and Thea met in the mid-1960s in New York's Greenwich Village. They hit it off. In 1967 Thea proposed marriage to Edie even though they knew it wasn't a possibility. The couple lived together as though they were married, buying a house together, sharing their earnings and living life. In 1975 Spyer was diagnosed with multiple sclerosis. Edie cared for Thea as her MS progressed, causing paralysis and forcing her into a wheelchair. When, in 2007, doctors told Thea that she had only one year to live, she reiterated her proposal to Edie. The couple flew to Toronto, and on May 22, 2007, they were wed in a ceremony officiated by Canada's first openly gay judge, Justice Harvey Brownstone.

Within a year, New York State, where the couple lived, officially recognized out-of-state same-sex marriages, although it took the state several more years to legalize such marriages performed in-state. With their Canadian marriage license and acceptance by

New York State, one major institution remained that refused to recognize their formal declaration of lifelong love and commitment: the United States government. As Edie would soon learn, this would have major tax implications.

Congress passed DOMA months before a national election, with solid bipartisan support. DOMA was signed into law by President Bill Clinton, on September 21, 1996. The law stated: "In determining the meaning of any Act of Congress, or of any ruling, regulation, or interpretation of the various administrative bureaus and agencies of the United States, the word 'marriage' means only a legal union between one man and one woman as husband and wife, and the word 'spouse' refers only to a person of the opposite sex who is a husband or a wife."

The passage of DOMA energized LGBTQ activists. In the years since his presidency—and in the course of his wife Hillary's subsequent campaigns for senate and president—Bill Clinton was often questioned or confronted about his support for DOMA. Finally, Clinton was forced to admit that he had been wrong to sign the legislation. In 2013 he wrote in the *Washington Post* that DOMA is "incompatible with our Constitution. Because Section 3 of the Act defines marriage as being between a man and a woman, same-sex couples who are legally married in nine states and the District of Columbia are denied the benefits of more than a thousand federal statutes and programs available to other married couples."

Thea Spyer died February 5, 2009, at the age of seventy-seven. After losing her wife, Edie suffered a heart attack. As she recovered, she learned that federal estate taxes on the value of what Thea had left her would cost her $363,000—but would have been $0 if the government recognized their marriage as legal. Edie, a lesbian rights activist for decades, decided to fight back. She sued the US government.

Edie prevailed in the federal district court and then in the federal appeals court. US Attorney General Eric Holder announced in February 2011 that the Obama administration would not be defending DOMA in court. You might think that would be the end of it. Enter BLAG, the five-member Bipartisan Legal Advisory Group of the US Congress. The three Republicans—House Speaker John Boehner, House Majority Leader Eric Cantor, and House Majority Whip Kevin McCarthy—voted to instruct the House Office of General Counsel to defend DOMA, since the Obama administration had declined. The House hired the George W. Bush administration's solicitor general, Paul Clement, to defend DOMA. The House spent $2.3 million in taxpayer funds on the case.[5]

United States v. Windsor was argued on March 27, 2013. Outside the Supreme Court, still wearing the engagement pin given to her by Thea back in 1967, Edie said, "I know that the spirit of my late spouse Thea Spyer is right here watching and listening."

In a profile in *Out* magazine, Edie recalled, "The first time we ever danced using the wheelchair—I would sit in her lap in the wheelchair—the song on the radio was, 'There's a place for us, there's a time for us.' I can't even sing it because I cry."

The song, "Somewhere" from *West Side Story*, begins:

Someday . . . Somewhere.
We'll find a new way of living . . .

In June 2013, in a resounding victory for marriage equality, the Supreme Court ruled that married same-sex couples were entitled to federal benefits, as it struck down the 1996 Defense of Marriage Act. When the 5-to-4 decision on DOMA was announced, an enormous cheer went up outside the courtroom, and the crowd started chanting "DOMA is dead!" as couples hugged and cried.

At a press conference, Edie Windsor reacted to the ruling in *United States v. Windsor*:

> I'm honored and humbled and overjoyed to be here today to represent not only the thousands of Americans whose lives have been adversely impacted by the Defense of Marriage Act, but those whose hopes and dreams have been constricted by the same discriminatory law. Children born today will grow up in a world without DOMA, and those same children who happen to be gay will be free to love and get married as Thea and I did, but with the same federal benefits, protections, and dignity as everyone else. If I had to survive Thea, what a glorious way to do it. And she would be so pleased.

Minutes after DOMA was struck down, the Supreme Court ruled that supporters of the ban on same-sex marriage in California did not have standing to appeal a lower-court ruling that overturned the Proposition 8 ban. This gave the green light for same-sex weddings to proceed in California, the most populous state in the nation.

The legal victories were milestones. But it was the LGBTQ rights movement that deserved the credit for changing social attitudes and challenging laws that ultimately made the court decisions possible.

Marriage equality had gone from distant dream to reality.

FLAMES OF INTOLERANCE

Conservatives have long used same-sex marriage as a reliable get-out-the-vote tool. Measures to restrict same-sex marriage were placed on ballots in large part to drive voter turnout to elect conservative candidates. President George W. Bush might owe his 2004 reelection to the fact that eleven states had proposed state constitutional amendments to ban marriage equality—notably the swing state of Ohio, where the marriage ban won with 61 percent of the vote that year, and Bush barely won with 51 percent, his smallest margin in any state. Had Bush lost Ohio, he would have lost the election to his Democratic opponent, Senator John Kerry.[6]

Then the tide changed. From 2013 to 2015, laws banning same-sex marriage were struck down in one state after another. But the flames of intolerance were not easily extinguished.

In February 2015 Roy Moore, chief justice of the Alabama Supreme Court, released an order that no same-sex marriage licenses be granted in the state. He was responding to a decision by a federal district court that struck down Alabama's ban on gay marriage. When the US Supreme Court declined to hear the state's appeal of the ruling, the ban was legally overturned, and Alabama became the thirty-seventh state to allow marriage equality—except for the counties that sided with a defiant Chief Justice Moore and continued to refuse to issue same-sex marriage licenses.

Moore is a radical conservative and a strident evangelical Christian. Back in 2003 he made national headlines when he placed a massive granite block, on which were carved the Ten Commandments, inside the Alabama Judicial Building in Montgomery. He defied a federal court order to remove the religious monument, which resulted in his removal from office. Despite being disgraced, Moore was reelected in 2012. He suggested at an evangelical Christian event that the First Amendment protects only Christians, as, he claimed, that was the religion of the nation's founders. On the TV program *Good Morning America*, he speculated what might follow were same-sex marriages allowed:

"Do they stop with one man and one man, or one woman and

one woman, or do they go to multiple marriages? Or do they go with marriages between men and their daughters, or women and their sons?"

Defying Moore's monumental intolerance, loving couples still wed in Alabama. The first couple to marry in Montgomery following the federal court ruling was Tori Sisson and Shanté Wolfe, both of whom adopted the surname Wolfe-Sisson. When I asked Tori how it felt to be the first couple married there after the Alabama ban was overturned, she said, "It feels like we need a nap."

Shanté explained their insistence on marrying in Alabama: "We said that we wouldn't go anywhere else because we work here, we pay our taxes here, and we're not going to go to another state just to come back and our union not be recognized. We've had several people tell us, 'Well, just go to New York, or just go somewhere else.' But no, we had faith that Alabama would move in a positive direction. And it has." Tori helped bring about this historic victory as the Alabama field organizer for the Human Rights Campaign, a national LGBTQ rights organization.

Intolerance persists, but people push back with a force more powerful: the force of movements, of grassroots organizing. It's what Rosa Parks did sixty years earlier in 1955, along with thousands of others, challenging segregation with the Montgomery bus boycott.

Bryan Stevenson, a Montgomery-based attorney who is founder and executive director of the Equal Justice Initiative, told me on *Democracy Now!*, "This is a state where you sometimes have to stand when other people are sitting. It's a place where you have to speak when other people are quiet . . . This is a state that's going to continually have to confront its resistance to complying with the Constitution and respecting the dignity and aspirations of all people."

HATE DOESN'T PAY

Bigotry isn't limited to the South. One month after same-sex couples married in Alabama, Republican Indiana Governor Mike Pence launched a wave of intolerance by signing into law Indiana's controversial Religious Freedom Restoration Act (RFRA) in March 2015.

The law's supporters claimed it protected religious freedom. Opponents called it a thinly veiled attack on the rights of LGBTQ people. The law allowed individuals and businesses to refuse service to LGBTQ people, based solely on their sexual orientation or gender identity. It provoked a national backlash, with prominent people, large corporations, and city and state governments condemning or boycotting Indiana.

Charles Barkley, former NBA basketball star and now a sports commentator, issued a statement declaring, "As long as antigay legislation exists in any state, I strongly believe big events such as the Final Four and Super Bowl should not be held in those states' cities." Indianapolis was hosting the Final Four basketball championship tournament April 4–6, 2015.

The University of Connecticut's men's basketball coach, Kevin Ollie, announced he wouldn't attend the games, respecting Connecticut Governor Dannel Malloy's travel ban forbidding state employees from using public funds to go to Indiana. Pat Haden, former NFL quarterback and current athletic director at the University of Southern California, announced he was boycotting a college football meeting held in Indianapolis at the same time as the Final Four. He tweeted: "I am the proud father of a gay son. In his honor, I will not be attending the CFP [College Football Playoff] committee meeting in Indy this week. #EmbraceDiversity." If the National Collegiate Athletic Association (NCAA) moved the games to another state, it would be an economic disaster for Indiana and a reputation killer for Governor Pence.

Speaking of sons, Governor Asa Hutchinson of Arkansas, where the legislature followed Indiana's by passing a similar RFRA law the same week, said he would not sign the bill into law. He cited his son Seth, a union organizer, who had signed a MoveOn.org petition against the law.

Seth Hutchinson wrote in a Facebook post that he was "proud to have made a small contribution to the overall effort to stop discrimination against the LGBT community in Arkansas."

"I love and respect my father very much, but sometimes we have political disagreements, just as many families do," he wrote. "Most importantly, I hope that the groundswell of grassroots opposition to HB 1228 and other similar discriminatory bills around the country will energize more Americans and help create a long-lasting drive for change in this country, on many issues." [7]

Governor Hutchinson had another reason to walk back his support for discrimination: the CEO of Walmart, the most powerful employer in Arkansas, asked the governor to veto the anti-LGBTQ bill.

Numerous institutions threw their economic clout into the battle against the discriminatory bills. The NCAA expressed deep concern about Indiana's law. Even the National Association for Stock Car Auto Racing (NASCAR) announced that it was "disappointed by the recent legislation passed in Indiana. We will not embrace nor participate in exclusion or intolerance. We are committed to diversity and inclusion within our sport."

New York and Washington joined Connecticut in banning state-funded travel to Indiana, as did New York City, Denver, Seattle, and San Francisco. Corporations from Nike, to Apple, to

Marriott International, denounced the law. Angie's List, the popular home-service referral website, halted a $40 million headquarters expansion in Indianapolis.

Under enormous pressure, after first refusing, Pence asked the state legislature to "fix" the bill, to "clarify" that the language in the law does not allow discrimination based on sexual orientation. Many opponents said they would settle on nothing less than a total repeal. As one protester's sign read, "You can't clarify hate."

Less than a week after he signed the original Religious Freedom Restoration Act in a private ceremony, Governor Pence, flanked by business leaders, signed a revision specifying that the law did not authorize anti-LGBTQ discrimination.

Bart Peterson, an executive at the pharmaceutical giant Eli Lilly and Company (and former Indianapolis mayor), hailed the change, saying, "For the first time ever, the words 'sexual orientation' and 'gender identity' appear in Indiana statute . . . in the context of nondiscrimination." Arkansas Governor Asa Hutchinson signed a similarly updated bill.

Following the signing of the revised bill, the ACLU said in a statement: "The events in Indiana over the last week represent a dramatic change in the way our country reacts to discrimination hiding under the guise of religion."

FREE AT LAST

On June 26, 2015, the US Supreme Court ruled that all fifty states must permit same-sex couples the "fundamental right to marry." The ruling put an end to same-sex marriage bans that remained in thirteen states—Arkansas, Georgia, Kentucky, Louisiana,

Michigan, Mississippi, most of Missouri, Nebraska, North Dakota, Ohio, South Dakota, Tennessee, and Texas. The court's decision impacted some seventy thousand couples living in those states, out of an estimated one million same-sex couples nationwide.

Writing for the majority, Justice Anthony Kennedy said, "Changed understandings of marriage are characteristic of a Nation where new dimensions of freedom become apparent to new generations." He added that it "demeans gays and lesbians for the State to lock them out of a central institution of the Nation's society." This was the Supreme Court's recognition of how the LGBTQ rights movement had permanently changed the human rights landscape.

President Obama hailed the landmark ruling but pointed out that not everyone was in agreement: "I know that Americans of good will continue to hold a wide range of views on this issue. Opposition, in some cases, has been based on sincere and deeply held beliefs. All of us who welcome today's news should be mindful of that fact, recognize different viewpoints, revere our deep commitment to religious freedom. But today should also give us hope that on the many issues with which we grapple, often painfully, real change is possible."

April DeBoer and Jayne Rowse were two of the plaintiffs in the Supreme Court's same-sex marriage case. They initially went to court in Michigan to win the right to jointly adopt each other's children. They then challenged the state's ban on same-sex marriage, since joint adoption in Michigan is tied to marriage. DeBoer told *Democracy Now!* a few days after the Supreme Court ruling, "We are happy that our family will finally be a legal, recognized family once Jayne and I put our wedding together and get married and second-parent adopt our children."

Jayne Rowse added that the court "recognized that we were

not second-class citizens anymore and that our children deserve protections like everyone else."

I asked Rowse if she ever thought this day would come. "I've been out since I was sixteen, and it was always a dream in the LGBTQ community, but I don't think any of us ever thought it would happen in our lifetime," she replied. "Hopefully in our kids' lifetimes, but not in ours."

Rowse and DeBoer were married in August 2015. Their wedding ceremony was officiated by US District judge Bernard Friedman, who heard arguments on the couple's lawsuit against the state of Michigan challenging the state's adoption code, which banned them from jointly adopting each other's children unless they were married. "Every citizen of the United States . . . owes you a big debt of gratitude," declared Judge Friedman before pronouncing the couple legally married.[8]

Achieving marriage equality for LGBTQ people was an enormous milestone in a much larger struggle. But there are many who feel that marriage is a conservative and patriarchal institution that just reinforces the status quo.

Katherine Franke, a professor of gender law at Columbia Law School and the author of *Wedlocked: The Perils of Marriage Equality*, writes, "As strangers to marriage for so long, we've created loving and committed forms of family, care, and attachment that far exceed, and often improve on, the narrow legal definition of marriage. Many of us are not ready to abandon those nonmarital ways of loving once we can legally marry."[9]

Democracy Now! hosted a debate between same-sex marriage critic Scot Nakagawa, a blogger and senior partner at the social justice think tank ChangeLab, and Marc Solomon, national campaign director of Freedom to Marry. Nakagawa explained: "The marriage issue, while very important and a step toward greater freedoms, is not the whole ball of wax, as there's much more that we need to fight for. I think we recognize that most people in our society do not live in traditional nuclear family arrangements. Most of us actually live outside of those arrangements and deserve to also have the protections of our government."

Nakagawa continued, "Marriage is an essentially conservative institution, and the demand for marriage is an essentially conservative demand. . . . It doesn't fundamentally change the way that society views family or the way government provides for families."

Marc Solomon countered that marriage is "something that a lot of same-sex couples really want, and want to be able to take care of their families and want the societal recognition. But there are also plenty of other needs that our community has, from employment nondiscrimination to youth suicide, to seniors who really don't have great care. So I think the challenge is to use the power and the momentum that we're building through the marriage fights to secure other gains."

Edie Windsor had earlier offered her perspective on this debate:

Many people ask me, "Why get married?" I was seventy-seven, Thea was seventy-five . . . It turns out marriage is different. And I've asked a number of long-range couples, gay couples, who then got married, "Was it different the next morning?" And the answer is always, "Yes, it's a huge difference." When our marriage appeared in the *New York Times*, we heard from literally hundreds of people—I mean, little playmates and schoolmates and colleagues and friends and relatives all congratulating us and sending love, because we were married. So it's a magic word. For anybody who doesn't understand why we want it and why we need it, okay, it is magic.

Nakagawa conceded that marriage "does kind of work like magic in making people feel as though relationships are legitimate." But, he added, "I hope we can look beyond that and start to see more and more kinds of family arrangements as legitimate.

"My objection is to the framing of [same-sex marriage] in the mainstream media—that it is the last great issue; that it is the future of the LGBT movement," he argued. "I think that what we need to do is speak beyond that and talk beyond marriage, about what the whole agenda is and where marriage fits into it."

Following the Supreme Court marriage equality decision, grassroots LGBTQ activists called for large, national organizations to also focus their attention and resources on other pressing issues, including lesbian and gay refugees and asylum seekers, the plight of homeless youth ostracized by their families, and the disproportionately high levels of violence experienced by transgender people.

Among those heeding this call are transgender people who are challenging the very notion of a gender binary. Real freedom, they say, means being free to be your true self.

BEYOND THE GENDER BINARY

At around midnight on June 5, 2011, CeCe McDonald, a twenty-three-year-old African American transgender woman, was walking with four of her friends past a Minneapolis bar called Schooner Tavern. They were on their way to pick up a few groceries. They often went at night to avoid the stares and homophobic and transphobic slurs that they endured routinely on the streets.

As they passed the bar, a group of cigarette-smoking white people began hurling insults. The group included forty-seven-year-old Dean Schmitz and his forty-year-old ex-girlfriend, Molly Flaherty.

"Look at that boy dressed as a girl, tucking his dick in!" spat Schmitz. "You niggers need to go back to Africa!" The torrent of insults continued: "Bitches with dicks!" "Faggot lovers!" "Rapists!" [10]

CeCe mustered her courage. "Excuse me," she shot back. "We are people, and you need to respect us."

Moments later, Flaherty swung a bottle and ripped open CeCe's face. Mayhem ensued. CeCe grabbed Flaherty's hair, and CeCe's friends swung fists and belts. The groups finally separated, and CeCe walked quickly away from the scene. She got half a block away when her friend called out, "Watch your back!"

CeCe turned and saw Schmitz charging toward her. He was high on meth, though she didn't know it. "Come here, bitch!" he shouted.

CeCe feared for her life. She moved backward and reached into her purse, where she grabbed fabric scissors that she used as a fashion student at Minneapolis Community & Technical College. As Schmitz lunged toward her, she plunged the scissors into him. It pierced a swastika tattoo on his chest—and his heart. Schmitz collapsed in a pool of blood on the sidewalk and died later. CeCe flagged down a police car and was promptly arrested.

CeCe McDonald's case helped turn a national spotlight on the violence and discrimination faced by transgender women of color. At the time, the murder rate for gay and transgender people in the United States was at an all-time high. The National Coalition of Anti-Violence Programs documented thirty hate-related murders of LGBTQ people in 2011; 40 percent of the victims were transgender women of color. A staggering 41 percent of people who are transgender or gender-nonconforming have attempted suicide, nearly nine times the national average. [11]

Rai'vyn Cross, one of CeCe's best friends, described the harassment that she and CeCe had faced for years. "We experience this on a daily basis when we wake up, when we go to sleep, if it's in a public place or if it's just outside, period. Transphobic slurs, racial slurs. I mean, we best deal with it just by just, you know, just wiping it off, just keep going on, just staying strong."

Nearly a year after the attack in Minneapolis, CeCe McDonald stood trial on charges of second-degree manslaughter. The judge in her case rejected key evidence, including information about Schmitz's swastika tattoo and his three prior convictions of assault. Facing up to eighty years in prison, CeCe McDonald took a plea deal that sentenced her to forty-one months behind bars. McDonald was held in a men's prison, even though she identifies as a woman.

In the eyes of her supporters, CeCe McDonald was jailed for defending herself against the bigotry and violence that transgender people face so often—and that's so rarely punished.

CeCe McDonald walked free after serving nineteen months in prison. Shortly after getting out of jail in 2014, she appeared on *Democracy Now!* with Laverne Cox, a transgender actress, producer, and activist who stars in the popular Netflix show *Orange Is the New Black*. She plays Sophia Burset, a transgender woman who is in prison for using credit card fraud to finance her gender transition. On the TV show, her real-life twin brother, M. Lamar, plays Sophia in flashbacks when she was a married husband and father, before her transition. Cox produced a documentary about McDonald called *Free CeCe*.

I asked CeCe how it felt to be out of jail. "I can just say it's a really, really good feeling to be back with everyone," she said, "and to actually use this platform that I have now to educate people and to inform people about the violence against trans women, about the prison-industrial complex, to let people know about hatred toward women and trans women, and just, you know, be more willing and open to help people understand what it's like for me and for other trans women who are in prison, and people in general who have to deal with the policies and the martial law of prison."

For Laverne Cox, CeCe's plight hit home. "So often our lives are treated as if they don't matter," Cox told me. "That's why CeCe's case has meant so much to me. I very easily could have been CeCe. Many times, I've walked down the streets of New York, and I've experienced harassment. I was kicked once on the street, and very easily that could have escalated into a situation that CeCe faced. And it's a situation that too many trans women of color face all over this country. The act of merely walking down the street is often a contested act, not only from the citizenry, but also from the police."

Trans lives have been routinely criminalized. Among all trans people, 16 percent have been incarcerated; among black trans persons, 47 percent have been jailed, while 30 percent of American Indian trans people, 21 percent of trans women, and 10 percent of trans men have been incarcerated. I asked Alisha Williams of the Sylvia Rivera Law Project how you change those numbers.

"We have a lot of legal remedies that reduce harm that people in prison are facing, but, really, the answer is to keep people out of prison and to provide safe spaces, safe access to health care, to employment, to education," Williams said.

Laverne Cox added:

> I think the bigger picture is: How do we begin to create spaces in our culture where we don't stigmatize trans identity, where we really create spaces of gender self-determination? It is so often acceptable to make fun of trans people, to ridicule trans people. When we look at the epidemic of violence against trans folk, so many people sort of think that our identities are inherently deceptive, our identities are inherently sort of suspect, and then we should be criminalized because of that . . .

How do we begin to create spaces where we accept trans people on trans people's own terms, and really listen and let trans people lead the discussions in terms of who we are and what the discussion about our lives should be?

Cox explained, "Gender is so deeply complicated. It's about more than genitalia. We assign people genders at birth. No one is born anything. We actually name and impose that on someone. And it's really important with trans folks to listen to how they describe their own experiences."

CeCe McDonald reflected, "It's rare that you hear about a trans woman living happily and long and having this glorious life where she dies of old age—natural causes or whatever." She cited Transgender Day of Remembrance, an annual observance on November 20 that honors the memory of those whose lives were lost in acts of anti-transgender violence. "We have to make Trans Day of Remembrance [a] Trans Day of Celebration."

During the 1969 Stonewall uprising, LGBTQ people who had been forced to live in the shadows fought to come out and reclaim their humanity. That spirit lives on in those fighting today for transgender rights.

"We need to celebrate our lives," said CeCe McDonald. "We need to celebrate being human."

CHAPTER 8

WHEN THE KILLER WEARS A BADGE

41 shots cut through the night
You're kneeling over his body in the vestibule
Praying for his life
Is it a gun, is it a knife
Is it a wallet, this is your life
It ain't no secret
It ain't no secret
No secret, my friend
You can get killed just for living
In your American skin.

—Bruce Springsteen, "American Skin (41 Shots)"

Amadou Diallo, a twenty-two-year-old immigrant from Guinea, was returning home after going out to get a meal after work. It was just after midnight on February 4, 1999. Diallo, a slight, hard-working man and a devout Muslim, sold socks, gloves, and videos on the street. He was saving for college and sent home money to his family in Africa. He shared an apartment with two other men in the Soundview neighborhood of the Bronx.

As Diallo stood outside his Bronx home about to go inside, an unmarked Ford Taurus rolled up. Four men in street clothes got out, with guns drawn. The men were members of the New York Police Department's notoriously aggressive Street Crimes Unit (SCU), the motto of which was "We Own the Night." As Diallo stood in the vestibule of his home, all four officers suddenly opened fire. Diallo died in a hail of forty-one bullets, nineteen of which hit him. The officers said they thought Diallo was holding a gun. It turned out that he was just holding his wallet. Diallo was unarmed and had no criminal record.

In the weeks following Diallo's killing, thousands of people marched in protest. A popular chant heard at the rallies went, "Police training 101! It's a wallet, not a gun!" Over eight hundred people were arrested outside New York police headquarters in a campaign of civil disobedience. The outrage ran deep, and the arrested included a who's who of New York City's politicians, religious leaders, seniors, and students. Among those who went to jail to protest the Diallo killing were former Mayor David Dinkins, Congressmen Charles Rangel and Gregory Meeks, NAACP President (and former Congressman) Kweisi Mfume, and actors Ruby Dee, Ossie Davis, and Susan Sarandon. Numerous protesters demanded that the four officers be arrested and fired from the force.

New York City mayor Rudolph Giuliani denounced the protests. "This is a great publicity stunt—can't you figure it out?" he told reporters.[1]

Amadou Diallo was buried in his native Guinea. Government ministers greeted his coffin at the airport in Conakry, and Guinea's minister of foreign affairs accompanied the casket three hundred miles to Diallo's village for burial. His funeral was attended by fifteen hundred people.

The NYPD Street Crimes Unit had a violent history. Three of the four officers who shot Diallo had been involved in previous shootings—an unusual distinction in a police force in which 90 percent of officers never fire their weapons in the line of duty.[2] Two of the officers, Sean Carroll and Edward McMellon, fired sixteen shots each, emptying their weapons at the unarmed man. Officer Kenneth Boss fired his gun five times, and Officer Richard Murphy fired four times. The SCU, which was supposedly focused on taking guns off the streets, had an extraordinary number of its cases thrown out of court. Of the two hundred felony gun cases that the SCU brought in Manhattan in 1997 and 1998, half were thrown out. And prosecutors threw out eighteen thousand arrests made by the NYPD in 1998—double the number thrown out in 1994.[3]

The SCU presaged Giuliani's notorious stop-and-frisk policy, in which police stop and question a pedestrian, and then frisk him or her for weapons and other contraband. The policy had a racist bias from the start: from 2002 to 2011, blacks and Latinos comprised 90 percent of those who were stopped. No gun was retrieved in 99.9 percent of stops.

Six weeks after the killing of Amadou Diallo, the four officers were charged with second-degree murder, depraved indifference to human life, and reckless endangerment. But in December a judge ordered the trial moved from the Bronx, which is two-thirds black and Hispanic, 150 miles north to Albany, the state capital, which is 89 percent white. One year later, after a four-week trial, all four officers were acquitted of all charges.

Saikou Diallo, Amadou's father, called the verdict "the second killing" of his son.

The NYPD Street Crimes Unit was disbanded in 2002, following sustained protests after Diallo's death and the acquittal of the police. The Diallo family sued the officers and the city, saying that racial profiling by police was responsible for Amadou's death. In 2004, five years after his killing, the family agreed to a $3 million settlement with the city.

In 2014, following a years-long campaign by community and civil rights groups, newly elected New York City Mayor Bill de Blasio ended the stop-and-frisk program.

In October 2015 Kadiatou Diallo, the mother of Amadou Diallo, spoke at a rally of thousands of people in New York City against police brutality. Some forty families from across the United States impacted by police violence participated in the event, part of three days of protest called Rise Up October. The crowd chanted, "Don't shoot! Hands up! Don't shoot! Hands up!" This was a reference to the killing of Michael Brown, an unarmed African American teenager killed by police in Ferguson, Missouri, in 2014. (More on this later.)

"My son didn't die in vain," Kadiatou Diallo addressed the crowd. "He died so that we can have change. But the change has been long coming. We are still waiting. How many more victims were unjustly killed since Amadou Diallo? We cannot even begin to count."

Filmmaker Quentin Tarantino also spoke briefly at the rally. "What am I doing here? I'm here because I am a human being with a conscience. And when I see murder, I cannot stand by, and I have to call the murdered the murdered, and I have to call the murderers the murderers."

In response to Tarantino's comments branding some police murderers, police organizations in New York, New Jersey, Pennsylvania, Los Angeles, and elsewhere called for a boycott of

Tarantino's films, and said they would refuse to provide security for his projects.

The reaction to Tarantino was similar to what happened to rock legend Bruce Springsteen, whose song "American Skin (41 Shots)" was about the Diallo killing. When Springsteen first performed the song in 2000, he was denounced by Mayor Rudolph Giuliani and the New York police organizations, which called on officers to boycott his shows. Bob Lucente, president of the New York Fraternal Order of Police, called this favorite son of New York and New Jersey a "dirtbag" and "floating fag."

Springsteen played the song at all ten of his Madison Square Garden concerts in 2000, and the Diallo family expressed their appreciation at one of the shows they attended. Springsteen also performed the song in Tampa, Florida, in 2012, one month after the killing of Trayvon Martin, an unarmed African American teenager, who was shot to death by George Zimmerman, a white vigilante. Following Zimmerman's acquittal on murder charges, Springsteen dedicated the song to Martin.[4]

The Diallo killing was part of a long history in the United States, dating back to lynching and slavery, in which black lives did not matter. The killing sparked a national movement to confront racism, change consciousness—and history: Black Lives Matter.

COPS, COLOR, AND CARNAGE

Thanks to bystander videos that often capture the scenes, the world is now seeing what many people of color have been experiencing on a frequent—even routine—basis. Yet even when videos exist, many African American victims of police violence have found that the doors of justice remain firmly closed. All too often, when a police officer kills an unarmed person of color, the local grand jury decides not to indict: Not for murder. Not for manslaughter. Not for assault. Not even for reckless endangerment. If the killer wears a blue uniform and a badge, prosecution is extremely rare. A *Washington Post* analysis of shootings by on-duty police officers in the last decade revealed that in thousands of shootings, just fifty-four officers were charged.

"In an overwhelming majority of the cases where an officer was charged, the person killed was unarmed," the *Post* reported. "When prosecutors pressed charges, the *Post* analysis found, there were typically other factors that made the case exceptional, including: a victim shot in the back, a video recording of the incident, incriminating testimony from other officers, or allegations of a coverup."[5] Yet even in these extreme cases, officers are rarely convicted.

ONE YEAR'S TOLL

Consider just some of the African Americans who were killed at the hands of police from mid-2014 to mid-2015. This list is representative but far from complete:[6]

ERIC GARNER, FORTY-THREE (STATEN ISLAND, NEW YORK, JULY 17, 2014). The unarmed African American man was killed after NYPD officer Daniel Pantaleo placed him in a chokehold for allegedly selling loose cigarettes. Garner gasped, "I can't breathe!" eleven times. His death was declared a homicide. Result: a grand jury declined to indict Pantaleo or any other officer for Garner's death.

JOHN CRAWFORD III, TWENTY-TWO (BEAVERCREEK, OHIO, AUGUST 5, 2014). The unarmed African American man was shot and killed by police inside a Walmart store as he was holding a toy BB gun that he picked up off the store shelf while talking to his family on his cell phone. Result: the officers involved in the shooting were not charged.

MICHAEL BROWN, EIGHTEEN (FERGUSON, MISSOURI, AUGUST 9, 2014). The unarmed African American teen was shot and killed by Ferguson police officer Darren Wilson. Result: a grand jury declined to charge Officer Wilson.

LAQUAN MCDONALD, SEVENTEEN (CHICAGO, ILLINOIS, OCTOBER 20, 2014). The African American teen, who was walking away from police, was shot sixteen times by white Chicago police officer Jason Van Dyke. In April 2015, in the midst of a close reelection campaign for Chicago Mayor Rahm Emanuel, the city negotiated a preemptive $5 million payment to McDonald's family. Result: In November 2015, when the video was released to the public by court order, Officer Van Dyke was charged with first-degree murder.

AKAI GURLEY, TWENTY-EIGHT (BROOKLYN, NEW YORK, NOVEMBER 20, 2014). The unarmed African American man was killed in a stairwell after being shot by rookie NYPD officer Peter Liang. Result: Liang was charged with second-degree manslaughter, criminally negligent homicide, second-degree assault, reckless endangerment, and two counts of official misconduct.

TAMIR RICE, TWELVE (CLEVELAND, OHIO, NOVEMBER 22, 2014). The unarmed African American boy was shot and killed by police officer Timothy Loehmann within two seconds after he and his partner arrived at a playground where Rice was playing with a toy gun. Result: In December 2015, an Ohio grand jury declined to indict the officers.

TONY ROBINSON, NINETEEN (MADISON, WISCONSIN, MARCH 6, 2015). The unarmed African American teen was shot and killed by a white Madison police officer, Matt Kenny, after allegedly disrupting traffic. Result: the district attorney declined to bring charges against Officer Kenny.

ERIC HARRIS, FORTY-FOUR (TULSA, OKLAHOMA, APRIL 2, 2015). The unarmed African American man was killed after a seventy-three-year-old reserve police officer, Robert Bates, claimed to have confused his gun for a Taser. Result: Bates was charged with manslaughter. The judge allowed Bates to take a vacation to the Bahamas after he was charged, but Bates later opted not to go because he didn't feel like he could be "fully there in mind and spirit."[7] In September 2015, Tulsa County sheriff Stanley Glanz resigned after being indicted by a grand jury for withholding details related to the Harris killing and for misusing a travel stipend.

WALTER SCOTT, FIFTY (NORTH CHARLESTON, SOUTH CAROLINA, APRIL 4, 2015). The unarmed African American man was shot and killed by Officer Michael Slager while running away from a traffic stop for a broken taillight. Result: after a bystander video emerged showing Slager shooting Scott in the back, the officer was charged with murder.

FREDDIE GRAY, TWENTY-FIVE (BALTIMORE, MARYLAND, APRIL 19, 2015). The unarmed African American man died in police custody from an injury to his spinal cord, which was 80 percent severed, a week after his arrest for running away from police. Result: six Baltimore police officers were charged with a range of crimes, including murder, assault, and false imprisonment.

SANDRA BLAND, TWENTY-EIGHT (WALLER COUNTY, TEXAS, JULY 13, 2015). The unarmed African American woman was pulled over by Texas state trooper Brian Encinia for allegedly failing to signal when changing lanes. Encinia ordered her out of her car and threatened, "I'll light you up" with a Taser. Bland was arrested and sent to jail, where she was found dead three days later, hanging from a trash bag. Authorities say she committed suicide, a claim her family rejects. Result: In December 2015, a Texas grand jury declined to indict anyone for Bland's death. Trooper Encinia was charged with perjury.

SAMUEL DUBOSE, FORTY-THREE (CINCINNATI, OHIO, JULY 19, 2015). The unarmed African American man was shot and killed by University of Cincinnati police officer Ray Tensing allegedly because DuBose was driving a car without a front license plate. Tensing claimed that his arm had been caught in the car, and he was dragged down the street, but his body cam video clearly debunked this. Result: Officer Tensing was charged with murder. In January 2016, the University of Cincinnati agreed to pay the DuBose family $4.85 million and provide tuition-free education to his twelve children.

On Saturday, August 9, 2014, at around noon, in the Saint Louis suburb of Ferguson, Missouri, a police officer named Darren Wilson shot and killed Michael Brown, an African American teenager. Brown was unarmed. At eighteen, he was just days away from starting college. He was walking down the middle of a quiet street with his friend Dorian Johnson when Wilson drove by in his police cruiser. Johnson said that Wilson pulled up in a squad car and said, "Get the f— on the sidewalk." Moments later Officer Wilson gunned down Brown.

Police left Michael Brown's bleeding corpse in the middle of the street for over four hours on that hot Saturday afternoon, behind police tape, as neighbors gathered and looked on in horror. Outraged citizens protested.

The protests grew day by day, night by night. Scores were arrested, as the Ferguson protests became a national story. In response, state and local law enforcement deployed a shocking array of military hardware. The battlefield scenes from this Saint Louis suburb helped expose how the Pentagon had been quietly unloading its surplus war-making materiel from Iraq and Afghanistan to thousands of cities and towns across the country. Since 9/11, over $5 billion worth of this gear, including armored personnel carriers, has been transferred. Missouri Governor Jay Nixon declared a state of emergency and deployed the National Guard, as scores were arrested, including at least nineteen journalists in the first ten days of protests. "Hands up! Don't shoot!" became the clarion call, as thousands of people in Ferguson and at solidarity protests around the world raised their hands when confronting the police, just as witnesses said Michael Brown raised his when he was killed.

Protesters demanded that Officer Darren Wilson be indicted for murder, to hold him accountable for the killing of Michael Brown, to end impunity for police officers who kill people of color. Robert P. "Bob" McCulloch, the prosecuting attorney for Saint Louis County, was in charge of the case. McCulloch's loyalty to the police was well known: his brother is a Saint Louis police sergeant, his mother was a clerk in the homicide division, and his father was a Saint Louis police officer who was killed in the line of duty when his son Bob was just twelve.[8] More than 100,000 people signed a petition demanding that McCulloch recuse himself from the case, and the NAACP immediately called for a special prosecutor, given the inherent conflict of interest that exists between prosecutors and the local police. McCulloch refused. As Ferguson seethed, the decision of whether or not to indict Officer Wilson was given to a secret grand jury.

THE NEW AMERICAN DREAM: "TO LIVE UNTIL I'M EIGHTEEN"

Following those initial protests in Missouri, I raced back to New York City to cover the march protesting the July 17 police killing of Eric Garner, a forty-three-year-old African American father of six. Both the Michael Brown case and the Eric Garner case involved a white police officer killing an unarmed African American man. In both cases, the local prosecutor was allowed to control the investigation and the decision about whether or not to charge the officer, using a grand jury. There was one crucial difference, however: Eric Garner's killing was captured on video.

In the video, NYPD Officer Daniel Pantaleo, assisted by several other officers, tackles Eric Garner and puts him in a chokehold. Garner puts his hands up, the international signal of surrender. You hear Garner cry out repeatedly, "I can't breathe!" He says it a total of eleven times before he goes limp.

Where did this video come from? A young man named Ramsey Orta was standing near Garner on the afternoon when the police moved in. Orta pointed his cell phone and recorded the whole thing. Pantaleo was caught red-handed. The evidence was there for everyone to see.

Two people were arrested in the wake of Garner's death, but not who you might have expected: Ramsey Orta, who shot the video, and his wife, Chrissie. Chrissie told a local television station that since Ramsey was identified as the videographer, they had been subjected to constant police harassment. Ramsey was arrested the day after the city medical examiner declared Garner's death a homicide.

I saw the Ortas at the Staten Island march that Saturday, about five weeks after Garner's death, standing near where he died. I asked them for comment, but they were too afraid to speak. They huddled on the same stoop that Ramsey was on when he filmed Garner's death.

At that march on Staten Island on August 23, 2014, many others were not afraid to speak. "The Staten Island [district attorney] should not be prosecuting this case," Constance Malcolm told me. "We need the feds to come in and take this case right now. We need accountability." Malcolm had her own story to tell: her unarmed eighteen-year-old African American son Ramarley was killed by police in her home in 2012. New York City settled with her family for $3.9 million.[9]

Imani Morrias was one of many children at the march. She said, "We need to show the community that these police officers need to be disciplined, and they need to be sentenced for all that they caused." Imani was twelve years old. She added, "They caused so much pain."

Not far from her, another young African American teen, Aniya, who only gave her first name, was marching solemnly. She was thirteen. I asked her what she hoped to accomplish with the protest: "To live until I'm eighteen."

Could this be the new American Dream: to not be shot by a police officer?

BATTLEFRONT FERGUSON

The organizing and the protests in Ferguson continued throughout the fall of 2014. On November 24, Saint Louis County prosecuting attorney Robert McCulloch announced that no criminal charges would be filed against Officer Darren Wilson. Inexplicably, McCulloch delayed release of the grand jury findings until nightfall. The prosecutor's press conference deeply insulted many, as he laboriously defended Wilson's actions, while attacking the character of the victim, Michael Brown. In January 2015 a Ferguson grand juror filed a lawsuit that accused McCulloch of presenting possible charges to the grand jury in a "muddled and untimely manner," and noted the case had a "stronger focus on the victim" than other cases. It also challenged "the implication that all grand jurors believed that there was no support for any charges" against Wilson. The juror challenged a lifetime ban preventing grand jury members from discussing the case.

Soon after McCulloch's announcement, Ferguson erupted. Buildings were set ablaze, burning to the ground. Cars were engulfed in flames. Aggressive riot police, ignoring much-touted "rules of engagement" agreements with protest organizers, fired tear-gas canisters at outraged residents.

"Black lives don't matter," one young man protesting in the freezing cold in Ferguson told me. I stood among the protesters with my *Democracy Now!* colleagues, choking as tear gas mixed with noxious smoke from raging fires nearby.

Another protester, Katrina Redmon, explained her frustration with the failure to indict Wilson: "He killed an unarmed black teenager. There is no excuse for that. A man was killed, and somebody walked away . . . We want answers. Because it seems like the only way you can get away with murder is if you got a badge."

I was interviewing the demonstrators outside the Ferguson police station, which was ringed with heavily armed riot police. As I reported from the middle of the protests, I watched as riot police and National Guard protected the white side of Ferguson. But the black side of town, along West Florissant Avenue, was ablaze. I saw almost no police there. As in August, Missouri Governor Jay Nixon had again declared a state of emergency, one week before the grand jury decision came down. Yet the National Guard troops he deployed were nowhere to be seen in this part of town. About a dozen businesses went up in flames.

Why was West Florissant Avenue left unguarded? Did the authorities let Ferguson burn?

In his 1968 speech "The Other America," Martin Luther King Jr. addressed fears of a forthcoming summer of riots like those that had consumed Newark, New Jersey, Detroit, and other black inner cities in 1967. King said:

"It is not enough for me to stand before you tonight and condemn riots. It would be morally irresponsible for me to do that without, at the same time, condemning the contingent, intolerable conditions that exist in our society. These conditions are the things that cause individuals to feel that they have no other alternative than to engage in violent rebellions to get attention. And I must say tonight that a riot is the language of the unheard."

Those unheard—the citizens of Ferguson who took to the streets for over a hundred days—were demanding justice. Solidarity protests involving thousands around the country and around the world amplified their demands, linking struggles, building a mass movement.

As one young man told me, shivering in the cold, his breath visible in the freezing night air as he faced off with riot police, "We're going to shake the heavens."

Just days before the renewed protests in Ferguson, another police killing occurred in Cleveland, Ohio. Twelve-year-old Tamir Rice had been playing with a toy gun in a public park on November 22. A caller to 911 alerted the police about a "guy with a pistol," but added, "It's probably fake"—a crucial detail that the dispatcher did not tell police. Cleveland police officers Timothy Loehmann and Frank Garmback careened into the park in a police cruiser. Within seconds, Loehmann leapt out of the car and fired at least twice, fatally wounding the boy. He died the next day. Surveillance footage, grainy and silent, captured it all. The officers then tackled Tamir's fourteen-year-old sister as she ran to be by her brother's side, handcuffed her, and threw her into the cruiser.

Reports have emerged that Loehmann was deemed unfit for police service more than two years earlier when he worked in the Cleveland suburb of Independence, Ohio. A letter from a superior there specifically criticizes Loehmann's performance in firearms training, saying, "He could not follow simple directions . . . his handgun performance was dismal." In 2014 the city of Cleveland paid $100,000 to settle an excessive-force case against Officer Garmback.

Seven months after Tamir was killed, in June 2015, citizen activists used a novel legal procedure to seek an indictment, given that the authorities had not. Cleveland municipal judge Ronald

Adrine heard their case and concluded that grounds existed to prosecute the officers. But months later, they still had not been charged.

Those seeking justice for Tamir Rice were disheartened when Cuyahoga County prosecutor Timothy McGinty released two "independent" reports in October 2015, which claimed that the use of deadly force was "objectively reasonable." McGinty tried to blunt criticism in his press release, writing, "We are not reaching any conclusions from these reports. The gathering of evidence continues, and the grand jury will evaluate it all."

On December 28, 2015, an Ohio grand jury declined to indict Cleveland police officers Timothy Loehmann and Frank Garmback in the death of Tamir Rice. Tamir's family released a statement saying: "In a time in which a nonindictment for two police officers who have killed an unarmed black child is business as usual, we mourn for Tamir, and for all of the black people who have been killed by the police without justice. In our view, this process demonstrates that race is still an extremely troubling and serious problem in our country and the criminal-justice system." [10]

As the fires in Ferguson smoldered in November 2014, the case of Eric Garner in New York City saw another disturbing development a few weeks later. Richmond County District Attorney Daniel Donovan stated, "After deliberation on the evidence presented in this matter, the grand jury found that there was no reasonable cause to vote an indictment."

Once again, a basic conflict of interest interfered with the administration of justice. The prosecutor is tasked with investigating the police. But the prosecutor depends on the police on a daily basis—without the police, the prosecutor would hardly be able to do his or her job. So you can expect the prosecutor to favor the police in any investigation of suspected criminal activity among officers. This isn't an absolute rule, but in city after city, grand juries, directed by prosecutors, fail to indict officers who have killed people. Daniel Donovan is no longer the Staten Island district attorney, though. Not long after his announcement on Garner, he entered the race to replace a member of Congress who had been indicted on tax evasion. Donovan won that election and moved on to Congress.

As news spread that Officer Daniel Pantaleo was cleared in the killing of Eric Garner, New York Mayor Bill de Blasio stood with African American leaders on Staten Island. "Our history requires that we say Black Lives Matter," he declared.

In July 2015 New York City agreed to pay $5.9 million to resolve a wrongful death claim from the family of Eric Garner. "Mr. Garner's death is a touchstone in the history of our city and in the history of the entire nation," said New York City comptroller Scott Stringer, in announcing the settlement. "It forced us to examine the state of race relations, and the relationship between our police force and the people they serve."[11]

ATHLETES TAKE A STAND

"Hands up! Don't shoot!" and "I can't breathe!" became mantras of the growing movement to stem police violence, and the systemic racism at the core of the problem. The phrases began appearing in popular culture, showing the speed and depth with which the movement was growing.

Professional athletes in the United States are followed closely by millions of fans. So, when basketball superstar LeBron James of the Cleveland Cavaliers warmed up before a game wearing a

T-shirt emblazoned "I Can't Breathe," people noticed. Including, we can assume, Prince William and Princess Kate, the Duke and Duchess of Cambridge, of the British royal family, who attended the game, seated in the front row.

Dave Zirin is a sports journalist who unflinchingly writes about the intersection of sports, politics, corporate interests, and high finance. He has written about the pressure on professional athletes to remain silent on political issues. He noted some of the athletes who engaged in Black Lives Matter protests. In addition to LeBron James, five or six other basketball players that same night wore "I Can't Breathe" T-shirts. In the National Football League, five Saint Louis Rams players, along with players from the Oakland Raiders and Washington Redskins, raised their arms in the "Hands up! Don't shoot!" gesture during games, while two more players from Detroit wrote "I can't breathe" on a wristband and cleats. Detroit Lions running back Reggie Bush wore an "I Can't Breathe" T-shirt during warm-ups, as did players from the Cleveland Browns and the San Diego Chargers. Two hockey players with the University of Oregon Ducks raised their arms during the national anthem, and a basketball player at Knox College lay on the court for four and a half minutes, one minute for each hour that the Ferguson police left Michael Brown's body on the hot pavement.

Zirin wrote, "Seeing the movement impinge upon the highly sanitized, deeply authoritarian world of sports is not only a reflection of just how widespread the outpouring of anger has been. These athletic protests also shape the movement, giving more people the confidence to get in the streets and puncturing the self-imposed bubbles of those who want to pretend that all is well in the world. It is politicizing sports fans and educating those who think that sports in general—and athletes in particular—have nothing to offer the struggle for a better world." In an escalation of the resistance, during halftime at the Super Bowl in February 2016, with one hundred million people watching, pop legend Beyoncé performed a musical homage to black power. Her backup dancers wore Black Panther–style berets and posed for a photo with their fists in the air. The previous day, Beyoncé released a music video, *Formation,* dealing with Hurricane Katrina and police brutality. The video ends with a camera panning to a wall graffitied with the words: "Stop shooting us."

BREAKING RANKS IN BALTIMORE

In the months that followed the deaths of Michael Brown, Eric Garner, and Tamir Rice, police killings of people of color continued unabated. In April 2015, Baltimore police arrested Freddie Gray, a twenty-five-year-old African American man. After "making eye contact" with a police lieutenant, Gray ran away. Police chased and tackled him and then dragged him into a police van as Gray shrieked in pain. Gray was not properly secured inside the van; he died of spinal injuries a week after he was arrested. Doctors said his spine was 80 percent severed at the neck.

A police union attorney justified Gray's arrest by claiming "[I]f you are in a high-crime area, and you flee from the police unprovoked, the police have the legal ability to pursue you." [12]

So running while black is now a capital offense.

Gray's death sparked days of riots and a national conversation about police brutality and the ways that America's inner cities have been bled of jobs and resources. A 2015 study by Harvard economists showed that Baltimore is the worst place in the United

States for a black boy to grow up if he dreams of having a better life than his parents did.[13]

Gene Ryan, president of the Fraternal Order of Police in Baltimore, compared the protesters to "a lynch mob."

Billy Murphy, attorney for the Gray family, expressed outrage, noting that blacks have long been the victims of lynchings at the hands of police. "It doesn't get more insensitive or insulting than that. These remarks illustrate why black people and the police don't get along."[14]

Then something remarkable happened: a glimmer of justice shined through the fog of smoke and tear gas in Baltimore.

Marilyn Mosby, the state's attorney (equivalent to a district attorney or prosecutor) for the City of Baltimore, announced that she had filed charges against six police officers involved in Gray's death. A thirty-five-year-old African American, she was the youngest state's attorney in a major American city. "I come from five generations of law enforcement," she said. "My father was an officer. My mother was an officer; several of my aunts and uncles. My recently departed and beloved grandfather was one of the founding members of the first black police organization in Massachusetts."

Mosby went on: "To those that are angry, hurt, or have their own experiences of injustice at the hands of police officers, I urge you to channel the energy peacefully as we prosecute this case. I have heard your calls for 'No justice, no peace'; however, your peace is sincerely needed, as I work to deliver justice on behalf of Freddie Gray."

She closed with what is certainly unique in the annals of prosecutorial oration: "Last, but certainly not least, to the youth of this city, I will seek justice on your behalf. This is your moment. Let's ensure that we have peaceful and productive rallies that will develop structural and systemic changes for generations to come.

You're at the forefront of this cause. And as young people, our time is now."

RACE AND REVOLUTION

On a winter's day, March 5, 1770, an angry crowd formed in Boston, then the capital of the Province of Massachusetts Bay. People were enraged by the extortionate taxes imposed by the British Parliament. To quell the public furor, the British sent troops, who violently quashed dissent. On that cold day, people had had enough. Word spread that a British private had beaten a young man with the butt of his musket. By late day, hundreds of Bostonians gathered, jeering the small crowd of redcoat soldiers arrayed with muskets loaded. The soldiers fired into the crowd, instantly killing Crispus Attucks and two others. Attucks was a man of African and Native American ancestry, and is considered the first casualty of the American Revolution, in what was to become known as the Boston Massacre. It took the indiscriminate murder of a man of color by armed agents of the state to launch the revolution.

Which brings me back to Ferguson, Missouri.

"Nearly seven months have passed since the shooting death of eighteen-year-old Michael Brown," US Attorney General Eric Holder said in March 2015. He was detailing the findings of two Justice Department investigations into the killing of the unarmed African American youth by Ferguson police officer Darren Wilson. "The facts do not support the filing of criminal charges against Officer Darren Wilson in this case. Michael Brown's death, though a tragedy, did not involve prosecutable conduct on the part of Officer Wilson." With those words, the outgoing attorney general laid to rest any prospect of a criminal trial sought by so many seeking justice. But Brown's death continues to send shock waves through his community and beyond.

Importantly, Holder went on to describe the findings of the second, broader report, *Investigation of the Ferguson Police Department*, from the DOJ's Civil Rights Division. "Local authorities consistently approached law enforcement not as a means for protecting public safety, but as a way to generate revenue," he stated. Ferguson, he said, was a "community where both policing and municipal-court practices were found to disproportionately harm African American residents . . . this harm frequently appears to stem, at least in part, from racial bias—both implicit and explicit."

Ferguson is one of about ninety municipalities in Saint Louis County, in the suburbs of the city of Saint Louis. Ferguson and many other towns in the region generate a significant portion of their annual budget by ticketing heavily for minor infractions.

"Despite making up 67 percent of the population," the DOJ report stated, "African Americans accounted for 85 percent of FPD's [Ferguson Police Department] traffic stops, 90 percent of FPD's citations, and 93 percent of FPD's arrests from 2012 to 2014."

Michael-John Voss, managing attorney at the nonprofit legal defense organization ArchCity Defenders, represents many of those harassed by these police stops. He told me, "What we have in Saint Louis, in the municipalities in Saint Louis County, is a modern debtors' prison. African Americans are disproportionately targeted by police . . . they are also exploited because of their financial inability to pay certain fines and costs related to that traffic stop. If they don't have the ability to pay, they become incarcerated." The fines mount, creating a vicious cycle, leaving the predominantly poor African American victims trapped by debt.

The one-hundred-page DOJ report included numerous disturbing cases of racist Ferguson police conduct: from use of the

N-word during violent arrests, to internal emails containing racist comments about President Barack Obama and First Lady Michelle Obama. One email depicted Obama as a chimpanzee; another predicted he would not last as president because "what black man holds a steady job for four years."

Further email exchanges revealed the extent to which revenues from infractions were pursued actively by city government. In one email, Police Chief Tom Jackson bragged "of the 80 St. Louis County Municipal Courts reporting revenue, only 8, including Ferguson, have collections greater than 1 million dollars."

Eric Holder announced that Ferguson and surrounding communities were being placed under federal supervision. They will change, or the Department of Justice will sue them to force change.

"It's not about making minor reforms and plodding along in the same direction," Ohio State University law professor Michelle Alexander, author of *The New Jim Crow: Mass Incarceration in the Age of Colorblindness*, told us on *Democracy Now!* "It's about mustering the courage to have a major reassessment of where we are as America, reckon with our racial history as well as our present, and build a broad-based movement rooted in the awareness of the dignity and humanity of us all."

From Crispus Attucks to Michael Brown almost 245 years later, two things remain clear: We never know what sparks a revolution. And black lives matter.

#BLACKLIVESMATTER

In July 2015, in the middle of a year of rebellions against police killings of people of color, I spoke with the three remarkable women who founded the Black Lives Matter movement: Alicia Garza, who is projects director for the National Domestic Workers Alliance; Opal Tometi, executive director of the Black Alliance for Just Immigration; and Patrisse Cullors, director of truth and reinvestment at the Ella Baker Center for Human Rights, and founder of Dignity and Power Now, a grassroots organization in Los Angeles fighting for incarcerated people and their families. These women represent the intersection of three powerful movements: Garza focuses on the fight for a $15 minimum wage, Tometi works on immigration issues, and Cullors is focused on the problem of mass incarceration.

They were inspired to act following the death of Trayvon Martin, the seventeen-year-old African American teen who was killed in Florida in 2012 by white vigilante George Zimmerman. Martin's death inspired Garza to send "love letters to black people"—a series of social media posts aimed at reassuring black people that their lives mattered. Her friend Cullors then created the #BlackLivesMatter hash tag.[15]

As Garza told *Democracy Now!*, #BlackLivesMatter "was born out of the incredible pain and rage that each of us feels and that black people across the world feel when any of our lives are taken unnecessarily, particularly in relationship to state-sanctioned violence." It was a response to "a real narrative around respectability politics: how if Trayvon had only pulled up his pants, and if we just vote, and if we just get a better education, then somehow we can save ourselves from untimely deaths, when the reality is that structural racism kills black people every single day." She noted that the Malcolm X Grassroots Movement, which defends human rights and promotes self-determination in communities of color, has documented that "every twenty-eight hours, a black person in this country is murdered by police, security guards, or vigilantes."

Opal Tometi is the daughter of two Nigerian immigrants. She sees the Black Lives Matter movement intersecting with many issues. "The reality," she said, "is that criminalization of people of color is impacting us, whether you're a citizen of the United States or you're not. And what we're seeing right now is the mass criminalization that is leaving low-income people of color, immigrant communities . . . particularly vulnerable to the whims of local law enforcement and Immigration and Customs Enforcement."

Tometi offered an alternative vision:

If black lives mattered, I believe that policing and immigration enforcement would not be the devastating force that it is in our communities. The reality is that it's rampant and that we have theories that basically criminalize all of our communities and leave us either brutalized at the hands of police in the street, it leaves us languishing in prison cells or detention centers, sometimes deported, and it leaves our communities in shambles . . . If "Black Lives Matter" was truly to be embraced and really actualized in this nation, we wouldn't see that. We would see a complete divestment from all apparatuses that criminalize our communities . . . And we would see a reinvestment in resources that would empower our communities and that would allow us to thrive.

The Black Lives Matter movement has grown to more than twenty-five chapters nationally. Black Lives Matter made waves on the 2016 presidential campaign trail, as activists disrupted events and demanded that the candidates address the issues at the core of their movement. At a Hillary Clinton campaign event in Keene,

New Hampshire, in 2015, four Black Lives Matter activists were denied entry to the venue.

"We went to New Hampshire with the intention of confronting Hillary Clinton. Unfortunately, when we got there, we were told that we couldn't come inside," Daunasia Yancey, founder of the Black Lives Matter chapter in Boston, told *Democracy Now!* CNN reporter Dan Merica had tweeted about their exclusion, which he was told was due to the room being at capacity. After that, Yancey explained, "Someone came out and invited us into an overflow room, where we could actually watch the forum. And then, one of her staffers came in and said, 'We could offer you a couple of minutes with her.' And we said, 'Absolutely,' so that we could ask her the questions that we had."

Candidates running for president are nearly impossible to reach—unless you are a major campaign donor. The candidates' public appearances are closely stage-managed. At campaign events in key primary states, however, where the candidates stump day in and day out, they sometimes have no choice but to speak with prospective voters. Black Lives Matter activists have been using these moments to challenge business as usual, bringing the issues of racism and inequality to a broad audience.

Yancey asked Clinton, "You and your family have been personally and politically responsible for policies that have caused health and human services disasters in impoverished communities of color through the domestic and international war on drugs that you championed as first lady, senator, and secretary of state. And so I just want to know how you feel about your role in that violence and how you plan to reverse it?"

Julius Jones, from the Black Lives Matter movement in Worcester, Massachusetts, also questioned Clinton: "How do you actually feel that's different than you did before? What were the mistakes? And how can those mistakes that you made be lessons for all of America for a moment of reflection on how we treat black people in this country?"

Clinton responded: "I don't believe you change hearts. I believe you change laws, you change allocation of resources, you change the way systems operate."

Black Lives Matter confronted other candidates at their speaking events, including Democrats Bernie Sanders and Martin O'Malley, and Republican Jeb Bush. Organizers vowed to continue disrupting presidential campaign events.

As the Black Lives Matter website states: "We have put our sweat equity and love for Black people into creating a political project: taking the hash tag off of social media and into the streets. The call for Black lives to matter is a rallying cry for *all* Black lives striving for liberation."

ENDING MASS INCARCERATION

The Black Lives Matter movement has brought attention to the grim fact that the United States is now the largest penal colony on Earth. America is home to 5 percent of the world's population but 25 percent of the world's prisoners. The US incarceration rate "dwarf[s] the rates of nearly every developed country, even surpassing highly repressive regimes like Russia, China, and Iran," writes Michelle Alexander in *The New Jim Crow: Mass Incarceration in the Age of Colorblindness.*

It wasn't always this way. America's prison population jumped from 500,000 in 1980 to 2.2 million today. This spike in imprisonment occurred during a period when the crime rate has been dropping steadily. Key drivers of the prison boom are the failed war on drugs and a for-profit prison industry that has lobbied heavily for money to build new facilities and policies to keep them full.

But that still doesn't explain America's insatiable appetite for locking up its citizens. Racism is a key feature of mass incarceration. Consider the fact that a black man has a one-in-three chance of serving time in prison in his life; for a Hispanic man, the chance is one in six, while a white man has just a one-in-nineteen chance of doing time. Alexander notes that "three out of four young black men (and nearly all those in the poorest neighborhoods) can expect to serve time in prison." [16]

Alexander argues that mass incarceration is a new form of social control, serving the same function as slavery and, later, Jim Crow laws. "This system of mass incarceration, in order to continue to grow, is adapting and is looking for new populations to bring under its control," she told *Democracy Now!* "And particularly the profit motive in the private prison industry is helping to drive much of that impulse. And so, when we talk about ending mass incarceration, we must, in the same breath, talk about ending mass deportation and the criminalization of immigrant communities in the United States today. You know, we see that the same racially divisive politics that gave rise to the war on drugs and the 'get tough' movement, those same racially divisive politics are now taking aim at immigrant communities and helping to ensure the continued expansion of the prison-industrial complex by including immigrants under its control.

"Unlike the old Jim Crow, there are no signs alerting us to the existence of this new caste system," she continued. "If this doesn't actually affect you directly, you can go your whole life and have no idea what is really going on. And so, if we are going to build this movement, we're going to have to pull back the curtain, speak courageous truths . . . and help to inspire a much broader awakening, so that the work of real movement building can get under way."

The Black Lives Matter movement helped catalyze an unusual convergence of people to push for an end to mass incarceration. In a 2015 speech, President Barack Obama praised the campaign for criminal justice reform from the left and right. "This is a cause that's bringing people in both houses of Congress together. It's created some unlikely bedfellows. You've got Van Jones and Newt Gingrich. You've got Americans for Tax Reform and the ACLU. You've got the NAACP and the Koch brothers."

Democracy Now! brought together several of those unlikely allies—who on any other day might be on our show vociferously opposing one another. Van Jones is president and cofounder of #cut50, a national bipartisan initiative to reduce the incarcerated population by 50 percent over the next ten years. He was President Obama's green jobs czar in 2009 and founded the nonprofit organization Green for All. Jones was ousted from his White House position later in 2009 following fierce criticism by Republicans. He is also a CNN political commentator. Mark Holden is senior vice president and general counsel for Koch Industries, where he's a close advisor to its leader, Charles Koch. Koch Industries is a supporter of the criminal justice group called the Coalition for Public Safety.

Van Jones explained, "We are in the middle of a very rare convergence. Both political parties, Republicans and Democrats, were stuck on stupid for thirty years, chasing each other off a cliff to put more and more people in prison. The way you showed you were a smart politician was you tried to one-up your opponent on how many people you wanted to put behind bars for petty offenses. And so, three strikes and you're out; two strikes and you're out; just, hey, if you're black, you're out—that became politics for both parties. Bill Clinton was a mass incarcerator. Let's not forget that."

Holden added, "What worked twenty or thirty years ago doesn't work today. And we have to have the intellectual honesty and courage and humility to correct that. In our businesses, we do that all the time when things aren't working. And I think, to Van's point, what we're seeing happen in the states is really a template for what should happen at the federal level, and making sure that everything we do enhances public safety and that it honors the Bill of Rights and treats everybody in the system as individuals with dignity and respect—particularly victims, law enforcement, the incarcerated, the accused and their families . . . It's morally, constitutionally, and fiscally the right thing to do to reform our criminal justice system."

Van Jones explained the unusual coalition:

I just want to address the elephant in the room, which is that for a lot of people who are in the listening audience, this is the first time they've actually heard from anybody associated with Koch Industries directly, and people are probably just shocked to hear what they just heard from someone who those of us on the left spend a lot of time fighting. And so, we have to deal with the question: How can this right-left thing even exist?

. . . It's because of two things. The core values of the Republican Party around liberty . . . are being completely violated. The core values of the Democratic Party around justice, social justice, racial justice, gender justice—totally being violated. So liberty and justice for all, both parties' political core values, are being violated by this massive system . . . And what we discovered by not talking *about* each other but by talking *to* each other—starting out in my life with me and Newt Gingrich and me and Mark— we realized there was this common ground.

Now, in a democracy, we don't have to agree on

everything . . . Nobody sitting in prison is sitting there saying, "Well, I hope the Republicans don't help. I hope that the Democrats and the Republicans don't work together." Anybody whose parents or child is locked up is not asking for more division. Let's fight where we don't agree. Let's fight hard where we don't agree. But where we do agree, let's fight together . . .

. . . I also will not turn down any helping hand for any of our sisters and brothers, of all colors, who are locked up unjustly. So I had to deal with that issue, because I know a lot of people are sitting here saying, "How can Amy Goodman put Koch Industries on the air?" And it's because there is a principled reason for them to be in the fight, a principled reason for us to be in the fight, and we've got to fight together . . .

This is an issue that is so horrible that it's actually brought the best out of both parties, in the same way it brought the worst out in both parties up until now.[17]

Jane Mayer, staff writer for *The New Yorker* and author of *Dark Money: The Hidden History of the Billionaires Behind the Rise of the Radical Right,* had a more cynical view of what the Koch brothers are doing. She told *Democracy Now!* "What they would like to do is get rid of many crimes that have to do with pollution, that have to do with corporate crimes, tax crimes. They want to weaken prosecution of companies like their own."

Mayer explained that the Koch brothers' concern for criminal justice reform is part of a rebranding campaign. "After they did not win the presidency in 2012, despite the money they put behind Mitt Romney, they went back to the drawing board. . . . They came to the conclusion that the public thought they were greedy and didn't trust them. . . . At that point, they launched a number of programs that have to do with doing good works for the poor."

THE NEW ABOLITIONISTS

The stark picture of America's race-based Gulag has led to calls not just for prison reform but also for abolition of prison altogether.

For over four decades, Angela Davis has been one of the most influential activists and intellectuals in the United States. An icon of the 1970s black liberation movement, her work around issues of gender, race, class, and prisons has influenced critical thought and social movements for years. She is a leading advocate for prison abolition, a position informed by her own experience as a fugitive on the FBI's top ten most wanted list forty years ago. Davis rose to national attention in 1969 when she was fired as a professor from the University of California at Los Angeles (UCLA) as a result of her membership in the Communist Party and her leading a campaign to defend three black prisoners at Soledad State Prison. She is professor emerita at the University of California, Santa Cruz, and the founder of the group Critical Resistance, a grassroots effort to end the prison-industrial complex.

Davis told *Democracy Now!*: "The effort to abolish imprisonment as the dominant mode of punishment and to shift resources from punishment to education, to housing, etcetera, in a way that is very similar to what Frederick Douglass might have argued with respect to the abolition of slavery. And, of course, here, we also have to mention W. E. B. DuBois, whose notion of abolition democracy is very much an inspiration for those of us who are struggling to abolish the prison-industrial complex today.

"I would like to see us engage in a national conversation on true alternatives to incarceration," she continued. "I'm not speaking about house arrest and probation and parole and so forth. I'm talking about ways of addressing social problems that are entirely disconnected from law enforcement.

"And that would mean an emphasis on education . . . Frederick Douglass taught himself how to read and write, because he recognized that there could be no liberation without education . . . We have to say, 'Education, not incarceration.' "

Davis argues for a broader vision of issues of crime and punishment. As she told me on *Democracy Now!* in 2010 on the fortieth anniversary of her arrest:

We have to return to the notion of abolition democracy. There were those who were struggling to simply get rid of prisons and assuming that freedom would be the negation of slavery. But there were those who recognized that there could be no freedom without economic equality, without political equality, without educational institutions. And even though we are under the impression that we abolished slavery, we're still living with those vestiges: the lack of an educational system that serves all people regardless of their economic background, the lack of a health care system, the lack of access to housing. And this is in large part the role that the prison has played. It has become a receptacle for those who have not been able to find a place in society. And this is true not only in the US but literally all over the world. This is why we are experiencing an expansion of the prison system in Europe, in Asia, in Africa, in Latin America. And this is very much connected to the rise in global capitalism.

"Prison abolition," Davis concludes, "is about building a new world."

CHAPTER 9

"THIS FLAG COMES DOWN TODAY"

On the evening of June 17, 2015, a dozen people gathered for their weekly Bible study at the Emanuel African Methodist Episcopal (AME) Church in Charleston, South Carolina. They were studying the book of Mark, chapter 4, verses 16–20, the Parable of the Sower. Reverend Clementa Pinckney, the pastor of the church, was there. He began preaching at age thirteen. By the age of twenty-three, he had been elected to the South Carolina House of Representatives, and then later to the state senate, where he still served. By his side was a retired minister, Reverend Daniel Simmons, seventy-four.

Leading the study that night was Myra Thompson, fifty-nine. Cynthia Graham Hurd, a fifty-four-year-old librarian who ran one of Charleston's largest branch libraries, was there along with two women who were also ministers in the AME church: Reverend Sharonda Coleman-Singleton, forty-five, a speech therapist and track

coach at Goose Creek High School; and Reverend DePayne Middleton-Doctor, forty-nine, a mother of four and an admissions coordi-
nator for Southern Wesleyan University. Middleton-Doctor received
her license to minister just that night. Seventy-year-old Ethel Lance,
a church sexton and a retired Charleston city employee, was there,
too. Felecia Sanders, fifty-eight, attended, along with her twenty-
six-year-old son, Tywanza, and her eleven-year-old granddaughter.
Tywanza's aunt, Susie Jackson, eighty-seven, an elder at the church,
joined the group, as did another parishioner, Polly Sheppard, seventy.

As they got started, one more person joined them. This late
arrival was twenty-one-year-old Dylann Storm Roof. As a young
white man, he might have stood out, but he was welcomed, in accord with the church's long-standing open-door practice. He asked
who the minister was and, after being told, sat next to Reverend
Pinckney for the hour. As they wrapped up their Bible study at nine
o'clock, Roof stood up, pulled out a .45-caliber Glock pistol, and
announced that he was there "to kill black people." He shot State
Senator Reverend Pinckney at point-blank range, killing him, and
then moved to the others, killing methodically. As he reloaded, Tywanza tried to talk Roof out of more bloodshed, to no avail.

Tywanza's mother, Felecia Sanders, slid under a round table,
pulling her granddaughter to her, telling her to "play dead." She
heard Roof tell the group, "I have to do it. You're raping our women
and taking over the country. You have to go." Sanders watched as
her son Tywanza was gunned down. He turned to her, "Mom, I've
been shot in the head. Why is he doing this?" [1] As Tywanza reached
to protect his aunt, Susie Jackson, Roof killed them both.

On his way out, Roof passed Polly Sheppard, who by then was
on her knees praying. She recounted later that Roof said, "I am going
to let you live so you can tell the story of what happened." Eight were

dead at the scene. Reverend Simmons died later in surgery from his wounds. Felecia Sanders, her granddaughter, and Sheppard survived, as did Reverend Pinckney's wife, Jennifer, and one of their daughters, who had been in Pinckney's office when the killings occurred.

Tywanza, the youngest victim of the massacre, was very active on social media. During that night's Bible study, in fact, he posted a short video to Snapchat. It showed the group sitting at one of the round tables, with Reverend Simmons speaking. Slightly obscured was the sandy-haired head of Dylann Roof. Earlier that evening, Tywanza had shared a video on Facebook from the independent media organization Brave New Films, *White Riots vs Black Protests*, along with the filmmaker's question: "Ever notice how the mainstream media treats black protesters and white rioters differently?" His frequent posts showed a deep awareness of the Black Lives Matter movement and the violence suffered by people of color, especially the threats to the lives of young black men like himself. In one of his earliest Instagram posts, Tywanza posted a quote from a sermon by Dr. Martin Luther King Jr.:

"The ultimate measure of a man is not where he stands in moments of comfort and convenience, but where he stands in times of challenge and controversy."

Tywanza Sanders showed where he stood in those terrible moments on June 17. He died trying to prevent more bloodshed, trying to comfort and protect his eighty-seven-year-old aunt.

Roof fled in a car and was apprehended the next day, 250 miles away in Shelby, North Carolina. A website called the Last Rhodesian surfaced, apparently created by Roof. It included a 2,400-word manifesto attributed to him, which read in part: "I chose Charleston because it is most historic city in my state, and at one time had the highest ratio of blacks to Whites in the country. We

have no skinheads, no real KKK, no one doing anything but talking on the internet. Well someone has to have the bravery to take
it to the real world, and I guess that has to be me." The website
included many photos of Roof brandishing a gun—a .45-caliber
Glock that is likely the murder weapon that was recovered from
his car—and wearing a jacket with the flags of the former apartheid states of Rhodesia and South Africa. Several photos feature
Roof holding a Confederate flag, a symbol of racism and hate. The
connection between the murders at Emanuel AME and the racist
heritage of slavery and the Confederacy were impossible to ignore.

This was not the first time that the Emanuel AME Church was
targeted by white supremacists. The church has a long history as a
central pillar in the city's African American community. Charleston
is a port city, and was where many kidnapped Africans first landed
after being torn from their homeland to be sold into bondage in
Charleston's infamous slave market. The African Methodist Episcopal Church was founded in 1816, in Philadelphia, as black parishioners there sought an independent church free of discrimination
and segregation. Facing similar oppression, freed blacks and slaves
in Charleston left the local Methodist congregation and formed a
parish of the new AME church later that same year. By 1818, they
had their own church building with over 1,400 members.

Not long after, one of the church's founders, Denmark Vesey,
a former slave who had bought his freedom, began planning a
major slave rebellion. Some estimates suggest the sophisticated
plan involved nine thousand slaves and free blacks—and even a
handful of white allies. But before the revolt could take place, the
plot was exposed, in 1822, and Vesey and thirty-four alleged co-
conspirators were hanged. Afterward, the church was burned to
the ground. Parishioners rebuilt and continued their worship until

1834, when independent black churches, along with the teaching of blacks, either free or enslaved, were outlawed entirely in South Carolina. After the Civil War, in 1865, the church started up again, continuing its long history as a beacon of civil rights. As the oldest AME church in the South, it became known as "Mother Emanuel." African American civil rights leaders Booker T. Washington and Martin Luther King are among the distinguished speakers who have addressed parishioners there.

While Mother Emanuel flourished, so too did racism in South Carolina. The Confederate battle flag was originally raised over the South Carolina State House in Columbia in 1961, supposedly to mark the hundredth anniversary of the start of the Civil War. In reality, it was a visceral reaction against the growing national civil rights movement. "It was a middle finger directed at the federal government," said Pulitzer Prize–winning *Washington Post* columnist Eugene Robinson. "It was flown there as a symbol of massive resistance to racial desegregation."[2]

After the NAACP launched a state boycott in 2000 to protest the flying of the Confederate flag, called by many "the Stars and Bars," a compromise was reached. The flag was removed from atop the state capitol dome and placed on a flagpole on statehouse grounds, as part of a Confederate war memorial. The NAACP was not appeased, however, and continued its boycott. It was joined by the NCAA, which refused to hold any championship basketball games in the state. Despite the boycott, which cost South Carolina millions of dollars in lost revenue, that flag, the symbol of the Confederacy, still held a place of honor in the Palmetto State.

When the senseless massacre of these nine innocent people in Charleston was linked to the imagery of the Confederate flag, the false argument that the flag represented cherished Southern cultural heritage fell away. The Confederate flag was exposed as the symbol of racism and violence that it has always been. As the late historian Howard Zinn wrote in 1993, "There is no flag large enough to cover the shame of killing innocent people."

On the Friday afternoon after the massacre, Dylann Storm Roof was led into a jailhouse video conference room, shackled, to appear remotely for his bond hearing. The magistrate allowed victims' family members to address the court and to speak directly to Roof himself. Through tears and grief, shocking and shaming the nation, they offered the alleged killer forgiveness. Nadine Collier, a daughter of Ethel Lance, addressed Roof:

"I just want everybody to know, to you, I forgive you. You took something very precious from me. I will never talk to her ever again, I will never be able to hold her again, but I forgive you, and have mercy on your soul. You hurt me. You hurt a lot of people. But God forgive you, and I forgive you."

Roof stood, visible in the courtroom on a flat-screen TV, motionless, blank faced.

One of the survivors, Felecia Sanders, addressed him as well:

"We welcomed you Wednesday night in our Bible study with open arms. You have killed some of the most beautiful people that I know. Every fiber in my body hurts, and I will never be the same. Tywanza Sanders is my son, but Tywanza was my hero. Tywanza was my hero. But, as we said in Bible study, we enjoyed you. But may God have mercy on you."[3]

Later, the family of Reverend DePayne Middleton-Doctor released a statement, labeling the massacre a terrorist attack, and calling for unity. The family said, in part:

What happened to our family is part of a larger attack on Black and Brown bodies. To impact change, we must recognize the connection between racism, hate crimes, and racialized policing. While the focus for this specific attack was on African Americans, we all have a responsibility to seek not only justice for the victims but an end to racial injustice.

We should put our faith to action, making a conscious decision to be more than empty drums that have long lost their melodies. In South Carolina, the Confederate flag—an unequivocal symbol of hate—remains on statehouse grounds. We must demand the flag be removed immediately. We cannot let icons of racism fly free within our society.[4]

The body of Senator Reverend Clementa Pinckney lay in state in the South Carolina State House in Columbia. He was one of the only African Americans ever to lie in the capitol rotunda. Even as South Carolina attempted to honor Pinckney in death, it could not hide the symbols of racial oppression that were everywhere. While other flags on the South Carolina State House were lowered to half-staff following the murders of the nine churchgoers, the Stars and Bars outside on the statehouse grounds flew high and proud as Pinckney's horse-drawn casket was brought to the capitol.

Indeed, there are so many monuments to the Confederacy in South Carolina's capital city that they are nearly impossible to avoid. Pinckney's body lay in state beside a statue of John C. Calhoun of South Carolina, the seventh US vice president and a leading advocate of slavery. Calhoun was a shrewd politician, and one of the architects of secession from the Union, although he died in 1850, before he could see his secessionist theories implemented fully. In 1838 Calhoun wrote, "Many in the South once believed that slavery was a moral and political evil. That folly and delusion are gone. We see it now in its true light, and regard it as the most safe and stable basis for free institutions in the world." He helped propel the United States into its devastating civil war, and in South Carolina, he is revered by some as a hero.

Emanuel AME Church is located on Calhoun Street. One block from the church in a city park, yet another statue of John Calhoun stands almost as high as Emanuel Church's steeple. It was placed on an extra-tall pedestal for fear that blacks would pull it down. Calls to remove the Confederate flag from the statehouse grounds, as well as demands that the name of Calhoun Street be changed, were met with the same discouraging refrain: memorials of the Confederacy, it turns out, have special status in South Carolina. As part of the compromise that allowed the flag to be moved off the capitol dome in 2000, the state legislature passed the Heritage Act. It prohibits tampering with Confederate memorials without the approval of a two-thirds majority vote of both houses of the state legislature. Since the Republican-controlled legislature would never agree to insult its Confederate past, attempts to remove the flag would be nearly impossible.

Reverend Pinckney's funeral was on Friday, June 26, 2015. It was moved to a nearby sports arena to accommodate the thousands who wanted to pay their respects. President Barack Obama gave the eulogy, in which he declared, "Removing the flag from this state's capitol would not be an act of political correctness. It would not be an insult to the valor of Confederate soldiers. It would simply be an acknowledgment that the cause for which they fought—the cause of slavery—was wrong."

Nelson Mandela said, "It always seems impossible until it's done." The day after Clementa Pinckney was laid to rest, on Saturday, the day of the funeral for Susie Jackson and Tywanza Sanders, the impossible happened.

"THIS FLAG COMES DOWN TODAY"

It was five thirty in the morning on June 27, 2015, ten days after the massacre at the Emanuel AME Church. The South Carolina State House glowed in the morning light. Bree Newsome, a thirty-year-old African American woman from Charlotte, North Carolina, walked toward the main entrance of the building. She was accompanied by Jimmy Tyson, a young white man from North Carolina, and others who scouted the grounds. They observed the scene around the statehouse, waiting until there were no guards visible. After about thirty minutes, Tyson and Newsome made their move. They walked swiftly toward the Confederate Monument, which stands directly in front of the main steps. The tall monument topped with a heroic image of a Confederate soldier pays tribute to those "who have glorified a fallen cause": slavery.

The two activists proceeded to the thirty-foot-high flagpole that stood directly behind the monument. The Confederate battle flag flapped lazily at the top. Tyson helped Newsome over a fence that surrounded the flagpole, and she donned climbing gear and began ascending the pole swiftly. Tyson watched her from below, ready to break her fall if she slipped. Guards noticed and began shouting at her to come down.

Reaching the top of the flagpole, she grabbed the Confederate flag and unhooked it.

"You come against me with hatred and oppression and violence. I come against you in the name of God!" Newsome declared as she clutched the symbol of the Confederacy. "This flag comes down today!"

She lowered herself slowly, along with the flag. As soon as she reached the ground, Newsome and Tyson were arrested.

Video of the protest went viral and was seen around the world. Her bail fund quickly raised more than $125,000. Ava DuVernay, director of the Oscar-nominated film *Selma*, was among the many to hail her, writing on Twitter, "I hope I get the call to direct the motion picture about a black superhero I admire. Her name is @BreeNewsome."

But within about an hour, two statehouse workers raised a new Confederate flag on the capitol grounds. Later that day, as Confederate flag supporters and antiracist counterprotesters gathered under the newly raised flag in Columbia, Bree Newsome and Jimmy Tyson faced a bond hearing at a nearby jail. As part of that compromise struck by the South Carolina legislature in 2000 to keep the Confederate flag flying next to the statehouse, lawmakers escalated the penalty for tampering with the flag. So Newsome and Tyson were charged with defacing state property, facing a penalty of up to three years in prison and a $5,000 fine.

I had come to South Carolina with a team of *Democracy Now!* producers to cover the aftermath of the church massacre. When we heard about this act of civil disobedience, we raced from Charleston to Columbia. I waited in the lobby of the jail for Newsome and Tyson to be released. About a dozen supporters milled about. I asked one of them, Tamika Lewis, about her reaction to Bree Newsome's protest. Like Newsome, she had traveled from Charlotte to be part of this action.

"To see that flag actually come down and all of the things that it represents being taken down by a strong black woman was one of the greatest symbolic images that one person could ever witness," she said. Another young woman, Karil Parker from Columbia, did not know Newsome but came to the jail because she was so inspired and wanted to show her support: "She has done what our governor hasn't had the courage to do, what our general assembly hasn't had the courage to do. She went up there and did what had to be done, when it needed to be done."

A MODERN ROSA PARKS

Bree Newsome knows her history.

"My ancestors came through Charleston, a slave market," she said on *Democracy Now!* a week after her protest on the flagpole. "The Confederate flag is a symbol of folks trying to hold us into the place of bondage that we had been before and our struggle the past one hundred fifty years of trying to come out of that place. I'm sure I was like a lot of people, sitting at home, looking at the flag flying. I wished I could just take it down, but had no idea if it was possible . . . I had even contemplated just on my own attempting to climb it, knowing full well that I wouldn't make it up the pole, and just let them arrest me, just to make that statement. I mean, that's how strongly I felt about it.

"And so," she continued, "when I ended up connecting with other activists there in North Carolina and found out that there were people who actually did know how to plan for how we could possibly scale the pole—and there were many roles to fill in the plan, and one included needing someone to actually climb up. And, of course, that was a high risk of arrest, we knew. After some prayer and really thinking about it, I decided to volunteer."

In preparation for her action, Newsome worked with professional climbers and practiced shimmying up basketball poles. About ten people ultimately helped her plan and train.[5]

Newsome knows that African American resistance to oppression has often provoked violence in response. "The retaliation piece was much scarier to me than arrest. I was even thinking about the possibility of being up on the flagpole and you never know who might walk by, quite frankly. You know, you could get shot." *

The media—and law enforcement—often treat violence against African Americans as something other than what it is. "One of the things that was so tough about the immediate aftermath of the [Charleston] massacre was not just the violence itself, but the apparent obfuscation about what had actually just happened—that it was a terrorist attack," Newsome said. "Yes, it's an issue of gun violence. Yes, it's an issue of the church being targeted. But it's specifically a *black* church. And I think it's important that we not remove it from the historical context . . . This exists in a long line of terrorist attacks against African Americans in this country. That's what domestic terrorism looks like in the United States."

I asked Newsome about her retweet of a quote by hip-hop artist Talib Kweli about protests in Baltimore in 2015. The protests were a response to the police killing of Freddie Gray, an unarmed black man whose offense was simply that he ran when he saw police. (See Chapter 8 for more on Gray.) In the rebellion that followed, a CVS pharmacy was burned, an image that the media broadcast endlessly.

Newsome retweeted: "CVS gets burned down. Every news outlet shows up. Seven black churches burned, one . . . burning right now. Silence."

She nodded knowingly. "When there was an uprising in Baltimore and a CVS burned, or a QuikTrip burned in Ferguson, I see tons of outrage—'How can you do this?' and 'It's horrible that they did that!' . . . But then all these black churches can burn [in the South], and it completely kind of goes under radar. Well, why is that? . . . Maybe the CVS burning does look like a really horrible thing, but you're not considering that this is a business that exists within an oppressed neighborhood where the people own nothing. They don't really benefit a whole lot from this economic situation. They've been protesting for a long time, and they've gone unheard.

"I do believe that all men are created equal, with inalienable rights endowed by our creator, absolutely," she continued. "And that flag is an affront to that value . . . Go back and read what was written by the people who created the Confederacy. They make it very clear that they seceded because they disagreed with that precept behind the Constitution. They don't believe that all people are created equal."

I asked Newsome about what she meant by what she'd said to the police while up on the flagpole: "You come against me with hatred and oppression and violence. I come against you in the name of God."

"I read the story of David and Goliath," she replied. "And David says to Goliath, 'You come against me with sword and spear and javelin, and I come against you in the name of the Lord.' And that, for me, as a black woman in America, I mean, that's what that moment felt like, because I come from a historically completely disempowered place. I think that's why it was so powerful to a lot of people, especially to black women, to see me up there holding that flag in that way."

Newsome reflected on her larger message. "It's not just about that Confederate flag. It's really about every person who has been oppressed, kind of like taking a stand against any kind of symbol of oppression."

Bree Newsome's powerful action grew out of her broader activism. She marched in Occupy Wall Street demonstrations. In North Carolina, she has been arrested in Moral Mondays protests, the movement that is standing up to regressive voting-rights laws and other issues. She continued, "I've done some work with Ignite North Carolina, which is organizing student leaders on campus. I've been involved in the Raise Up campaign, helping fast-food workers unionize and raise wages. And then I'm also with a very grassroots, very organic group called the Tribe in Charlotte [which] is seriously just community members—a lot of people are teachers, some artists—just coming together and really trying to develop self-sufficiency, helping our community to be in a place where we're not so dependent on systems that don't value our lives."

I asked Newsome what she thinks about comparisons that have been made between her and Rosa Parks, the civil rights icon who launched the 1955 Montgomery bus boycott. "Rosa Parks probably didn't feel like Rosa Parks. Rosa Parks was probably thinking, you know, 'I'm an organizer doing what organizers do.' "

Bree Newsome is also a singer and hip-hop artist. She performed a verse of one of her pieces, "#StayStrong: A Love Song to Freedom Fighters," on *Democracy Now!*:

> *Y'all be quoting King while you pushing a button*
> *to drop some bombs on some babies like you ain't doing nothing*
> *that's why you ain't got no jurisdiction with me*
> *can't handcuff knowledge, so Ms. Bree stay free*
> *I went through college, in the hood I be*
> *spreading love to my brothers and my sister I keep.*

Newsome explained the lyrics:

> In the aftermath of Ferguson, there was a lot of "How would Dr. King feel about you rabble-rousers in the street?" specifically

to the young people. I just find that so completely odious and offensive, because a lot of times, when people call for peace, what they're really just calling for is order. What they're really calling for is just for people to go back to business as usual, which is actually violence. People think that violence is only when something is on fire, only when a gun is being fired. But Gandhi himself said poverty is the worst form of violence. Poverty is violence. Our kids being shuffled from schools into prison is violence. Kids being hungry is violence. We live with violence every single day. The violence doesn't begin just when the CVS is burned.

On July 9, 2015, following a call by South Carolina Republican Governor Nikki Haley to remove the Confederate flag from the statehouse grounds, the South Carolina legislature held thirteen hours of contentious debate on the issue. The bill passed by a vote of 93 to 27. Governor Haley signed it into law, and the next day—three weeks after the Charleston massacre, and two weeks after Bree Newsome scaled a flagpole and removed the flag—the Confederate flag that flew on the statehouse grounds was formally lowered and moved to a museum.

Bree Newsome wrote after her release from jail:

"It is important to remember that our struggle doesn't end when the flag comes down. The Confederacy is a southern thing, but white supremacy is not. Our generation has taken up the banner to fight battles many thought were won long ago. We must fight with all vigor now so that our grandchildren aren't still fighting these battles in another 50 years. Black Lives Matter. This is nonnegotiable."[6] In November 2015, the charges against Bree Newsome and Jimmy Tyson were dropped.

"THE PERPETRATOR HAS BEEN ARRESTED, BUT THE KILLER IS STILL AT LARGE"

The Reverend Dr. William J. Barber II is the president of the North Carolina NAACP. He heard about the slaughter in Charleston while in jail that day, where he frequently finds himself. "About ten of us had been arrested in the statehouse in North Carolina for challenging extremist politicians who have passed the worst voter-suppression law in the country," he said on *Democracy Now!* Barber has led the Moral Mondays movement, with hundreds to thousands of people protesting weekly against the entire legislative agenda being pursued by North Carolina's Republican-controlled state government.

For Barber, showing that Black Lives Matter is more than re-moving the "vulgar" Confederate flag. He suggested that passing policy would be a more lasting memorial to Clementa Pinckney and the other victims in the Emanuel AME Church massacre.

"Reverend Pinckney was not just opposed to the flag. He was opposed to the denial of Medicaid expansion," Barber continued. "He was opposed to those who have celebrated the ending of the Voting Rights Act. He was opposed to the lack of funding for pub-lic education. He wanted to see living wages raised."

Addressing Republican South Carolina state representative Doug Brannon on *Democracy Now!*, Barber said, "Let's put to-gether an omnibus bill in the name of the nine martyrs, and all of the things Reverend Pinckney was standing for. If we say we love him and his colleagues, let's put all of those things in one big omni-bus bill and pass that and bring it to the funeral."

In the wake of the Charleston massacre, Walmart, Amazon,

and other major retailers pulled Confederate paraphernalia from their shelves. Alabama Governor Robert Bentley ordered that the four flags on that state's capitol grounds be removed. In other states, the debates started. Several governors, such as Republican Nathan Deal of Georgia and Democrat Terry McAuliffe of Virginia, blocked access to special license plates that include the Confederate flag imagery. In Mississippi, the last state that actually has the Confederate Stars and Bars as a part of its state flag, a movement is growing to change the flag, removing that vestige of the Confederacy. A referendum to do that failed in 2001, but organizers in Mississippi think that the times have changed and that a revote could succeed.

The current Mississippi flag is becoming increasingly difficult to fly in public: in October 2015, following student protests, the student senate at the University of Mississippi voted overwhelmingly to remove the state flag from campus. Removing the flag would be particularly significant for Ole Miss, a school with a deep-rooted history of white supremacy. It was there in 1962 that white students rioted over the registration of African American student James Meredith, an incident that became a flashpoint in the civil rights struggle. He was the first African American student to integrate the University of Mississippi.

Allen Coon, president of the University of Mississippi College Democrats and a sponsor of the vote to remove the state flag, told *Democracy Now!* that the flag "represents a heritage of hate. It represents a heritage of white supremacy. It represents a heritage that this university has, in which this university actively oppressed people of color attempting to receive an education . . . We're trying to create a safe, tolerant academic space for all students." Three other public universities—Jackson State University, Mississippi

Valley State University, and Alcorn State University—had previously stopped flying the Mississippi state flag.

Remarkably, as the controversy raged over the Confederate flag, Republicans in Congress blocked a measure to take down all flags from the US Capitol that contain a Confederate flag as a component, such as the state flag of Mississippi. House Democrats also put forth several bills and amendments that would have prohibited the display of Confederate flags at national cemeteries run by the National Park Service. Again, the Republicans, in control of both houses of Congress, managed to stifle those efforts through parliamentary maneuvers.

Democratic New York Congressman Hakeem Jeffries declared, "The members of the Republican conference who support the Confederate battle flag apparently argue that this is about heritage and tradition. What exactly is the tradition the Confederate battle flag is meant to represent? Is it slavery? Rape? Kidnap? Genocide? Treason? Or all of the above?"

The fight for equality, waged two hundred years ago by the founders of Charleston's Emanuel AME Church, continues. As Reverend Barber says, systemic change is essential: "The perpetrator has been arrested, but the killer is still at large."

In the final hour of life for Senator Reverend Clementa Pinckney and the eight others who were killed on June 17, 2015, they studied the Bible, the Parable of the Sower. The basic point of the parable is that seeds—metaphorically, ideas planted in good soil or soil that is ready—will grow. The parable appears in the first published words of escaped slave-turned-activist Frederick Douglass. On Tuesday, November 8, 1842, Douglass sent a letter to his friend and mentor William Lloyd Garrison, who published the letter in his abolitionist newspaper the *Liberator*. Douglass escaped the brutality of slavery in 1838, at the age of twenty and, with the support of the underground railway, made his way to New Bedford, Massachusetts. There he lived, worked, and raised a family, under an assumed name, as a free black man—but always under threat of being kidnapped and returned to slavery under the terms of the Fugitive Slave Act.

In 1841 Douglass gave an impassioned address to a Quaker community on the island of Nantucket. The speech was so powerful that it launched Douglass into the forefront of the abolitionist movement as one of its most compelling orators. By late 1842, he was speaking constantly, helping to build the movement to end slavery. The letter to Garrison that Douglass wrote included remarkable details about how they organized: in town halls and churches, with three lectures per day, to standing-room crowds. He wrote about a day of lectures in New Bedford, where he was joined by two other speakers, also free black men: Charles Lenox Remond and Jeremiah Burke Sanderson.

Sanderson, after reading scripture from the Bible, "proceeded to make some remarks on the general question of human rights," Douglass wrote. "These, too, seemed to sink deep into the hearts of the gathered multitude. Not a word was lost; it was good seed, sown in good ground, by a careful hand; it must, it will bring forth fruit." That last sentence is from the Parable of the Sower, almost verbatim. Douglass was a religious man; he too had had enough of being forced to stand in the back of the white-dominated church every Sunday. So, like Denmark Vesey twenty-six years earlier, Douglass quit the oppressive congregation and joined the AME Church in New Bedford.

The immediate goal of the New Bedford lectures in late 1842 was to save an escaped slave from being returned to his master in Virginia. George Latimer had escaped to Boston, but he was caught by his previous owner and jailed, awaiting a return to slavery. Douglass believed that Latimer would not be forced back to work but rather, would be tortured to death in front of the other slaves to serve as a lesson to those considering escape.

Douglass and the abolitionist movement began a massive organizing drive. Funds were raised, and Latimer was purchased from his owner, freeing him from the threat of returning to Virginia. Although Latimer had been saved, the movement carried on, spurred by the oratory and organizing of Douglass and others, focusing pressure on the Massachusetts legislature. By spring 1843, activists forced legislation banning the state from supporting or participating in the apprehension of escaped slaves or involvement with slavery in any way.

By 1845, Douglass had written his first book, *Narrative of the Life of Frederick Douglass, an American Slave,* subjecting himself to great publicity, and thus, the very real danger of abduction and return to his former slave master. He went into exile in Great Britain, speaking and organizing. Supporters there raised funds to buy his freedom so that he could return to the United States truly free—free to fight slavery. Douglass went on to found his own newspaper, the *North Star,* and actively supported civil rights and women's rights, including suffrage. He served as an advisor to six presidents.

Douglass's first printed words back in 1842 included the very last words that Clementa Pinckney and his colleagues studied: the words of that parable. The sower is the organizer. Movements matter, and we can't know when or if our efforts will succeed, when that magic moment will take place, when movements take root, force change, and make history.

"The arc of the moral universe is long," Martin Luther King Jr. said in 1967, paraphrasing early nineteenth-century Massachusetts abolitionist Theodore Parker, "but it bends toward justice." From Denmark Vesey, to Frederick Douglass, to Harriet Tubman, and A. Philip Randolph, Rosa Parks, Emmet Till, Malcolm X, and King, to the thousands in the streets of Ferguson and Staten Island, the language has varied, but the refrain has been constant and unrelenting: black lives matter.

CHAPTER 10

DISABLING THE ENABLERS

In 2014 President Barack Obama admitted, "In the immediate aftermath of 9/11, we did some things that were wrong . . . We tortured some folks." It was a simple, stunning acknowledgment of what human rights advocates had been insisting had routinely occurred at the hands of US interrogators.

For years, there has been a steady stream of evidence giving horrifying details of the US torture program. *Democracy Now!* has doggedly followed the trail of America's torturers through the testimony of victims, attorneys, and former interrogators. A grim picture has emerged of how torture became standard operating procedure, unapologetically authorized at the highest levels. Today there is finally a measure of official acknowledgment of what happened, though no one has been held accountable for what many human rights advocates insist are war crimes.

One story that *Democracy Now!* has investigated over the last decade stands out for its twisted and disturbing plotline: how healers participated in torture. The American Psychological Association (APA), the world's largest body of psychologists, and some of its top practitioners have been key players in the torture program. For years, the APA disputed the reporting by *Democracy Now!* and others about the complicity of psychologists in torture. Lately, the tables have been turned on them.

Psychologists have been at the center of some of the most sadistic interrogations. Two CIA-contracted psychologists, James Elmer Mitchell and Bruce Jessen, designed the torture tactics used on detainees held at secret CIA black sites, the network of secret prisons around the globe where interrogations and torture were carried out. Mitchell and Jessen helped to reverse engineer what they formerly taught to US troops to enable captured soldiers to resist torture techniques once used by Soviet and Chinese interrogators to extract false confessions. This torture resistance program taught to American soldiers was known as Search, Evade, Resist, and Escape (SERE).

In a twist, the CIA put Mitchell and Jessen in charge of training interrogators in how to use the brutal techniques, including waterboarding, at its network of black sites. Mitchell was present at the interrogation of Al Qaeda lieutenant Abu Zubaydah in a CIA safe house in Thailand.

Reporter Katherine Eban, who wrote about the incident for *Vanity Fair*, told *Democracy Now!* in 2007, "Mitchell showed up at the safe house, along with the chief psychologist for the counterterrorism center, Dr. R. Scott Shumate, who, I should mention, was a member of the APA's task force on interrogation policy. Mitchell said that 'We're going to use these harsh interrogation tactics in order to extract all the possible information from Zubaydah.'

And among those, as I mentioned, was a coffin in which they were planning to bury him alive . . . Shumate protested the tactics and subsequently told associates, as we had learned, that he thought it was a mistake for the CIA to hire contractors.

"Nonetheless, at the time, Mitchell said that the interrogators were going to be Zubaydah's god, and that they would basically bestow privileges or take them away, depending on his level of co-operation. And basically, his philosophy . . . is to completely break down a detainee through white noise, through complete separa-tion of his personality, to completely unmoor him and make him completely dependent on his interrogators. And it was through that psychic breakdown he had planned to extract as much intel-ligence as possible."

Their company, Mitchell Jessen & Associates, is "booming," said Eban. By 2007, they reportedly had 120 employees in their offices in Spokane, Washington. Mitchell and Jessen issued a state-ment in response to questions from *Vanity Fair* saying, "We are proud of the work we have done for our country."

In December 2007 the *New York Times* revealed that the CIA had secretly destroyed videotapes of two interrogations. One of them was the interrogation of Abu Zubaydah. It is widely sus-pected that the CIA was trying to protect its agents—including its psychologists—from charges that they had participated in war crimes.

THE ENABLERS

In 2007 my *Democracy Now!* colleagues and I attended the an-nual convention of the American Psychological Association. We came in search of answers to a disturbing question: How had psychologists become leading enablers of torture?

In the post-9/11 era, the George W. Bush administration had gone looking for health care professionals to participate in so-called enhanced interrogations—a euphemism for torture—at Guantánamo Bay and other secret interrogation centers and prisons around the world. They needed to certify that interrogations were "safe, legal and effective." According to Physicians for Human Rights, Bush's Justice Department used the "spurious legal rationale that the techniques would not be considered torture so long as health professionals certified they were not." [1] Most healers were not buying the snake oil that Bush was peddling.

In 2006 the American Psychiatric Association and the American Medical Association both barred their members from taking part in military interrogations. Even the Society for Ethnomusicology took a stand against torture, in response to reports that the US military was blaring music to torment prisoners at Abu Ghraib prison in Iraq and at Guantánamo.

But the 148,000-member APA stood alone among major health care associations in being willing to participate in interrogations at military and CIA facilities.

Psychologists had become "the last ones willing to do this dirty work," charged Steven Reisner, PhD, a psychologist at Columbia University and New York University Medical School. He cofounded Coalition for an Ethical Psychology, a group of dissident psychologists who were demanding that the APA declare a moratorium on psychologist participation in all military and CIA interrogations. Reisner has twice run for president of the APA on a platform calling for an end to APA support for military interrogations.

First, do no harm. This basic tenet of medicine applies to psychologists. The idea that those charged with caring for patient health were implicated in abuses was chilling and cried out for closer scrutiny.

At the APA convention, we tried to film some of the sessions. It's what journalists do, from the White House, to city hall, to Occupy Wall Street. We were fully credentialed by the APA to cover its meeting.

We discovered quickly that the APA leadership mimicked the obsessive secrecy of the military. An APA official ordered me to shut off my recording equipment, allegedly due to privacy concerns of some of the panelists who worked with the military. Later, at a town hall meeting about interrogations that took place during the convention, APA officials threatened to call security to eject me and my colleagues if we did not stop filming. I broke away from the handlers and dashed for the podium.

Grabbing the microphone, over the objections of senior APA officials standing near me, I posed a question to the assembled APA members: Did they agree to such secrecy?

Pandemonium broke out. The psychologists, who were unaware of the media restrictions, were outraged. They began shouting at the officials who were trying to muzzle me.

The curtain had suddenly been pulled back on APA leaders, who were accustomed to doing as they pleased. After tense consultations, APA officials backed down—reluctantly—and allowed the filming to continue.

At a climactic meeting with APA leaders, Reisner and other dissident psychologists proposed a moratorium on psychologist participation in military interrogations. Our cameras rolled as the issue came up for a vote. The scene inside the cavernous Moscone

Center in San Francisco was surreal: uniformed military were out in force. Men and women in desert camo and navy whites worked the APA Council of Representatives, and officers in crisp dress uniforms stepped to the microphones.

Military psychologists insisted that they helped make interrogations safe, ethical, and legal. They cited instances where psychologists allegedly intervened to stop abuse.

"If we remove psychologists from these facilities, people are going to die!" boomed Colonel Larry James of the US Army, then chief psychologist at Guantánamo Bay and a member of the APA governing body.

"People are already dying!" shouted a psychologist in the audience.

Dr. Laurie Wagner, a Dallas psychologist and the past president of the APA Division of Psychoanalysis, shot back, "If psychologists have to be there in order to keep detainees from being killed, then those conditions are so horrendous that the only moral and ethical thing to do is to protest it by leaving it."

Moments later, the APA governing body approved a measure condemning "torture and cruel, inhuman, or degrading treatment or punishment," and prohibiting psychologists from participating in nineteen specific torture techniques. But the APA leadership inserted a curious caveat at the last minute: some techniques, such as isolation and sleep deprivation, were barred only when "used in a manner that represents significant pain or suffering or in a manner that a reasonable person would judge to cause lasting harm."

This appeared to leave room for "enhanced interrogation" techniques—such as near drowning, or waterboarding—authorized by President Bush in July 2007 for use at CIA black sites. Bush was determined to allow the CIA to torture, and the APA was just as determined to help. A broader resolution, which would have brought the association into line with its professional counterparts by banning members from participating in any interrogations at detention centers, failed.

Boston psychoanalyst Stephen Soldz, an organizer of the interrogation moratorium, was outraged. He noted that "Do no harm" is part of the Hippocratic oath taken by physicians, and is a cardinal principle of psychology. "By endorsing that it is an ethical thing for psychologists to do harm as long as it doesn't cause 'significant pain and suffering and long-lasting impairment'—this is a very sad day for psychology," he declared

RELENTLESS DISSIDENTS

Democracy Now! has closely chronicled the antitorture movement among psychologists. The ranks of the movement have swelled, as groups such as Physicians for Human Rights teamed up with the Coalition for an Ethical Psychology to push for change within the APA.

Psychologist Jean Maria Arrigo was a member of the APA's Presidential Task Force on Psychological Ethics and National Security in 2005, also known as the PENS Task Force. She later blew the whistle. Arrigo figured out that many of the people on the task force had close ties to the military. In 2006 reporter Mark Benjamin revealed the extent of the ties in *Salon*: six of the nine voting members of the task force worked in or closely with the military or the CIA. Several of them held command positions for psychologists in places where psychologist abuses had been reported.

Arrigo charged that the PENS Task Force was not interested in revealing the truth about psychologists and torture. It was attempting to cover up the truth.

When Arrigo exposed the APA's connection to torturers, she became a target of personal attacks from APA leaders. Following *Democracy Now!*'s coverage of the convention, APA president Gerald Koocher published an open letter addressed to me that attempted to smear Arrigo by questioning her "personal biases and troubled past." Koocher claimed that Arrigo's "personal difficulties" stemmed partly from her father's having committed suicide. It was one of many bizarre distortions and attempts to discredit her: Arrigo's father was, in fact, alive and well in California.

As APA leaders waged psychological warfare against their opponents, the dissidents pressed ahead. For psychologist Steven Reisner, the mission to end torture was personal: his parents were Holocaust survivors, and his father escaped from Poland to Russia, only to endure harsh interrogations there.

"What the suffering of the Holocaust gives those of us who are touched by it," he told me, "is the requirement that we stay separate from any authority and keep attention to fighting where such things might take place on any level. I am an activist against oppression and cruelty in the name of anything."

President George W. Bush had carefully crafted a legal rationale authorizing "enhanced interrogation techniques," and American torturers—including its psychologists—got down to work. From the US prison camp in Guantánamo Bay, to the dungeons of Abu Ghraib prison in Iraq, to Bagram Air Base in Afghanistan, countless hundreds, if not thousands, of people were subjected to torture in the name of the "Global War on Terror" since 9/11.

But with the exception of a few low-level soldiers at Abu Ghraib, not one person has been held accountable. The only high-level person sent to prison over torture was CIA analyst John Kiriakou—not for conducting torture but for exposing it, as a whistleblower. (See chapter 2, "The Whistleblowers.")

Professional psychologists were a key to maintaining the legal facade behind which these heinous acts were conducted. It was psychologists who trained and advised the interrogators and supervised the progress of "breaking" prisoners. This cooperation in turn was dependent on an official seal of approval from the American Psychological Association.

The APA and the military have actually been linked since birth. "The roots of contemporary psychology are in war and defense efforts," Steven Breckler, then head of the APA science directorate, told us. Psychology as a science distinct from psychiatry (psychiatrists, who are physicians, can prescribe drugs, and psychologists cannot) came into prominence with World War II, when the US military turned to psychologists for testing and evaluation of soldiers. Psychology "got a big boost" from the war, said Breckler. In the 1950s, nearly all federal funding for social science came from the military, and psychologists have been working closely with the military and intelligence agencies ever since.

The APA remains umbilically connected to the Pentagon. While the number of military psychologists in the APA is small—there are only about five hundred members of the APA's Society of Military Psychology, which also includes civilians who work with the military—they have outsized influence in the organization. That's because military money talks. The APA aggressively lobbies for funding from the military services, the Department of Homeland Security, the Defense Advanced Research Projects Agency (DARPA), and the DOD Counterintelligence Field

Activity (CIFA), to name a few. DOD spends several hundred million dollars on behavioral, cognitive, and social science research each year.

THE RECKONING

In 2014 Pulitzer Prize–winning *New York Times* journalist James Risen disclosed a damning email trail showing collusion between the APA and CIA in crafting the APA ethics policies that gave cover to psychologists involved in interrogations. Risen wrote about the collusion in his book, *Pay Any Price: Greed, Power and Endless War*.

In response to Risen's book, the growing pressure from rank-and-file psychologists, and continuing revelations about the APA's role in supporting torture, the association's board of directors commissioned an independent review by former assistant US attorney David Hoffman.

In July 2015 the 542-page Hoffman Report (officially titled *Report to the Special Committee of the Board of Directors of the American Psychological Association: Independent Review Relating to APA Ethics Guidelines, National Security Interrogations, and Torture*) was released. It contained explosive revelations that undermined the APA's repeated decade-long denials that some of its members were complicit in torture. It confirmed what whistle-blowers and dissident psychologists had long charged: the APA colluded actively with the US Department of Defense and the CIA, manipulating the association's policies, meetings, and members in order to continue its participation in and sanctioning of the Pentagon's torture program. The Hoffman Report also included an entire section headed "Arrigo and *Democracy Now!* fallout:

August–September 2007" about the ongoing coverage and revelations about the APA and torture on *Democracy Now!*

Stephen Soldz, who is a professor at the Boston Graduate School of Psychoanalysis, told *Democracy Now!*, "Since at least 2005, there's been a major debate in the [APA] and the profession about the role of psychologists in national security interrogations and torture. The association has denied it . . . The report says that the association was wrong; the so-called dissidents, the critics, were right."

The Hoffman Report delved into the practices of the PENS Task Force, which was convened ostensibly to determine the ethical standards for psychologists overseeing interrogations. But as PENS Task Force member Jean Maria Arrigo revealed, the task force issued a report after just two and a half days of deliberations that psychologists were playing a "valuable and ethical role" in assisting the military.

"I was appointed to be duped," Arrigo told *Democracy Now!* "The manipulation began very early on. So, for instance, I was seated between, on the one side, Morgan Banks, a US Army colonel who was the head of the BSCT psychologists [Behavioral Science Consultation Team, which worked on Guantánamo Bay], and on the other side, the now-President Barry Anton." Arrigo detailed how the task force was essentially run by Pentagon psychologists, some of them in uniform. While she was told not to take notes, she did anyway (she has since created the PENS Task Force archives at the University of Colorado at Boulder). Arrigo was lied to about the PENS process, and APA leaders suggested that her concerns about torture would be addressed at a future meeting.

A disturbing question remains: Why did the APA sell its soul to the military?

Part of the answer is that torture is profitable.

"In some ways, DoD is like a rich, powerful uncle to APA," stated the Hoffman Report. "The substantial financial benefits in the form of employment, grants, and contracts that DoD provided to psychologists around the country had a strong influence on APA's actions relating to the PENS Task Force (and therefore 'relating to torture'), since preserving and improving APA's relationship with DoD (including the benefits to psychology that flowed from it) formed an important part of the motive behind APA's actions." [2]

Reporter Katherine Eban wrote on the *Vanity Fair* website, "The report details how APA officials colluded secretly with defense department officials, plotted to deflect critics, used procedural sleight-of-hand to bury ethics complaints against participating psychologists, ignored blatant conflicts of interest, kept their communications secret, and even tried to destroy the email trail when things got too close for comfort." [3]

Among the torture profiteers were former CIA contractors and APA members James Mitchell and Bruce Jessen. "Mitchell and Jessen not only designed and monitored the torture, but undertook it with sleeves rolled up, an effort for which their company Mitchell Jessen & Associates was awarded $180 million in contracts by the CIA, $81 million of which was paid by the time the agreement was terminated," Eban reported. [4]

The Hoffman Report sent shock waves through the APA. The director of the APA Ethics Office, Stephen Behnke, considered the "chief of staff" of the APA-Pentagon-CIA collusion, was forced out, followed by the "retirements" in July 2015 of APA CEO Dr. Norman Anderson, Deputy CEO Dr. Michael Honaker, and the executive director for public and member communications, Rhea Farberman.

APA President-elect Nadine Kaslow and past president Susan McDaniel issued a public apology following the Hoffman Report. Addressing the "dissident" psychologists opposed to torture, they wrote, "We deeply regret the fact that some APA members and other critics were privately and publicly discounted for raising concerns. What happened never should have."

The APA followed with a letter to psychologists around the world: "We are strongly aware that these events have cast a pall on psychology and psychologists in all countries, with the potential to negatively affect perceptions of the integrity of our discipline worldwide. For this we are deeply sorry."

Apologies are a start. Accountability should follow. When asked if there should be indictments, Stephen Soldz said, "There should be a legal investigation." He is calling for the FBI and the Justice Department to investigate.

Only if torture's enablers are held accountable will it remove "this stain on our collective integrity," as APA Presidents Kaslow and McDaniel wrote.

PSYCHOLOGISTS' CONFESSION

For nearly a decade, dissident psychologists had been organizing and waging a fierce, lonely battle to reclaim the soul of their healing profession from a corrupt professional association. A decade of resolutions and finally a legal report that took down the entire leadership of the organization—this is what it took to get a ban on torture.

This struggle came to a climactic head at the APA annual convention held in Toronto in August 2015. It had been ten years since the sham PENS Task Force and a month since the Hoffman Report.

The psychologists' moment of reckoning had finally arrived. *Democracy Now!* traveled to Toronto to cover the historic session.

The APA's Council of Representatives voted 156–1 (six members also abstained from voting) to adopt a policy barring psychologists from participating in national security interrogations.[5] The resolution also put the APA on the side of international law by barring psychologists from working at Guantánamo Bay, CIA black sites, and other settings deemed illegal under the Geneva Conventions of the UN Convention Against Torture, unless they are working directly for the persons being detained or for an independent third party working to protect human rights. The sole dissenter was retired colonel Larry James, former top army intelligence psychologist at Guantánamo and Abu Ghraib prison in Iraq and more recently the dean of the School of Professional Psychology at Wright State University in Dayton, Ohio.

Peter Kinderman, president-elect of the British Psychological Society, observed the vote. He remarked wryly to me, "This represents American psychologists rejoining the seventeenth century and repudiating torture as a means of state power."

I was standing next to Stephen Soldz, the longtime crusader against torture. He was wearing a button, "First, do no harm." I asked him what the vote banning psychologists from interrogation meant.

"This is the result of nearly a decade of effort by hundreds and thousands of people," he told me. "When the membership of the APA spoke in 2008 in a referendum, they voted fifty-nine percent to get psychologists out of Guantánamo and CIA black sites—but a small group of APA insiders undermined that. This reverses that, after seven years of deceit. So it's a victory for our movement. But I also want to emphasize that it's a victory for the anti-torture movement. The APA has moved from being complicit in

THE SWORD AND THE SHIELD

Democracy Now! has far outlived its original nine-month projected life span covering the 1996 presidential race as the only daily election show in public broadcasting. It has been my privilege these past two decades to be part of the largest independent media collaboration in the country, bringing out the voices of people building movements that have changed the world.

Independent media is the oxygen of a democracy. It is not brought to you by the oil or gas or coal companies when we talk about climate change. It's not brought to you by the weapons manufacturers when we talk about war and peace. It's not brought to you by the insurance industry or big pharma when we talk about health care.

I see the media as a huge kitchen table that stretches across the globe that we all sit around and debate and discuss the most important issues of the day: war and peace, life and death.

Anything less than that is a disservice to the servicemen and women of this country.

People on military bases can't have these debates. They rely on us in civilian society to have the discussions that lead to the decisions about whether they live or die, whether they kill or are killed.

Anything less than that is a disservice to a democratic society.

GOING TO WHERE THE SILENCE IS

I think back to the event that cemented my lifelong commitment to independent media—where I experienced its power, its importance, and the responsibility that journalists have to go to where the silence is. It happened in 1991, when I survived a massacre in occupied East Timor, a tiny country on the other side of the world.

In 1975 President Gerald Ford and Secretary of State Henry Kissinger traveled to Indonesia and met with the long-reigning dictator Suharto, who had presided over the killing of perhaps more than a million of his own people from 1965 to 1967. During their trip, Kissinger and Ford gave Suharto the go-ahead for Indonesia to invade East Timor, about three hundred miles north of Australia.

As the president and secretary of state flew out of Indonesia to meet with Philippines dictator Ferdinand Marcos, the Indonesian military invaded East Timor by land, air, and sea. It was December 7, 1975. Ninety percent of the weapons used in the invasion were from the United States. Indonesia closed East Timor to the outside world and commenced one of the great slaughters of the twentieth century.

I first got a chance to go to East Timor in 1990 with my colleague, the remarkably brave journalist Allan Nairn. What we
found there was a hell on Earth. Everywhere we went, the military
was surveilling the people, disappearing many. One-third of the
population had been killed. It was truly terrifying.

We returned to East Timor in October 1991. Allan was writing
for the *New Yorker*. I was doing a radio documentary for Pacifica.
For the first time, the United Nations had brokered a deal with
Indonesia to send in a delegation to investigate the human rights
situation. We wanted to see if the Timorese were going to be able
to talk to the UN delegation.

When we arrived, we went to the main church in Dili, the capital of East Timor. A mass was being held, and the women were crying. We didn't know if it was the standard sorrow of this occupied
country or if something terrible had just happened. After mass, we
learned that the Indonesian military had surrounded the church
the night before and shot into it, killing a young man named Sebastião Gomes. Many young people had taken refuge in the churches
of East Timor so they could speak to the UN delegation. They
didn't want to be arrested. The church was the only place where
they could assemble.

The next day there was a funeral for Sebastião. A thousand
people came out. Following the service, they walked to the cemetery. We'd never seen anything like it. In this land with no freedom
of assembly, no freedom of the press, no freedom of speech, the
people of East Timor put up their hands in the V sign and shouted,
"Viva East Timor! Viva independence! Viva Sebastião!"

Amid this unprecedented act of defiance, they buried Sebastião
Gomes.

Allan and I traveled around East Timor seeing how the Indonesian military was preparing for the UN delegation. Everywhere we

heard the same story. They told the villagers, "If you speak to the UN delegation, we will kill you after they leave and put your body in a mass grave." Bishop Carlos Filipe Ximenes Belo, who would win the Nobel Peace Prize in 1996, told us that the line most commonly used was, "We will kill your family until the seventh generation." A nationwide death threat had been issued.

We learned that the delegation would not be coming. We found out later that it had been canceled at the behest of the United States.

On the two-week anniversary of Sebastião's death, the people of East Timor decided to march once again, retracing their steps to the cemetery.

It was early in the morning on November 12, 1991. So many people turned out for mass in the main Catholic church that the priests had to hold communion outside under the trees. Afterward, people streamed into the street. But this time students unfurled banners that they had written on bedsheets, hidden under their Catholic school blouses. You'd see an older woman in her traditional Timorese garb holding up one end of a sign and a girl in her Catholic school uniform holding up the other.

They marched through the streets of Dili through a geography of pain. Every other building had a story: perhaps it was a military barracks where prisoners were killed. Or the back of a hotel where Timorese were held. Or officers' homes where Timorese women were raped.

We followed thousands of East Timorese as they marched through the streets of Dili and made their way to the cemetery, the same place where Sebastião and so many other victims were buried. The peaceful protesters were risking so much. The Indonesian military had lined the route.

At the cemetery we asked the marchers, "Why are you doing this?"

"For my mother," one responded.

"For my father."

"For my village—it was wiped out."

Then from the direction the procession had come, we saw hundreds of Indonesian soldiers marching down the dirt road holding their US M16 rifles at the ready position. We were in the middle of the crowd, interviewing people. Allan suggested we walk to the front, because although we knew they had committed many massacres in the past, they'd never done it in front of Western journalists.

We had always hidden our equipment, because if people were caught talking to journalists, they could be arrested, disappeared, or killed. But this time we took out our equipment. We wanted to make clear who we were. I put on my headphones. I held up my microphone like a flag. Allan put the camera above his head, and we walked to the front of the crowd. The people were trapped because there were high walls on either side of the road. People at the back could run away. Some could run through a small opening in the cemetery wall.

MASSACRE

The Indonesian soldiers marched up, ten to twelve abreast. It got very quiet. They rounded the corner, and—without any warning, without any hesitation, without any provocation—the soldiers swept past us and opened fire on the crowd, gunning people down from right to left. The first to go down was a little boy behind us. He just exploded from the gun-fire. The soldiers kept shooting. A group of them came at me and they took my microphone, waving it in my face as if to say, "This is what we don't want."

They slammed me to the ground. Allan took a photograph of the soldiers opening fire. He threw himself on top of me to protect me, but then they took their M16s like baseball bats and slammed them against his head until they fractured his skull. We were lying on the ground. Allan was covered in blood. They were killing everyone around us.

A group of soldiers that weren't killing the others lined up in firing squad fashion and put their guns to our heads. They'd stripped us now of everything. The only thing I had left was my passport. They were shouting, "Australia? Australia?" and *"Politik! Politik!"* as if to say we were political if we were witnessing this, and they wanted to know if we were from Australia.

We understood what was at stake with this question. Just before Indonesia invaded East Timor, Indonesian soldiers executed five Australia-based television journalists who were covering events leading up to the invasion. On December 8, 1975, Australian journalist Roger East, the only other Western reporter left in East Timor, was dragged out of a radio station in Dili. As he shouted, "I'm from Australia!" they dragged him down to the harbor and shot him dead.

The Australian government hardly protested the killing of its journalists. We believe that's because years later, Indonesia and Australia would sign the Timor Gap Treaty, dividing up occupied Timor's oil between them. Oil is the source of so much pain in the world.

I threw my passport at the soldiers. We shouted, "No, we're from America! America!" They kicked me in the stomach. When I got my breath back, I shouted again, "America, America!" More soldiers joined the firing squad line.

At some point, they lowered their guns from our heads. We believe it was because we were from the same country that their weapons were from. They would have to pay a price for killing us that they had never had to pay for killing the Timorese. They moved on.

A Red Cross Jeep pulled up. The driver got out. They had beaten an old Timorese man into a ditch. Every time he picked up his head in prayer, they took the butts of their rifles and smashed his face. Then they had moved on to kill others. The Red Cross driver picked him up and put him in the Jeep.

We climbed into the Jeep. Scores of Timorese jumped on top of us as we rode on top of the vehicle. We drove away from this killing field to the hospital, where the doctors and nurses were working furiously to save those who had not died immediately.

There were incredibly brave young people who could have run. But when one of their friends or sisters or brothers had fallen, they would stop and hold them so they wouldn't die alone. The hospital was overflowing. When the doctors and nurses saw us, they started to cry. Not because we were in worse shape than the Timorese— we weren't. It was what we symbolized to them as Americans, as Westerners—not just to people in Timor but also to people all over the world.

They see us in two ways: as the sword and the shield. The sword, because the United States provides weapons to human-rights-abusing regimes like the Indonesian government, or uses the weapons itself, like in Iraq or Afghanistan.

But they also see the American people as a shield. That day, they saw that shield bloodied. It just deepened their despair.

We made it to the compound of Bishop Belo. Thousands of terrified people were taking refuge there. We certainly had not succeeded in stopping the killing: the Indonesian military killed 270 people that day. And this was not one of the larger massacres in Timor.

We could still hear gunshots. We knew the only way to stop the killing was if we left the country and got word to the outside world. There was one plane leaving that day. The bishop helped me clean up Allan. He gave him a new shirt. I took Allan's bloody shirt and wrapped it around my waist under a towel. We had someone take pictures of us. We knew the Indonesian military would deny there was a massacre, but at least they would have to explain what happened to us. I hid the film on my body. We could not take anything with us because soldiers had surrounded our hotel.

Allan's head was just glistening with blood, as if he were wearing a red bathing cap under his matted dark mop of hair. If we could clean him up and get to the airport fast enough, maybe we could get out on the only plane leaving that day.

The city was now shut down. We raced to the airport, where soldiers behind the counter started to shout. Did they realize we'd been at the massacre site? Had they officially decided not to kill us there, and now they wanted us out? We didn't know, but we demanded to get on the flight.

On the tarmac, we walked very slowly to the plane, escorted by the military. Pain was shooting through Allan's body. I didn't want it to be obvious that he was badly injured, so I kept pausing to say I was admiring the view of this beautiful country. We were the last ones on the plane. When we got on board and the door closed, the flight attendants handed me a silver bowl with water and said gently, "Clean him."

We were able to fly to West Timor, which is part of Indonesia, and on to Bali, where Allan made a phone call to Western media. I took the towel that I had wrapped around my waist and wiped the blood off the phone as he spoke. He said, "There's been a massacre."

Then we boarded an international flight to the United States that stopped in Guam, a US territory. We had to argue with the airline officials to let us on the flight, because they were concerned that our condition would scare the other passengers.

Once we took off and were no longer on Indonesian soil, the flight attendants asked over the loudspeaker if there was a physician on the plane. Doctors checked Allan and urged us to go to the US naval hospital on Guam, but we said no. We knew they would restrict our access there. So we requested to go to a civilian hospital. An ambulance from Guam Memorial Hospital met us at the gate. Once at the hospital, while doctors were stitching Allan's head, he had the phone to his ear as we fielded calls from media around the world. Allan would occasionally shout out in pain in the midst of an interview as doctors closed up his head. He never stopped talking.

An ambulance took us to the cable network station that linked up with CNN. While we were at the hospital, someone got my film developed, and we were then able to show the photographs on the broadcast as we were interviewed and explained how scores of people had been killed. The Indonesian military denied that a massacre had taken place.

Allan was operated on again in Washington, DC. We then held a news conference at the National Press Club. We described what we saw: Indonesian soldiers armed with US M16s gunned down innocent civilians. From the beginning of the invasion of East Timor in 1975, the Indonesian military was armed, trained, and financed by the United States.

The massacre was the first time that the major nightly network newscasts in the United States mentioned East Timor since the day after Indonesia had invaded sixteen years before, despite the fact that this was one of the worst genocides of the late twentieth century.

Compare that to Pol Pot's Cambodia, where the genocide from 1975 to 1979 was proportionally similar. Hundreds of articles exposing Pol Pot's atrocities appeared in the US media. The difference? Cambodia was an official enemy of the United States; Indonesia was a close ally. The president and the secretary of state denounced Pol Pot's Cambodia regularly, and the press echoed that criticism. But what about when the United States remains silent on atrocities and supports the regime in power?

We need a media that does not simply serve as a stenographer to those in power.

The massacre took place November 12, 1991. Eight years later, the people of East Timor voted for their freedom in a UN-supervised referendum. For the next three years, the United Nations would run East Timor as it transitioned. On May 20, 2002, East Timor became the newest nation in the world.

Allan Nairn and I returned to Timor for this celebration of independence. One hundred thousand people gathered outside of Dili in a place called Tasitolu. UN Secretary General Kofi Annan and world dignitaries gave speeches. Finally, Xanana Gusmão—the rebel leader of occupied East Timor who had been imprisoned by the Indonesians for years and was now the founding president—addressed the crowd in many languages. He then unfurled the flag of the Democratic Republic of East Timor.

As fireworks lit the sky, you could see the light reflected in the tear-streaked faces of the people of Timor. They had resisted, and they had won—at an unbelievably high price. One-third of their population—two hundred thousand people—was killed. Yet this nation of survivors had prevailed.

As they celebrated their victory, the Timorese thanked people, especially those from the most powerful countries, for pressuring their governments to stop supplying weapons to human-rights-abusing regimes.

The Timorese have always served as a remarkable lesson to me. Whether we are doctors, nurses, professors, lawyers, farmers, or businesspeople; whether we're librarians, journalists, or students; whether we're artists, employed, or unemployed—we have a decision to make every hour of every day: whether we want to represent the sword or the shield.

Democracy Now!

ACKNOWLEDGMENTS

There would be no *Democracy Now!* without the many incredibly dedicated people who have helped to transform it from a daily election show in 1996 to the largest public media collaboration in the country today.

A huge thank you to those who have taken that daily journey with me, especially my cohost, award-winning journalist Juan González, who has been there from the beginning.

My heartfelt gratitude goes to the remarkable team at *Democracy Now!*, who work day and night. Julie Crosby has kept our organization on a firm foundation and steered us through countless challenges and dynamic growth; without her intelligence, her heart, and her dedication, our work would be impossible. Our daily, global, grassroots news hour is produced by a remarkable team, led by the unflappable and insightful Mike Burke, including Sam Alcoff, Laura Gottesdiener, Deena Guzder, Robby Karran, Amy Littlefield, Hany Massoud, Aaron Mate, Nermeen Shaikh, Carla Wills, and Charina Nadura; special thanks to Nermeen, also, for cohosting for many years. We have an incredible team who pulls together the broadcast each morning, including Mike DiFilippo, Miguel Nogueira,

Becca Staley, Hugh Gran, David Prude, Vesta Goodarz, Jon Randolph, Kieran Meadows, Anna Ozbek; and our colleagues who work to keep the whole operation running smoothly, from social media to development, outreach and archives, among whom are Brendan Allen, Miriam Barnard, Ariel Boone, Naqi Cruz, Simin Farkhondeh, Angie Karran, Malik Nickens, Isis Phillips, and Rob Young. A special thank you to Neil Shibata, whose dedication to the written word makes our daily transcripts available to readers around the world.

Democracy Now!'s Spanish-language team carefully translates our daily headlines in text and audio for the world. Spanning many countries, this amazing group includes Clara Ibarra, Andres Conteris, Igor Moreno Unanua, and the inimitable Chuck Scurich. And a special *arigato* to our dedicated group of volunteers who maintain *Democracy Now!* Japan (democracynow.jp) under the dedicated leadership of Makiko Nakano.

We continue to be inspired by the very talented journalists who have worked with us and continue as friends and colleagues as they pursue their work around the world. They are our DNA (*Democracy Now!* Alumni): Renee Feltz, Sharif Abdel Kouddous, Anjali Kamat, Nicole Salazar, Ana Nogueira, Elizabeth Press, John Hamilton, Maria Carrion, Jaisal Noor, Ryan Devereaux, Franklin Lopez, Julie Drizin, Dan Coughlin, David Love, Richard Rowley, Jacquie Soohen, Jeremy Scahill, Yoruba Richen, Jessica Lee, Jon Gerberg, Nemo Allen, and Steve Martinez.

We thank Patrick Lannan, Andy Tuch, Laurie Betlach, Randall Wallace, Janet MacGillivray Wallace, Diana Cohn and Craig Merrilees, Hans Schoepflin, Israel and Edith Taub, Tony Tabatznik, Len Goodman, Barbara and Martha Fleischman, Larry and Mary Ann Tucker, Steve Silberstein, Shel Kaphan and Ericka Locke, Rob Glaser, Martin Collier, Joe Zimlich, Jean Beard, Edith Penty, Roy Singham and the Thoughtworkers, and the late Irma Weiss.

Deep thanks to Karen Ranucci, who has worked in every capacity at *Democracy Now!*, including orchestrating the building of our green, LEED Platinum-certified broadcast TV/radio/internet studio, and who continues her commitment, ensuring the future of *Democracy Now!* And to Michael Ratner, a dear friend and president emeritus of The Center for Constitutional Rights, whose work inspires us all.

Our gratitude to those on whose shoulders we stand, including Bill Moyers, present at the creation of public television and a stalwart supporter to this day; DeeDee Halleck, godmother of community television;

and the late Samori Marksman, a pan-Africanist who, as WBAI's program director, taught me so much about the history of Africa and the Caribbean, and how a local radio station can be the gateway to a rich world.

Also deep appreciation for the friendship and support of my colleague Brenda Murad, and to Caren Spruch, Elisabeth Benjamin, Maria Carrion, Allan Nairn, Julie Cohen, my news mews crew Fred Padgett, Isabel Jenkins, Miquel Rowell and Mario Delgado and the next generation, including Ceci, Rory, Sara, Aliza, Gabriela, Estrella, Leila, Maria, Ksenija, Oskar, Will, Jack and Ryan, Leila, Rafah, Ana, Jake, Paige, Gehrig, Reese, AnaLouisa, Ismael, Sofian, Zakariah, Qasim, Esteban, Arthur, Nina, Olivia, Sonia, Dakota, and Kevin.

Loving thanks to our family, as always, who provide constant support, including Dan and Steve, along with Yujin Weng, Sue Minter, Ruth Levine, and all the incredible nieces and nephews: Jasper, Ariel, Eli, Sarah, and Anna. Also Denis's mother, Patricia Moynihan; his brothers Tim, Sean, and Mike; sister, Deirdre; sisters-in-law Mary, Kate, and Amy; the nieces and nephews Quinn, Liam, Maren, Nora, Evan, Maeve, and Fergus; and, for her support, caring, and tolerance for frequent absences, Denis's wife, Trish Schoch. And to the memory of our dear parents, George and Dorrie Goodman, and Michael Moynihan.

Thanks to Jonathan Karp, our publisher at Simon & Schuster, who believed in this book. Thanks also to our editor, Ben Loehnen, for his thoughtful guidance and patience and for shepherding this project to completion, and to Amar Deol and Jonathan Evans for keeping us on track. As always, gratitude to our agent, Luke Janklow, and his associate, Claire Dippel, for their counsel and for finding the right home for this book.

We also thank Glenn Mott, Chris Richcreek, and T.R. "Rocky" Shepard III at King Features for their work in supporting our weekly column over the past decade.

Capturing the spirit of two decades of *Democracy Now!* was a daunting task. A profound thank you to David Goodman and Denis Moynihan for helping me find the right words.

NOTES

CHAPTER 1: THE WAR AND PEACE REPORT

1. "Pat Buchanan in His Own Words," Fairness & Accuracy in Reporting, last modified February 26, 1996, http://fair.org/press-release/pat-buchanan-in-his-own-words.
2. "Pat Buchanan in United We Stand America Conference," On the Issues, last modified April 17, 2013, www.ontheissues.org/Archive/UWSA_Conference_Pat_Buchanan.htm

CHAPTER 2: THE WHISTLEBLOWERS

1. John Pilger, "The Siege of Julian Assange Is a Farce—A Special Investigation," Johnpilger.com, November 16, 2014, http://johnpilger.com/articles/the-siege-of-julian-assange-is-a-farce-a-special-investigation.

2. "2012-05-30 UK Supreme Court Rules Against Assange Appeal," WL Central, May 30, 2012, www.wlcentral.org/node/2624.

3. "2012-05-29 Four Days After Julian Assange Verdict, US Secretary Clinton to Visit Sweden," WL Central, May 29, 2012, http://wlcentral.org/node/2623.

4. "Cable: 10SANAA4_a, General Petraeus' Meeting with Saleh on Security Assistance, AQAP Strikes," WikiLeaks, January 4, 2010, https://wikileaks.org/plusd/cables/10SANAA4_a.html.

5. UPI, "Clinton on a WikiLeaks 'Apology Tour,'" January 10, 2011, www.upi.com/Top_News/World-News/2011/01/10/Clinton-on-a-WikiLeaks-apology-tour/30541294675421.

6. Matthew Schofield, "WikiLeaks: Iraqi Children in U.S. Raid Shot in Head, U.N. Says," *McClatchyDC*, August 31, 2011, www.mcclatchydc.com/news/special-reports/article24696685.html.

7. Ibid.

8. Morgan Marquis-Boire, Glenn Greenwald, and Micah Lee, "XKEY-SCORE: NSA's Google for the World's Private Communications," the Intercept, July 1, 2015, https://theintercept.com/2015/07/01/nsas-google-worlds-private-communications.

9. Dan Froomkin, "NSA's Bulk Collection of Phone Records Is Illegal, Appeals Court Says," the Intercept, May 7, 2015, https://theintercept.com/2015/05/07/appellate-court-rules-nsas-bulk-collection-phone-records-illegal.

10. David Leigh, "US Embassy Cables Leak Sparks Global Diplomatic Crisis," *Guardian* (UK), November 28, 2010, www.theguardian.com/world/2010/nov/28/us-embassy-cable-leak-diplomacy-crisis.

11. Jack Mirkinson, "Daniel Ellsberg Calls Edward Snowden a 'Hero,' Says NSA Leak Was Most Important in American History," *Huffington Post*, June 10, 2013, www.huffingtonpost.com/2013/06/10/edward-snowden-daniel-ellsberg-whistleblower-history_n_3413545.html.

12. Maureen Dowd, "Where's the Justice at Justice?," *New York Times*, August 16, 2014, www.nytimes.com/2014/08/17/opinion/sunday/maureen-dowd-wheres-the-justice-at-justice.html?_r=0.

13. Leigh, "US Embassy Cables Leak."

14. Spencer Ackerman, "Petraeus Leaks: Obama's Leniency Reveals 'Profound Double Standard,' Lawyer Says," *Guardian*, March 16, 2015, http://www.theguardian.com/us-news/2015/mar/16/obama-double-standard-petraeus-leaks.

15. Thomas Gibbons-Neff and Dan Lamothe, "Pentagon Chief's Use of Personal Email Will Prompt Senate Review," *Washington Post,* December 17, 2015, https://www.washingtonpost.com/news/checkpoint/wp/2015/12/17/pentagon-chief-used-personal-email-account-for-some-official-business/.

16. Matt Apuzzo and Michael S. Schmidt, "Obama's Comments About Clinton's Emails Rankle Some in the F.B.I.," *New York Times*, October 16, 2015, www.nytimes.com/2015/10/17/us/politics/obamas-comments-on-clinton-emails-collide-with-fbi-inquiry.html.

17. Ellen Nakashima and Adam Goldman, "Leak Investigation Stalls amid Fears of Confirming U.S.-Israel Operation," *Washington Post*, March 10, 2015, www.washingtonpost.com/world/national-security/leak-investigation-stalls-amid-fears-of-confirming-joint-us-israel-operation/2015/03/10/2a348b1e-c36c-11e4-9ec2-b418f57a4a99_story.html.

18. Nia-Malika Henderson, "Feinstein on Petraeus: 'This Man Has Suffered Enough,' " *Washington Post,* January 11, 2015, www.washingtonpost.com/news/post-politics/wp/2015/01/11/feinstein-on-petraeus-this-man-has-suffered-enough.

19. David Folkenflik, " '*New York Times*' Editor: Losing Snowden Scoop 'Really Painful,' " NPR, June 5, 2014, www.npr.org/2014/06/05/319233332/new-york-times-editor-losing-snowden-scoop-really-painful.

20. Isabell Hülsen and Holger Stark, " 'We Were Arrogant': Interview with *New York Times* Editor Baquet," Spiegel Online International, January 23, 2015, www.spiegel.de/international/business/spiegel-interview-with-chief-new-york-times-editor-dean-baquet-a-1014704.html.

21. The "Puzzle Palace" is a nickname for the NSA and the title of the first in-depth book examining the workings of the agency, written

by investigative reporter James Bamford, *The Puzzle Palace: A Report on America's Most Secret Agency* (Boston: Houghton Mifflin, 1982).

22. James Bamford, "The Agency That Could Be Big Brother," *New York Times*, December 25, 2005, www.nytimes.com/2005/12/25/weekinre view/the-agency-that-could-be-big-brother.html.

23. *Democracy Now!*, June 10, 2013.

CHAPTER 4: STOPPING THE MACHINERY OF DEATH

1. Brenda Goodman, "As Execution Nears, Last Push from Inmate's Supporters," *New York Times,* July 15, 2007, www.nytimes .com/2007/07/15/us/15execute.html.

2. Jen Marlowe, Martina Davis-Correia, and Troy Anthony Davis, *I Am Troy Davis* (New York: Haymarket, 2013), 40–43.

3. Amy Goodman, "Troy Davis and the Meaning of 'Actual Innocence,' " Truthdig, August 18, 2009, www.truthdig.com/report /item/20090818_troy_davis_and_the_meaning_of_actual _innocence.

4. Amy Goodman, "Troy Davis, Victim of Judicial Lynching," *Guardian* (UK), September 14, 2011, www.theguardian.com/commentisfree /cifamerica/2011/sep/14/troy-davis-death-penalty-lynching.

5. Brendan Lowe, "Will Georgia Kill an Innocent Man?," *Time*, July 13, 2007, http://content.time.com/time/nation/article/0,8599,1643384,00 .html.

6. Marlowe, Davis-Correia, and Davis, *Troy Davis*, 153.

7. Ehab Zahriyeh, "Execution Methods Around the World," Al Jazeera America, April 30, 2014, http://america.aljazeera.com/articles/2014 /4/30/execution-methods.html.

8. "Methods of Execution," Death Penalty Worldwide, Cornell University Law School, June 22, 2012, www.deathpenaltyworldwide.org /methods-of-execution.cfm.

9. "Facts About the Death Penalty," Death Penalty Information Center, last modified December 9, 2015, www.deathpenaltyinfo.org/documents /FactSheet.pdf.

10. "Death Penalty and Race," Amnesty International USA, accessed December 15, 2015, www.amnestyusa.org/our-work/issues/death-penalty/us-death-penalty-facts/death-penalty-and-race.

11. Angel Harris, "Replacing the Noose with a Needle: The Legacy of Lynching in the United States," American Civil Liberties Union, February 18, 2015, www.aclu.org/blog/speakeasy/replacing-noose-needle-legacy-lynching-united-states.

12. Katie Fretland, "Records Show Oklahoma Officials Wanted Perks for Helping Texas in Search for Scarce Lethal Injections," *Colorado Independent*, March 18, 2014, http://www.coloradoindependent.com/146553/oklahoma-scrambles-to-find-lethal-injections-for-two-imminent-executions.

13. Tom McNichol, "Death by Nitrogen: Will This New Method of Execution Save the Death Penalty?," *Slate*, May 22, 2014, http://www.slate.com/articles/news_and_politics/jurisprudence/2014/05/death_by_nitrogen_gas_will_the_new_method_of_execution_save_the_death_penalty.html.

14. Kim Bellware, "Oklahoma Adds Nitrogen Gas Chamber to Its Execution Methods," *Huffington Post*, April 17, 2015, www.huffingtonpost.com/2015/04/17/oklahoma-gas-execution_n_7089416.html.

15. Steven W. Hawkins, "A Death Knell for the Death Penalty?," MSNBC, October 12, 2015, www.msnbc.com/msnbc/death-knell-the-death-penalty.

16. "Part I: History of the Death Penalty," Death Penalty Information Center, accessed December 16, 2015, www.deathpenaltyinfo.org/part-i-history-death-penalty.

17. "Part II: History of the Death Penalty," Death Penalty Information Center, accessed December 16, 2015, www.deathpenaltyinfo.org/part-ii-history-death-penalty.

18. "Innocence: List of Those Freed from Death Row," Death Penalty Information Center, last modified October 12, 2015, www.deathpenaltyinfo.org/innocence-list-those-freed-death-row.

19. *Democracy Now!*, December 27, 2000.

20. Ed Pilkington, "Loner on a Mission to Make Conservative Nebraska Ditch the Death Penalty," *Guardian* (UK), May 23, 2015, www.the

guardian.com/us-news/2015/may/23/loner-mission-conservative
-nebraska-ditch-death-penalty.

21. Chris McDaniel and Tasneem Nashrulla, "This Is the Man in India Who Is Selling States Illegally Imported Execution Drugs," BuzzFeed, October 20, 2015, www.buzzfeed.com/chrismcdaniel/this-is-the -man-in-india-who-is-selling-states-illegally-imp#.luV9gp4d7.

CHAPTER 5: THE RISE OF THE 99 PERCENT

1. Ishaan Tharoor, "From Europe with Love: U.S. 'Indignados' Occupy Wall Street," *Time*, October 5, 2011, http://world.time .com/2011/10/05/from-europe-with-love-the-u-s-indignados-have -arrived.

2. Nick Pinto, "City Settles Lawsuit Over the Destruction of the Occupy Wall Street Library," *Village Voice*, April 09, 2013, www.villagevoice .com/news/city-settles-lawsuit-over-the-destruction-of-the-occupy -wall-street-library-6706963.

3. Murray Wardrop, " 'Occupy' Is Most Commonly Used Word in English Language Media, Claims Study," *Telegraph* (UK), November 10, 2011, www.telegraph.co.uk/news/newstopics/howaboutthat/8881273 /Occupy-is-most-commonly-used-word-in-English-language-media -claims-study.html.

4. One executive did go to jail. Kareem Serageldin was a trader with Credit Suisse and was convicted of "mismarking" hundreds of millions in investments, hiding losses as the global financial crisis deepened. He was sentenced to thirty months in federal prison, which he spent at a low-security prison run by the for-profit GEO Group.

5. *The Low-Wage Drag on Our Economy*, Democratic staff, U.S. House Committee on Education and the Workforce, May 2013, http://demo crats.edworkforce.house.gov/sites/democrats.edworkforce.house.gov /files/documents/WalMartReport-May2013.pdf.

6. *Walmart on Tax Day: How Taxpayers Subsidize America's Biggest Employer and Richest Family* (Washington, DC: Americans for Tax Fairness, April 2014), http://www.americansfortaxfairness.org/files /Walmart-on-Tax-Day-Americans-for-Tax-Fairness-1.pdf.

7. Deborah Wang, "How Seattle Agonized Over and Passed the $15 Minimum Wage," KUOW.org, March 28, 2015, http://kuow.org/post /how-seattle-agonized-over-and-passed-15-minimum-wage.

8. Ibid.

9. Kenneth Lovett, "Andrew Cuomo Rejects Assembly Democrats' Plan to Raise Minimum Wage to $15 an Hour in 2018," *New York Daily News*, March 12, 2015, www.nydailynews.com/news/politics /cuomo-rejects-assembly-dems-plan-15-hour-minimum-wage-article -1.2146491.

10. Andrew Cuomo, "Andrew M. Cuomo: Fast-Food Workers Deserve a Raise," *New York Times*, May 6, 2015, www.nytimes.com/2015/05/07 /opinion/andrew-m-cuomo-fast-food-workers-deserve-a-raise.html? _r=0.

11. Steven Greenhouse and Jana Kasperkevic, "Fight for $15 Swells Into Largest Protest by Low-Wage Workers in US History," *Guardian* (UK), April 15, 2015, www.theguardian.com/us-news/2015/apr/15 /fight-for-15-minimum-wage-protests-new-york-los-angeles-atlanta -boston.

12. Editorial board, "A Big Victory for Fast-Food Workers in New York," *New York Times*, July 23, 2015, www.nytimes.com/2015/07/24 /opinion/a-big-victory-for-fast-food-workers-in-new-york.html.

CHAPTER 6: CLIMATE JUSTICE

1. NASA, "Scientific Consensus: Earth's Climate Is Warming," Climate Change: Vital Signs of the Planet, http://climate.nasa.gov/scientific -consensus/.

2. Neela Banerjee, "Exxon's Oil Industry Peers Knew About Climate Dangers in the 1970s, Too," InsideClimate News, December 22, 2015, http://insideclimatenews.org/news/22122015/exxon-mobile-oil -industry-peers-knew-about-climate-change-dangers-1970s-american -petroleum-institute-api-shell-chevron-texaco.

3. *Democracy Now!*, June 9, 2009.

CHAPTER 7: THE LGBTQ REVOLUTION

1. Lillian Faderman, *Odd Girls and Twilight Lovers: A History of Lesbian Life in Twentieth-Century America* (New York: Columbia University Press, 1991), 195.

2. David Carter, *Stonewall: The Riots That Sparked the Gay Revolution* (New York: St. Martin's Press, 2010), 160.

3. "Day of Desperation," AIDS Coalition to Unleash Power (ACT UP) website, last accessed December 16, 2015, www.actupny.org/diva/syn Desperation.html.

4. Greg Jobin-Leeds, *When We Fight, We Win!: Twenty-First-Century Social Movements and the Activists That Are Transforming Our World* (New York: New Press, 2016), 9.

5. Derek Wallbank, "Boehner's House: $2.3 Mln Defending DOMA in Losing Court Fight," Bloomberg News, June 26, 2013.

6. Paul Taylor, "Wedge Issues on the Ballot," Pew Research Center, July 26, 2006, www.pewresearch.org/2006/07/26/wedge-issues-on-the -ballot.

7. Jeremy Diamond, "Arkansas Gov. Asa Hutchinson Influenced by Son, Seth," CNN, April 1, 2015, www.cnn.com/2015/04/01/politics/asa -hutchinson-arkansas-governor-religious-freedom.

8. Oralandar Brand-Williams, "DeBoer and Rowse Exchange Vows in 'Historic' Wedding," *Detroit News*, August 23, 2015, http://www.de troitnews.com/story/news/local/oakland-county/2015/08/22/deboer -rowse-exchange-vows-historic-wedding/32212729/.

9. Katherine M. Franke, "Marriage Is a Mixed Blessing," *New York Times*, June 23, 2011, http://www.nytimes.com/2011/06/24/opinion /24franke.html.

10. Sabrina Rubin Erdely, "The Transgender Crucible," *Rolling Stone*, July 30, 2014, www.rollingstone.com/culture/news/the-transgender -crucible-20140730.

11. Emily Alpert Reyes, "Transgender Study Looks at 'Exceptionally High' Suicide-Attempt Rate," *Los Angeles Times*, January 28, 2014, http:// articles.latimes.com/2014/jan/28/local/la-me-ln-suicide-attempts -alarming-transgender-20140127.

CHAPTER 8: WHEN THE KILLER WEARS A BADGE

1. Michael Cooper, "Dinkins Among 14 Arrested in Protest of Police Shooting," *New York Times*, March 16, 1999, www.nytimes.com /1999/03/16/nyregion/dinkins-among-14-arrested-in-protest-of -police-shooting.html.

2. Michael Cooper, "Officers in Bronx Fire 41 Shots, And an Unarmed Man Is Killed," *New York Times*, February 5, 1999, www.nytimes .com/1999/02/05/nyregion/officers-in-bronx-fire-41-shots-and-an -unarmed-man-is-killed.html?pagewanted=all.

3. Timothy Lynch, *We Own the Night: Amadou Diallo's Deadly Encounter with New York City's Street Crimes Unit*, Cato Institute Briefing Papers, no. 56 (Washington, DC: Cato Institute, March 31, 2000), 5, http://object.cato.org/sites/cato.org/files/pubs/pdf/bp56.pdf.

4. Dave Lifton, "15 Years Ago: Bruce Springsteen Angers New York Police Department," Ultimate Classic Rock, June 8, 2015, http://ulti mateclassicrock.com/bruce-springsteen-angers-new-york-police.

5. Kimberly Kindy and Kimbriell Kelly, "Thousands Dead, Few Prosecuted," *Washington Post*, April 11, 2015, www.washingtonpost.com /sf/investigative/2015/04/11/thousands-dead-few-prosecuted.

6. Nicholas Quah and Laura E. Davis, "Here's a Timeline of Unarmed Black People Killed by Police over Past Year," BuzzFeed, May 1, 2015, www.buzzfeed.com/nicholasquah/heres-a-timeline-of-unarmed-black -men-killed-by-police-over#.qyb57BdAz.

7. Rebecca Cantrell, "Reserve Deputy Who Shot Eric Harris Canceled Trip to Bahamas," KFORcom, May 12, 2015, http://kfor.com /2015/05/12/reserve-deputy-who-shot-eric-harris-canceled-trip-to -bahamas/.

8. Peter James Hudson, "Who Killed Robert McCulloch's Father?," *Los Angeles Review of Books*, September 18, 2014, https://lareviewof books.org/essay/killed-robert-mccullochs-father.

9. Carla Murphy, "8 Questions for Constance Malcolm, Grieving Mother Turned Activist," *Colorlines*, February 13, 2015, http://www .colorlines.com/articles/8-questions-constance-malcolm-grieving -mother-turned-activist.

10. Ashley Fantz, Steve Almasy, and Catherine E. Shoichet, "Tamir Rice Shooting: No Charges For Officers," CNN, December 28, 2015, http://www.cnn.com/2015/12/28/us/tamir-rice-shooting/.

11. Kevin Conlon, "NYC Official: City Settles with Eric Garner's Estate for $5.9 Million," CNN, July 14, 2015, www.cnn.com/2015/07/13/us/garner-nyc-settlement.

12. Eliott C. McLaughlin and Ed Payne, "Arresting Officers Provide Statements in Freddie Gray Death," CNN, April 22, 2015, www.cnn.com/2015/04/22/us/baltimore-freddie-gray-death.

13. Emily Badger, "Confirmed: Baltimore Is a Terrible Place to Grow up as a Poor Black Boy," *Washington Post*, May 7, 2015, www.businessinsider.com/confirmed-baltimore-is-a-terrible-place-to-grow-up-as-a-poor-black-boy-2015-5.

14. Colin Campbell and Justin George, "Baltimore Police Union President Likens Protests to 'Lynch Mob,' " *Baltimore Sun*, April 22, 2015, www.baltimoresun.com/news/maryland/baltimore-city/bs-md-ci-fop-news-conference-20150422-story.html.

15. Alicia Garza and L. A. Kaufmann, "A Love Note to Our Folks," *N+1*, January 20, 2015, https://nplusonemag.com/online-only/online-only/a-love-note-to-our-folks.

16. Michelle Alexander, *The New Jim Crow: Mass Incarceration in the Age of Colorblindness*, (New York: New Press, 2011), 6.

17. *Democracy Now!*, July 15, 2015.

CHAPTER 9: "THIS FLAG COMES DOWN TODAY"

1. Abby Phillip and DeNeen L. Brown, "3 Survivors of the Charleston Church Shooting Grapple with Their Grief," *Washington Post*, June 24, 2015, www.washingtonpost.com/national/3-survivors-of-the-charleston-church-shooting-grapple-with-grief/2015/06/24/0ba48c26-19f2-11e5-93b7-5eddc056ad8a_story.html.

2. Anna Bruzgulis, "Confederate Flag Wasn't Flown at South Carolina Statehouse Until 1961, Pundit Claims," PolitiFact, June 22, 2015, www.politifact.com/punditfact/statements/2015/jun/22/eugene-robinson/confederate-flag-wasnt-flown-south-carolina-state-.

3. Elahe Izadi, "The Powerful Words of Forgiveness Delivered to Dylann Roof by Victims' Relatives," *Washington Post*, June 19, 2015, https://www.washingtonpost.com/news/post-nation/wp/2015/06/19/hate-wont-win-the-powerful-words-delivered-to-dylann-roof-by-victims-relatives/.

4. "Family of Rev. Depayne Middleton Call for Unity and Justice," Advancement Project, June 19, 2015, http://www.advancementproject.org/news/entry/family-of-rev.-depayne-middleton-call-for-unity-and-justice.

5. Beth Walton, "Bree Newsome Calls Western North Carolina to Action," Asheville *Citizen-Times*, July 13, 2015, www.citizen-times.com/story/news/local/2015/07/12/bree-newsome-calls-western-north-carolina-action/30050717.

6. Goldie Taylor, "Exclusive: Bree Newsome Speaks for the First Time After Courageous Act of Civil Disobedience," *Blue Nation Review*, June 29, 2015, http://bluenationreview.com/exclusive-bree-newsome-speaks-for-the-first-time-after-courageous-act-of-civil-disobedience.

CHAPTER 10: DISABLING THE ENABLERS

1. Allen Keller et al., "Doing Harm: Health Professionals' Central Role in the CIA Torture Program," Physicians for Human Rights, December 2014, 5, https://s3.amazonaws.com/PHR_Reports/doing-harm-health-professionals-central-role-in-the-cia-torture-program.pdf.

2. David H. Hoffman et al., *Report to the Special Committee of the Board of Directors of the American Psychological Association: Independent Review Relating to APA Ethics Guidelines, National Security Interrogations, And Torture* (Chicago: Sidley Austin LLP, July 2, 2015), 68, www.apa.org/independent-review/APA-FINAL-Report-7.2.15.pdf.

3. Katherine Eban, "Torture, American-Style: The Role of Money in Interrogations," *Vanity Fair*, July 14, 2015, www.vanityfair.com/news/2015/07/torture-american-style-hoffman-report.

4. Ibid.

5. Lauren Walker, "The Man Who Voted Against Banning Psychologists From National Security Interrogations," *Newsweek*, August 11, 2015, http://www.newsweek.com/man-who-voted-against-banning-psychologists-national-security-interrogations-361996.